INTERNATIONAL DEVELOPMENT IN FOCUS

Technology Transfer and Innovation for Low-Carbon Development

MIRIA A. PIGATO, SIMON J. BLACK, DAMIEN DUSSAUX, ZHIMIN MAO,
MILES MCKENNA, RYAN RAFATY, AND SIMON TOUBOUL

 **WORLD BANK GROUP**

Contents

Foreword

In the rising tide of bad news about climate change, it is easy to feel pessimistic. The task of halving emissions by 2030 seems insurmountable. The stakes are high, the threat to global development is serious, and the road to success is murky, at best.

This book provides a ray of hope for the global effort to tackle climate change. It shows that decades of rapid innovation and targeted investment in low-carbon technology (LCT) are paying off. The tools we need to curb most emissions are at our fingertips—in the form of commercially proven LCT that is becoming less expensive and more widely available each year. In fact, two-thirds of the emissions reductions needed by 2030 can be achieved through the mass deployment of existing technology in just four sectors: energy, industry, transport, and buildings.

Yet this book also highlights the degree to which the world's most vulnerable economies are excluded from the promise of these technological solutions. Huge swaths of the globe—especially the poorest countries—are almost completely absent from the LCT market as buyers, sellers, or innovators. Low-income countries accounted for just 0.01 percent of global LCT exports and 0.3 percent of global LCT imports in 2015–16. High-income countries produced 80 percent of all LCT innovations between 2010 and 2015.

Most future emissions are expected to come from developing countries. People in the poorest countries already are at the highest risk for climate-related disasters. With so much at stake, this raises an obvious question: Why aren't more low-income countries adopting readily available LCT solutions?

The answer involves the most fundamental challenges of development. Transferring technology is a process of collaboration and learning that requires human, physical, financial, and organizational capital—inputs that are scarce in developing countries, particularly in low-income economies. To boost LCT to the necessary scale, developing countries encounter several obstacles. The up-front costs of LCT are high. Using them effectively requires complementary investment in infrastructure, such as power grids and transmission lines. And their success ultimately requires governments to create policies that displace entrenched firms and fossil-fuel based technology while providing long-term incentives for decarbonization.

Given these obstacles, there is an urgent need to facilitate the transfer of technology to developing countries. This requires getting energy prices right, building human and institutional capital, supporting LCT investment through de-risking mechanisms, and introducing policies that support the uptake of LCT. This is the central message of this book: It is technically feasible to contain global warming to 1.5 degrees Celsius by using existing LCT—but only if it is deployed on a massive scale in developing countries.

Achieving the Paris Agreement goals is perhaps the greatest challenge of our time. To solve it, national and international strategies for low-carbon development should be strategic, comprehensive, and bold. The recommendations in this volume can help governments design smart, equitable, and politically feasible policies that put countries on the fastest path to a low-carbon future.

Ceyla Pazarbasioglu
Vice President, Equitable Growth, Finance and Institutions
World Bank Group

Acknowledgments

Technology Transfer and Innovation for Low-Carbon Development was prepared by a team led by Miria A. Pigato and comprising Simon J. Black, Damien Dussaux, Zhimin Mao, Miles McKenna, Ryan Rafaty, and Simon Touboul. The team worked under the guidance of Marcello Estevão.

The team is grateful to Inchul Hwang and Naoko Kojo for their contributions to chapter 1 and chapter 4, respectively, and to peer reviewers Xavier Cirera, Mark Dutz, Stephane Hallegatte, and Deepak Mishra.

The team also benefitted from comments and advice from Guillermo Arenas, Carter Brandon, Dominik Englert, Phillip Hannam, Dirk Heine, Henry Lee, William Maloney, Mariana Mazzucato, Denis Medvedev, Antonio Nucifora, Joseph Rebello, Michele Ruta, Erin Scronce, Stephen Stretton, Frauke Urban, Gonzalo Varela, and Rupert Way.

The team is grateful to Lucy Mukuka, Zakia Nekaien-Nowrouz, and Ivana Ticha for their assistance during the preparation of the report. The financial contribution of the Korean Global Facility on Growth for Development is gratefully acknowledged.

About the Authors

Simon J. Black is an economist in the World Bank's Climate Change Group. Previously, he was the climate economist of the United Kingdom's Foreign and Commonwealth Office, a diplomatic service economist (Fast Stream), and a private sector macroeconomist, and served on the United Kingdom's delegation to the United Nations Framework Convention on Climate Change in the run-up to the Paris Agreement. He holds a master's degree in international political economy from the London School of Economics and Political Science and a master's degree in international development from Harvard University, where he was a Frank Knox Fellow.

Damien Dussaux is a researcher at the Centre for Industrial Economics at MINES ParisTech, PSL University, and a visiting fellow at the Grantham Research Institute on Climate Change and the Environment at the London School of Economics and Political Science. His research interests include the environmental impacts of international trade, the competitiveness impacts of environmental policies, international technology diffusion, and the circular economy. Damien completed his PhD thesis "The effects of environmental regulations on waste trade, clean innovation, and competitiveness in a globalized world" at MINES ParisTech, PSL Research University. Damien graduated as an environmental science engineer from AgroParisTech and has a master's degree in environmental and energy economics from AgroParisTech, Paris.

Zhimin Mao is a young professional at the World Bank. Previously, she was a postdoctoral fellow in the Environment and Natural Resources Program at Harvard Kennedy School's Belfer Center for Science and International Affairs, where she focused on China's low-carbon development. Before joining the Belfer Center, Zhimin was a PhD fellow at the Pardee RAND Graduate School and an assistant policy analyst at the RAND Corporation. Her RAND experience focused on energy, environmental policy, and international development. She has also worked at the International Institute of Applied Systems Analysis; the Heinz Center for Science, Economics and Environment; the University Corporation for Atmospheric Research; and the Asian Development Bank.

Miles McKenna is an associate economist at the International Finance Corporation. His work focuses on improving private sector diagnostics and strategic engagement to deepen development impact in IFC client countries. He previously worked as an analyst in the World Bank's Macroeconomics, Trade, and Investment Global Practice, where he assessed opportunities for sustainable economic growth and regional integration through global value chains, trade facilitation, and private sector–led initiatives to improve standards and sustainability. Before joining the World Bank Group, he lectured at Xiamen University. Miles holds an MSc in global energy and climate policy from SOAS University of London.

Miria A. Pigato is a lead economist and climate lead in the World Bank's Macroeconomics, Trade, and Investment Global Practice. Before assuming this position in 2016, she served as practice and sector manager of the Macroeconomics and Fiscal Management Global Practice. She led senior policy dialogue on growth, climate, macro, fiscal, and trade policy and supervised more than 60 development policy operations for Africa, the Caribbean, Central Asia, Eastern Europe, the Middle East, and South Asia. Currently, she co-leads the Secretariat of the Coalition of Finance Ministers for Climate Action, a group of more than 50 finance ministers committed to taking collective and domestic action on climate change. She holds a master's degree in economics from the London School of Economics and Political Science and a PhD in economics from University College London.

Ryan Rafaty is a postdoctoral research fellow at Climate Econometrics, Nuffield College, University of Oxford. He is also a senior research officer at the Institute for New Economic Thinking at the Oxford Martin School, where he works with the Post-Carbon Transition Project. His research focuses on the design, evaluation, and political economy of climate change mitigation policies from a comparative, historical perspective. He has published articles in *Science, Nature Climate Change*, and other journals. Previously, Ryan was a consultant in the World Bank's Macroeconomics, Trade and Investment Global Practice; deputy research director at the Climate Leadership Council; and an editor at the *Cambridge Review of International Affairs*, among other roles. He completed his PhD in politics at King's College, University of Cambridge, in 2017. His dissertation provided a macrocomparative assessment of the politics and environmental performance of low-carbon energy transition policies in OECD countries over three decades, with a focus on the Scandinavian countries and Germany.

Simon Touboul is a PhD student in economics at the Centre for Industrial Economics at MINES ParisTech, PSL University. His thesis focuses on technological innovation and adaptation to climate change. Simon's research interests are the impact of climate finance on climate change adaptation technologies, the effect of extreme weather events on climate change adaptation technologies, and the international diffusion of climate change adaptation technologies. He has worked with the World Bank, the Grantham Research Institute on Climate Change and the Environment at the London School of Economics and Political Science, and the University of Cambridge. Simon holds a master's degree in environmental and energy economics from AgroParisTech, Paris-Saclay University.

Executive Summary

INTRODUCTION

This report is a call to action. It argues that most of the emissions reductions required to achieve the Paris Agreement goals can be reached through the global deployment of existing and commercially proven low-carbon technologies (LCTs). Deploying them at the necessary scale will not be easy, but the evidence clearly indicates that it can be done, and this report describes how.

Technological revolutions have increased the world's wealth to a level that was once unimaginable but at the cost of accelerating climate change and ecological devastation.[1] To limit global warming to between 1.5 and 2.0 degrees Celsius, in line with the Paris Agreement, the world's greenhouse gas (GHG) emissions must decline to net zero by 2050 and become negative in the second half of this century. Achieving this target will require a rapid and systemic transformation of the energy sector, starting with energy conservation and efficiency and the progressive replacement of fossil fuels with renewable energy. It will also require the widespread deployment and mass-scale transfer of low-carbon technologies[2] from high-income countries to the developing world, which this report refers to as the North and South, respectively.[3] Although countries in the North have produced the bulk of global GHG emissions, most of future emissions are expected to occur in the South, underscoring the urgency of accelerating North-South LCT transfer.

Without new mitigation policies, emissions are likely to increase to about 65 gigatons of carbon dioxide equivalent ($GtCO_2e$) by 2030. This amount is roughly 41 $GtCO_2e$ higher than the maximum level—24 $GtCO_2e$—necessary to contain global warming to 1.5 degrees (UNEP 2017). However, most of the necessary emissions reductions can be achieved by deploying existing, commercially proven LCTs globally, while stopping deforestation. Expanding the use of existing LCT in four major sectors—energy, industry, transportation, and construction—could narrow the emission gap by almost two-thirds (figure ES.1).

FIGURE ES.1

GHG emissions abatement potential across sectors by 2030

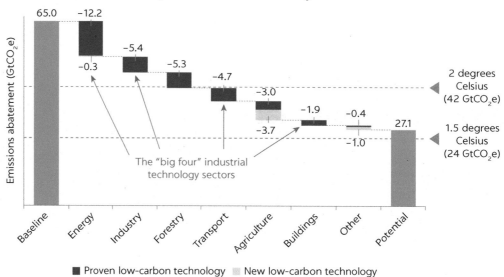

Source: Based on data from UNEP 2017.
Note: Global warming can be contained to 1.5 degrees Celsius by 2030 (lower horizontal line) or to 2 degrees Celsius (higher horizontal line). GHG = greenhouse gas; $GtCO_2e$ = gigatons of carbon dioxide equivalent; LCT = low-carbon technology.

Like other forms of technology, the process of developing, adapting, and deploying LCT requires large up-front capital investment, but the returns to that investment are influenced by the presence of complementary infrastructure and the conduciveness of the policy framework. Moreover, the capital sunk into the incumbent fossil-fuel value chains and established high-carbon industries creates both economic incentives and political pressure to maintain the carbon-intensive status quo. The uncertainty regarding prospective policy changes, such as the introduction of carbon pricing or the elimination of fossil-fuel subsidies creates disincentives to invest in LCTs. Without access to adequate policy support and long-term financing, investments will continue to be biased toward conventional, high-carbon technologies.

Historically, energy transitions have been gradual processes that take at least 50 years. However, several examples of faster transitions create hope for the swift deployment of LCT. These include the rapid adoption of nuclear power in France and the spread of combined heat and power plants in Denmark in the late 1970s and early 1980s. Well-designed policies and investments have helped reduce the cost of renewable-energy technologies: between 2010 and 2018, the costs per gigawatt of installed capacity fell by almost 80 percent for utility solar photovoltaic, 54 percent for energy storage, and 22 percent for onshore wind (IEA 2019). Estimates of the unsubsidized cost of renewable energy technologies relative to existing coal generation suggest that renewable-energy technologies are among the least expensive in the United States—and the cost of wind and solar may be even lower when explicit or implicit subsidies are included (Gillingham and Stock 2018). Meanwhile, the average time taken to install one gigawatt of renewable energy dropped from 2.6 years in 2013 to 1.9 in 2018. While further reductions in capital and time costs will be necessary to speed the deployment of LCT across the South, these trends are encouraging.

Beyond combatting climate change, the global transfer of LCT represents a major development opportunity for low- and middle-income countries

Over the past two centuries, cross-national differences in the adoption rate of new technologies have accounted for as much as 75 percent of the divergence in per capita incomes between developed and developing economies (Comin and Mestieri 2018). Policies to accelerate the deployment and adoption of LCT can expand energy supply and improve energy security, enhancing economic prospects by accelerating productivity growth while improving the public welfare through gains in utility access and environmental quality. Fast-growing LCT sectors also provide opportunities for firms in developing countries to integrate into global value chains, creating new drivers of economic growth and job creation. Countries with the absorptive capacity and competencies to adopt LCT and innovate are more likely to attract foreign direct investment (FDI), accelerate technological advancement, boost productivity through spillovers, and capitalize on increased export competitiveness.

Transferring LCT is a process of collaboration, learning, and adaptation

Effective technology transfer encompasses not only physical hardware (e.g., solar panels and wind turbines) but also the technical know-how and capabilities necessary to understand, operate, and maintain new technologies, as well as institutional and policy arrangements that facilitate technological uptake and encourage local innovation (Lema and Lema 2012; Sampath and Roffe 2012; Cirera and Maloney 2017). Thus, LCT transfer is a process of learning and interactive collaboration. To be sustainable, it requires the capabilities to deploy, operate, maintain, adapt, improve, and reproduce the transferred technology and, ultimately, the capacity to invent new technologies. This process can be visualized as the "technology-transfer staircase" (figure ES.2), which shows the different stages of technology transfer, from the importation of foreign technologies by firms and households (adoption and diffusion) to the adaptation of those technologies to the local context (imitation and collaborative innovation) to the domestic creation of new technologies (indigenous invention). The first two steps of the ladder rely on imports, but the next three offer the possibility of developing and producing technologies for export.

FIGURE ES.2

The technology-transfer staircase

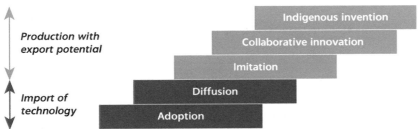

Note: The figure shows different stages of technology transfer, from importing a foreign technology to domestic production with the potential for further innovation. The technology-transfer staircase is an homage to, but separate from, the capabilities escalator of firm and state capabilities needed to achieve higher levels of innovation sophistication (Cirera and Maloney 2017).

Firms and households benefit from imported technology, but local firms initially lack the ability to significantly modify or reproduce it. As domestic capabilities develop, countries become able to diffuse imported technology more widely across economic sectors. Eventually, domestic firms acquire the capacity to imitate foreign products and production methods, but they still rely on intellectual property developed and owned abroad. Collaborative innovation between domestic and foreign firms (for example, through joint ventures) begins to create the domestic capacity to develop original technologies, conferring some degree of local control and ownership over the technological upgrading process. Ultimately, the country's domestic research and development capacity evolves to the point that it can produce, commercialize, and potentially export technologies based largely or entirely on locally owned intellectual property. However, progression up the technology staircase is not automatic, and countries can languish for years or even decades at the lower steps.

Climbing the technology staircase requires an increasingly complex system of capabilities

Progressing to higher levels of technological sophistication requires complementary inputs, including human, physical, financial, institutional, and organizational capital, which are often scarce in developing countries. This scarcity largely explains why so many countries in the South underinvest in importing and diffusing foreign technologies. As a country progresses up the staircase, firms and workers require ever-increasing skill levels, culminating in the capacity to develop new and original products. Meanwhile, governments must provide the institutional and administrative framework necessary to support the economy's growing technological complexity, including public investment in education and physical capital (figure ES.3).

FIGURE ES.3

National capabilities that influence technology transfer

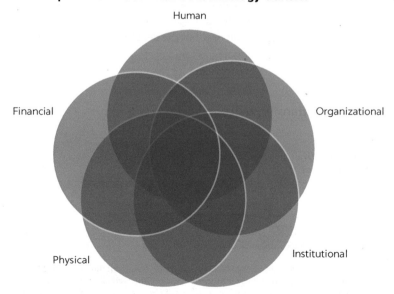

Reaching the last step of the staircase presents significant challenges for both public and private sectors. This report finds that, across countries, human capital is the strongest predictor of high performance in LCT trade and innovation, followed by institutional and physical capital.[4] Economies with greater endowments of human, institutional and physical capital tend to import and export more LCTs and to innovate more. Human capital also appears to be among the most important factors for accelerating LCT transfer *within* countries. Moreover, countries that have growing economies, large markets, and a deep base of productive capital are better positioned to make the large upfront capital investments required to diffuse, produce, and export LCT. Organizational and institutional capital appear to matter more for importing than for exporting LCT. Finally, financial-sector development marginally encourages LCT imports, but the observed effect is surprisingly small. This finding indicates that strategies to improve educational outcomes, increase the infrastructure stock, or build institutional capacity may be more effective in accelerating LCT transfer than efforts to deepen the financial sector.

Recognizing the pivotal role of North-South LCT transfer in reducing GHG emissions, this report is designed to assist client governments in defining national strategies to facilitate LCT adoption, absorption, and innovation. The next section of this executive summary describes evolving trends in international LCT transfer, as proxied by trade, FDI, and patent data. The analysis is complemented by a case study on the rise of the electric vehicle (EV) industry in China, which has successfully leveraged domestic policies to produce, and export LCT. This example and other cases from the international literature offer lessons for how policymakers can help adopt, deploy, and produce LCT in the context of their capacity constraints and development objectives. The final section concludes the executive summary with a concise review of policy options for accelerating North-South LCT transfer.

KEY FINDINGS

LCT represents a growing share of global trade, but the world's poorest countries are the least able to benefit from trade in LCT

This report finds that LCT represented roughly 4 percent of global trade in 2016, but its growth rate has outpaced the growth rate of global trade over the past several decades. LCT exports grew at a compound annual growth rate of 11.1 percent from 1990–2016, exceeding the growth rates of total exports (9.7 percent), merchandise exports (6.0 percent), and all high-technology exports (3.4 percent). The North accounted for more than 70 percent of total LCT exports and 62 percent of imports by value in 2016.

Within the South, low-income countries accounted for just 0.01 percent and 0.3 percent of total LCT exports and imports respectively in 2015–16. South–South trade in LCT has increased, but it has yet to have a transformational effect on low-income economies. Moreover, although the South has become more integrated into LCT trade networks, the world's poorest countries remain on the periphery. South–North LCT trade flows have also grown, albeit from a negligible base, but only a few countries participate in this trade pattern.

TABLE ES.1 **Top-10 LCT exporters, 2016**

ECONOMY	TOTAL LCT EXPORTS (US$, BILLIONS)	SHARE OF LCT EXPORTS (%)
All economies	*698.5*	*100.0*
China	117.6	16.8
Germany	87.5	12.5
United States	77.1	11.0
Japan	51.3	7.3
Korea, Rep.	45.0	6.4
Italy	23.8	3.4
Hong Kong SAR, China	20.8	3.0
Taiwan, China	20.1	2.9
United Kingdom	19.7	2.8
Singapore	19.3	2.8

Source: World Bank World Integrated Trade Solution (database); https://wits.worldbank.org/.
Note: SAR = Special Administrative Region.

China is the world's largest importer and exporter of LCT. In 2016, China accounted for 15.9 percent of total LCT imports, ranking ahead of the United States (13.2 percent) and Germany (6.9 percent). China also accounted for 16.8 percent of LCT exports in 2016, (table ES.1) and 56 percent of the total value of South–North LCT exports. By contrast, Brazil, India, and South Africa accounted for a combined 4.3 percent of South–North LCT exports.

With the notable exception of India, LCT exports from countries in the South tend to be concentrated in a small number of goods and markets. For example, South Africa's top LCT exports consistently account for over half its total LCT exports, most of which are destined for Germany. Similarly, China and Mexico's top-five LCT exports accounted for over half of their total LCT exports in 2017. In terms of imports, India is the only country to import more LCT from the South—primarily China and other upper-middle-income countries—than from the North. This pattern appears to indicate the India is not importing the most advanced technologies from high-income countries, but is instead importing more suitable or affordable technologies from its peers in developing countries.

FDI is a critical channel for technology transfer to developing countries, and countries with larger markets and more sophisticated capabilities attract greater FDI in renewable energy

After growing steadily before the 2008–09 financial crisis, FDI in renewable energy has become highly volatile.[5] FDI in renewable energy totaled US$82.5 billion in 2018, with one-third of investments originating from countries in the South.[6] China has quietly emerged as the global leader in renewable energy investment, and in 2018 it overtook Germany as the top foreign direct investor in renewable energy. China accounts for 45 percent of total global investment in renewable energy, and its total investments in the sector (including both FDI and domestic projects) exceeded the combined total investment of all other

TABLE ES.2 **Total renewable-energy FDI by destination, source, and subsector, 2003–18**

DESTINATIONS	RE INVESTMENT (US$, BILLIONS)	TOP-THREE SOURCE ECONOMIES	TOP-THREE SUBSECTORS
India	29.9	China, United States, United Kingdom	Solar, wind, other
Brazil	27.5	United States, Spain, France	Biomass, wind, solar
Mexico	26.2	Spain, United States, Italy	Solar, wind, hydro
South Africa	14.3	Italy, Ireland, Saudi Arabia	Solar, wind, biomass
China	14.2	United States; Canada; Hong Kong SAR, China	Wind, solar, biomass
Korea, Rep.	4.2	Germany, United States, Japan	Biomass, solar, other

Source: Calculations based on fDi Markets (database) https://www.fdiintelligence.com/fdi-markets.
Note: FDI = foreign direct investment; RE = renewable energy.

countries in 2017 (REN21 2018). South–South investment accounted for 14.1 percent of all renewable energy investment between 2003 and 2018. Most of this investment has gone toward large hydropower projects, and many developing countries—notably China—have cultivated expertise in hydroelectric technologies.

Countries with large domestic markets and more sophisticated capabilities tend to attract more FDI in renewable energy while the poorest countries have attracted much less investment and had fewer opportunities to benefit from technological spillovers. Between 2003 and 2018, India was the largest recipient of FDI in renewable energy, followed by Brazil and Mexico (table ES.2).

Only 13.2 percent of renewable energy investment in the top three countries went to manufacturing, and most was focused on electricity production. These three countries are not major exporters of LCT, suggesting that inbound FDI has not yet transformed their production and export dynamics. Notably, China received relatively little FDI in renewable energy over the period.

Innovation in LCT is growing faster than innovation in other technologies, but almost no new LCT is being transferred to low-income countries

Between 1990 and 2015, the annual growth rate of LCT patents averaged about 8 percent per year, twice the average growth rate for all technologies.[7] High-income countries produced at least 80 percent of LCT innovations in all technological fields over the period. Japan produced the largest share, followed by the United States, Germany, the Republic of Korea, and China (figure ES.4). This order was broadly similar across technological fields. However, lower-middle-income and low-income countries produced almost no LCT innovations during the period.

China has become a global leader in LCT innovation, but China's share of LCT inventions remains small relative to its share of global carbon emissions. Moreover, only a small percentage of China's LCT patents is transferred abroad,[8] raising questions about the quality of these inventions.

Between 2010 and 2015, roughly 71 percent of all patent transfers occurred between countries in the North. Only 23 percent of LCT patent transfers went from high-income to middle-income countries, and only 4 percent went from middle-income to high-income countries. Almost no patents were transferred

FIGURE ES.4

Share of LCT innovations, by country

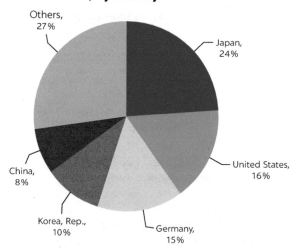

Source: Calculations based on PATSTAT (database), https://www.epo.org/index.html.

to or from low-income countries. Within countries in the South, China received the largest number of inbound LCT patents. Between 2010 and 2015, firms from the North filed more than 90 percent of the inbound LCT patents in China.

Restrictive FDI policies and tariffs inhibit LCT transfer—but nontariff barriers may encourage it

Econometric analysis of patent data from 75 countries observed during 2006–15[9] suggests that restrictive trade and FDI policies unequivocally discourage technology transfer. However, nontariff barriers tend to *increase* technology transfer by encouraging firms to interact with foreign markets through FDI rather than trade. Nontariff barriers—such as import quotas—set a limit on the goods that can be imported. When the import quota is met, FDI becomes the only way to further exploit the technology that produces those goods. Subsidies that encourage foreign firms to enter the domestic market have a similar effect. By contrast, controls on the movement of capital and people have a substantial negative impact on LCT patents transferred by both high-income and developing countries.

Because FDI tends to be more knowledge-intensive than trade in capital goods, the positive effect of nontariff barriers on FDI more than compensates for the negative effect of nontariff barriers on trade. Nontariff barriers tend to be most effective in promoting technology transfer through an increase in FDI in countries that have large domestic markets, which make FDI in domestic production more profitable. In addition, countries with growing populations tend to receive more patent transfers from the South, whereas wealthier countries receive more transfers from both the North and the South.

The influence of other policy variables is more ambiguous. In principle, strong protections for intellectual property rights (IPR) can encourage market entry by foreign firms, whose intellectual assets are shielded from imitation by domestic competitors. IPR protections, however, can also enhance the market power of patent holders, creating monopolistic price distortions that disadvantage local competitors. The analysis presented in this report finds that strong IPR protections have no significant effect on LCT transfer from either high-income or developing countries.

Local technological capacity has similarly complex implications for patent transfer. Although some local capacity is necessary to exploit transferred technology, a very high degree of local capacity can increase the risk of imitation, potentially deterring foreign patent holders from transferring their technologies. Strong IPR protections can mitigate this risk, but only partially. Likewise, stringent environmental protections can encourage innovation and boost LCT transfer, but they can also increase public investment in research and development, which may crowd out private investment and discourage technology transfer.

China's success in the electric vehicles market illustrates both the challenges and the rewards of reaching the final step on the technology-transfer staircase

China's initial push into the electric vehicle (EV) market was driven by a combination of domestic objectives targeting pollution control, energy security, and economic growth. Building on a decade-long process of investing in research and development, the government launched an ambitious pilot program in 2009 designed to promote the development of EVs in several cities and regions. This program, known as "Ten Cities, Thousand Vehicles," was centralized, but the pilot cities had significant leeway to establish rollout models that reflected their circumstances, with variation in models yielding important lessons to guide national rollout.

Multiple structural, technical, and market constraints prevented the program from achieving its anticipated outcomes. For example, firms realized that the creation of a national EV industry would require developing uniform industrial standards for battery types and designs for public buses, all of which were missing. It also became clear that the transition from conventional vehicles to EVs would require better incentives, as well as close coordination among auto manufacturers, battery developers, infrastructure providers, and consumers. Reacting quickly to the program's initial failure, the government significantly increased subsidies to EV manufacturers and developed a network of charging facilities and services based on unified standards. Working closely with the government and local authorities, the EV firms focused on producing cheaper, better-designed models tailored to the preferences of Chinese consumers. This time the program succeeded and, by 2015, China had become the world's largest EV market. In 2007, only 100 EVs were sold worldwide; by 2018, this figure had reached 2 million, with China accounting for half of the total.

Several lessons can be gleaned from this experience. First, the Chinese government's vision and support—including the construction of infrastructure networks—were essential to enable EV producers to overcome the entrenched dominance of conventional vehicles. Second, industrial policies were vital to support EV development and deployment. For example, China's strategy of encouraging municipal governments to invest in charging facilities and applying favorable tax and regulatory treatment to EVs played a major role in accelerating EV uptake. Third, contrary to China's traditional automotive market, which is dominated by joint ventures between foreign and domestic companies, the EV market was dominated by wholly domestic firms. China's EV industry was not a product of the "Trade Technology for Market" policy. Under this policy, foreign companies in strategic sectors are required to share their technology as a condition to gain access to the Chinese consumer market, which Chinese critics have long argued encourages Chinese firms to rely on outdated imported technologies instead of investing in domestic research. By contrast, the growth of the EV industry was driven by the capacity of domestic firms to innovate and to tailor their products to the specific circumstances of the Chinese market.

China's success in the EV market ultimately hinged on the government's ability to learn from failure and persevere until it found an approach that worked, but the costs of sustaining the creation of the EV industry were astronomical. In 2016, subsidies for battery-powered vehicle models were about US$2,000 per vehicle in California, US$4,500 in Sweden, and US$8,000 in China (Yang et al. 2016). China was able to afford this level of subsidization, but most countries cannot. Moreover, even China eventually changed course again: After realizing that its EV subsidies were excessive and untargeted, it decided to phase them out almost entirely by 2020 and to replace them with several targeted regulatory initiatives.

China's EV experience provides some insights into the challenges of delivering EVs to a mass market through centralized leadership and industrial policies. Other countries—such as the United States, Germany, India, and Sweden—have adopted different models, with various degrees of success. Markets are driven by the interaction of individual firms within the context of national regulatory frameworks, and box ES.1 analyzes the experience of two comparably successful EV companies, one in China and one in the United States. These two companies employed two very different strategies, highlighting the ongoing process of experimentation that characterizes the EV market.

BOX ES.1

Two paths to leadership in the global electric vehicle market

Electric vehicle (EV) manufacturers Build Your Dreams (BYD), a Chinese company, and Tesla, a U.S. company, provide a case study of how two different business strategies enabled these firms to become leaders in the global EV market.

Founded in Shenzhen in the mid-1990s, BYD embraced the Chinese government's vision of transitioning to low-carbon energy, which entailed promoting a massive increase in EV production and sales. BYD currently owns 30 percent of China's EV market and is the largest producer of plug-in vehicles globally. Tesla's mission is "to accelerate the world's transition to a sustainable energy future." Tesla currently dominates the U.S. EV market, and its Model 3 was the best-selling electric car in the world in 2018.

continued

Box ES.1, *continued*

Although the leaders of BYD and Tesla are both innovators capable of influencing entire industries, the differences between their business strategies during the past decade are striking. BYD closely guarded its technology, whereas Tesla made its patents publicly available. BYD initially positioned itself in the low-end market; Tesla began at the high end. BYD imitated foreign technologies and exploited a niche market that foreign automakers were exiting; Tesla partnered with established conventional vehicle manufacturers to alleviate the constraints imposed by its limited automotive experience. Whereas Tesla has been criticized for overpromising and underdelivering and has suffered serious financial problems, BYD has overdelivered on its objectives and expanded rapidly in both the domestic and international markets. BYD's profitability, however, has hinged on its access to Chinese government subsidies, which have been far more generous than those available to Tesla.

Although both companies were successful, Tesla may contribute more than BYD to the development of a global EV market with its "open innovation" approach to intellectual property rights. Open innovation—coupled with a strategic focus on alliances and partnerships—appears to offer EV firms a means to thrive in a world of global competition and rapid technological change.

POLICY IMPLICATIONS

The five chapters of this report yield multiple recommendations for facilitating the transfer, adoption, production and creation of LCT. Each country has its own development objectives and faces its own unique constraints. Countries with limited capabilities may prefer to focus on leveraging LCT to expand energy access, improve energy efficiency, or help domestic firms become more cost-competitive. Countries with higher levels of capability may be more willing to assimilate imported technology and eventually develop their own LCT industries. The global transfer of LCT is not only a necessity to achieve climate objectives but also an opportunity to achieve development goals. The policies needed to deploy LCT could also raise output, employment and competitiveness while yielding ancillary welfare benefits, such as reduced air and water pollution. Moreover, adopting LCT offers an opportunity for economies seeking export-led growth to become LCT producers and exporters.

Establish effective policies to get energy prices right while building human, physical, and institutional capital

Across countries, the policy environment for LCT must be aligned with their overall development objectives. For example, by reducing or eliminating fossil fuel subsidies and implementing carbon pricing, governments can systematically shift the incentives faced by firms and households toward low-carbon energy. But carbon pricing often faces significant political opposition, and other measures may be needed to accelerate the deployment and production of LCT. Investing in human capital and in low-carbon infrastructure—including public transportation and energy infrastructure—is vital to boost the capabilities of firms and households to embrace LCT.

Support private investment in LCT deployment through de-risking mechanisms

Although returns to investment in technology in developing countries should be higher than in developed countries, country-specific risks—both actual and perceived—reduce expected returns across all types of LCT investment. High financing costs may render investment in LCT infeasible. Given the insufficient supply of long-term private capital to support decarbonization, public support is crucial. De-risking instruments, including loan guarantees, public equity co-investments, and political risk insurance, can help address the underlying causes of policy risk and accelerate private investment in LCT.

Introduce demand-pull policies to create a market for LCT

Policies that support the demand for technologies—demand-pull policies—can be especially effective in encouraging the uptake of LCT. Direct subsidies and feed-in tariffs have proven effective in making renewable energies cost-competitive with fossil fuel technologies, though they often entail considerable costs. Public outreach campaigns designed to raise awareness of the costs and risks associated with climate change can foster positive social norms around consumption. Regulatory standards and labeling requirements can help overcome informational constraints. Governments can also increase LCT demand directly through their public procurement and investment policies, and they can provide financing to help firms and household transition to LCT. Partnerships between the government, public utilities, the private sector, and academic institutions can build the human capital necessary to support LCT deployment and supply LCT directly to low-income households as part of broader efforts to achieve energy-access and distributional-equity objectives.

Demand-pull policies tend to be most effective in large markets. Market size influences both the production and deployment of LCT, and countries with large consumer markets are well-positioned to leverage demand to advance their LCT goals. However, demand-pull policies can also be effective in smaller countries, especially if they pool their market size through policy harmonization and regional integration.

Focus on technology-push policies to drive innovation and support LCT production and exports

Supply-side policies that encourage technology innovation—technology-push policies—are especially appropriate for countries seeking to spur LCT innovation, production, and exports. Determining which policies will work in which context, however, remains a key challenge for innovation policy in general and for LCT production and exports in particular. Developing countries seeking to innovate, produce, and export LCT require sophisticated national capabilities, long-term strategic planning, and an especially aggressive mix of demand-pull and technology-push policies. Countries that reach this stage are likely to experience accelerated productivity growth, as LCTs tend to be more complex than other technologies, with dense backward and forward linkages across multiple value chains. Consequently, the value of capturing part of a complex and growing sector may outweigh the risk-adjusted costs of investing in LCT. Within this context, governments should adopt a policy approach designed to create—rather than pick—winners, which can reduce the risk of generating distortive rents. For example, governments can support intermediaries such as accelerators and technology centers that help firms and workers develop the capabilities to innovate, including the necessary managerial and absorptive capacity, rather than directly supporting specific firms.

Poorer countries tend to face more and deeper market failures involving technology, and they often have less domestic capacity to address those failures effectively. As these countries develop, policymakers should alter their LCT policies to reflect their expanding national capabilities, as well as other dynamic country- and technology-specific variables. However, the combination of technology-related market failures and limited national capabilities can leave low-income countries stuck in a "technology trap."[10] Increasing external assistance for LCT transfer may be necessary to free low-income countries from the technology trap.

Use environmental provisions in multilateral trade and investment initiatives to accelerate LCT transfer

Bilateral and regional trade agreements can enable trade liberalization and environmental protection to support and reinforce each other. The number of such agreements has soared over the past three decades, as has the number of environmental provisions they contain (Monteiro and Trachman, forthcoming). Committing to a clear path of sequenced reforms to support environmental objectives can boost economic and welfare gains and the inclusion of environmental provisions in trade agreements correlates with increased trade flows (Berger et al. 2020). Trade agreements have also helped to drive bilateral and multilateral cooperation on issues such as product standards and environmental subsidies.

Multilateral trade liberalization is vital to accelerate LCT transfer. In 2014, 46 members of the World Trade Organization (WTO) initiated negotiations for an Environmental Goods Agreement (EGA) designed to remove barriers to trade in goods with positive environmental or climate change impacts. However, these negotiations stalled in 2016. Completing the EGA could accelerate LCT transfer worldwide. Although reaching consensus on a list of environmental goods is likely to be a challenge, unilateral tariff reductions offer an immediate incentive to increase trade in LCT-intensive goods and services. Econometric analysis suggests that low-income countries would experience the greatest increase in LCT imports and the largest welfare gains from the elimination of tariffs on LCT (de Melo and Solleder 2018)—including expanded access to clean, lower-cost energy—which would disproportionately benefit low-income households (Mahlstein and McDaniel 2017).

International investment agreements could accelerate LCT transfer to developing countries by reducing FDI restrictions and stimulating both foreign and domestic investment. International investment agreements should, however, include a degree of flexibility to accommodate the "increased ambition" mandated by the Paris Agreement.[11] For example, they should allow for the periodic tightening of mitigation and adaptation policies in the Nationally Determined Contributions (NDCs), and they should include correction mechanisms that enable countries to adjust their policies in response to new information about environmental risks. Finally, international investment agreements could encourage countries to provide greater policy certainty by clearly communicating their long-term climate objectives and transparently integrating them into their long-term macroeconomic and sectoral development strategies.

Adopt new IPR agreements for accelerating the transfer of LCT

The international experience underscores the importance of IPR protections to promote the development of new technologies but the urgency for the rapid deployment of LCT to avert the catastrophic impact of climate change provides a compelling rational for sharing the intellectual property that underpins LCT. Firms are interested in both profiting from the diffusion of their innovation and avoiding expropriation by imitating firms. To balance these interests, industries with historically high rates of patenting and records of operating in environments with complementary technologies—such as aircraft manufacturing, semiconductors, mobile telecommunications, and electricity metering—have managed to accelerate innovation and diffusion simultaneously by adopting technology-standards agreements and cooperative IPR arrangements, including cross-licensing (Iliev and Neuhoff 2009).

Patent pools, which are agreements between two or more patent owners to collectively manage IPRs, have the potential to accelerate LCT transfer, following the example of the biomedical and pharmaceutical industries. However, this approach would need to be incorporated into the international IPR architecture and linked to appropriate sources of financing. In the near term, a "club" of countries could take the lead by creating collaborative patent pools to facilitate the cost-efficient transfer of the most promising LCT (Maskus 2010).

Mobilize the UNFCCC to facilitate the transfer of LCT to the poorest countries

International institutions and donor countries could play a much larger role in facilitating transfer of LCT to the poorest countries, including via the UNFCCC process. Increasing the amount of resources allocated to publicizing successful examples of technology transfer could provide critical knowledge for policymakers striving to promote LCT transfer and innovation. In addition, a much stronger commitment by upper-middle-income and high-income countries to explicitly include technology-transfer objectives in their NDCs would signal their commitment to facilitating the spread of LCT.

The UNFCCC has yet to formulate a comprehensive international framework to address the challenges of South-South LCT transfer. While this pattern of LCT transfer is likely to accelerate in the medium term even in the absence of a comprehensive international policy framework, a consistent focus on the unique dynamics of South–South LCT transfer within the existing framework could have a highly positive impact. The poorest countries have the most to gain from South–South LCT transfer, and the UNFCCC has a key role to play in overcoming their pervasive market failures and domestic financial and institutional capacity constraints. Low- and lower-middle-income countries should lobby the UNFCCC and the WTO to develop cooperative and differentiated IPR arrangements designed to promote LCT transfer, following the example set by the health sector for HIV-AIDS medicines. Cooperative IPR arrangements such as cross-licensing, patent pooling, technology-standards agreements, and other forms of technology sharing could have the greatest positive impact in the poorest countries with the least access to finance.

Finally, resources from the Green Climate Fund could be used to meet the full cost of acquiring the IPRs to LCT, which should be provided to developing countries at no cost. This recommendation was initially put forward by the working group on the Durban Platform for Enhanced Action in 2015.[12] However, due to a lack of consensus among participant nations, the final version of the Paris Agreement did not include this provision. Instead, the agreement relies on technology networks and alliances to promote the diffusion and dissemination of green technologies. Given the critical importance of accelerating LCT transfer to developing countries, the Green Climate Fund could leverage its unique network, institutional capacities, and financial resources to acquire ownership and dissemination rights to patent-protected LCTs and make them available to the poorest countries. Technology donations, aided by voluntary patent-pool agreements, could minimize the cost of this approach.

CONCLUSIONS

Achieving the Paris Agreement goals presents an immense challenge, reflecting both the global dependence on fossil fuels and the tremendous barriers to the deployment of LCT in developing countries. The five chapters of this report document the limited but encouraging progress achieved in LCT transfer, highlight key obstacles to LCT deployment and innovation, and present practical recommendations. The overarching conclusions of the analysis can be summarized as follows:

- National strategies for low-carbon development should be strategic, comprehensive, and bold. Key elements of a successful national strategy would include: (i) phasing out subsidies for fossil fuels and implementing an economy-wide price on carbon; (ii) building the technological capabilities necessary to adopt, imitate, and ultimately create LCT; (iii) strengthening regulatory frameworks to boost investor confidence in the political commitment to low-carbon growth; (iv) adopting demand-pull policies such as feed-in tariffs, fiscal incentives, public outreach campaigns, and policies to strengthen LCT-intensive public procurement, investment, and financing; and (iv) implementing technology-push measures to support LCT innovation, production, and exports, particularly in countries with adequate capabilities.
- The international climate architecture should be strengthened to favor the least-developed countries. Effectively strengthening the climate architecture would require: (i) balancing appropriate IPR protections with the necessity to facilitate cost-efficient LCT transfer; (ii) supporting the creation of patent pools, as well as other cooperative IPR agreements; and (iii) advocating for the introduction of environmental provisions into multilateral trade and investment initiatives designed to accelerate LCT transfer.

NOTES

1. "Global warming" refers to the long-term warming of the planet. "Climate change" includes global warming and broader related changes such as sea-level rise, glacial decline, ice melt, and shifts in agricultural conditions.

2. LCTs include renewable wind energy (offshore and onshore), solar energy (on- and off-grid solar photovoltaic and solar thermal), energy-efficiency technologies used in buildings, industrial processes, vehicles, heating and cooling, lighting, and appliances. This report deals exclusively with LCTs related to climate-change mitigation. The Intergovernmental Panel of Climate Change defines low-carbon development as "policies and strategies that mitigate GHGs while achieving, at the same time, social and economic development goals" (Metz et al. 2000).

3. In this report, "North" refers broadly to high-income countries as defined by the World Bank, while "South" refers to all other countries.

4. The report (refer to chapter 5) uses a multivariate regression analysis (controlling for country and year fixed effects) for identifying the factors that are critical for moving LCT trade up the technology staircase.

5. UNCTAD (2010) defines "low-carbon foreign investment" as the transfer of technologies, practices, or products by multinational firms to host countries—through equity and nonequity forms of participation—such that the firms' operations, products, and services generate significantly lower GHG emissions than would prevail in the industry under business-as-usual circumstances.

6. The report uses FDI data on investments in renewable energy recorded in the *Financial Times' fDi Markets* database, one of the few databases to specifically classify investments in the renewable energy sector.

7. Patent counts are a common metric for innovation, and technology transfer can be measured by counting the number of patents an inventor from one country files in a different country. This report uses patent counts and patent-transfer data from the PATSTAT database maintained by the European Patent Office (EPO) to analyze LCT innovation and transfer.

8. As measured by patent data. See: Medvedev 2019.

9. Refer to chapter 3.

10. Poor countries with low scientific infrastructure and widening education and skills gaps are said to be in a "technology trap," implying that they continue to operate in the lowest technology ladder, far off the global technology frontier (Fofack 2008).

11. To ensure that foreign firms receive fair and equitable treatment in the countries in which they are investing.

12. "[F]unds from the Green Climate Fund will be utilized to meet the full costs of IPRs of environmentally sound technologies and know-how and such technologies will be provided to developing country Parties free of cost in order to enhance their actions to address climate change and its adverse impacts." (Quoted in Rimmer 2019).

REFERENCES

Berger, A, C Brandi, J. F. Morin, and J. Schwab, 2020. "The Trade Effects of Environmental Provisions in Preferential Trade Agreements. In *International Trade, Investment, and the Sustainable Development Goals*, edited by C. Beverelli, J. Kurtz, and D. Raess. Cambridge: Cambridge University Press.

Cirera, X., and W. Maloney. 2017. *The Innovation Paradox: Developing-Country Capabilities and the Unrealized Promise of Technological Catch-Up.* Washington, DC: World Bank.

Comin, D., and M. Mestieri. 2018. "If Technology Has Arrived Everywhere, Why Has Income Diverged?" *American Economic Journal: Macroeconomics* 10 (3): 137–78.

de Melo, J., and J.-M. Solleder. 2018. "Barriers to Trade in Environmental Goods: How Important They Are and What Should Developing Countries Expect from Their Removal." FERDI Working Paper P235, Fondation pour les Études et Recherches sur le Développement International. https://ferdi.fr/en/publications/barriers-to-trade-in-environmental-goods -how-important-they-are-and-what-should-developing-countries-expect-from-their -removal-3454990a-0916-4a0e-abfc-c3736653a799.

Fofack, H. 2008. *Technology Trap and Poverty Trap in Sub-Saharan Africa*. Policy Research Working Paper 4582. Washington, DC: World Bank. http://documents.worldbank.org /curated/en/169021468198874707/Technology-trap-and-poverty-trap-in-Sub-Saharan -Africa.

Gillingham, K., and J. H. Stock. 2018. "The Cost of Reducing Greenhouse Gas Emissions." *Journal of Economic Perspectives* 32 (4): 53–72.

IEA (International Energy Agency). 2019. "Global Energy and CO$_2$ Status Report 2018." IEA, Paris.

Iliev, I., and K. Neuhoff. 2009. "Intellectual Property: Cross-Licensing, Patent Pools and Cooperative Standards as a Channel for Climate Change Technology Cooperation." International Support for Domestic Action, Climate Strategies, London.

Lema, R., and A. Lema. 2012. "Technology Transfer? The Rise of China and India in Green Technology Sectors." *Innovation and Development* 2 (1): 23–44.

Mahlstein, K., and C. McDaniel. 2017. "The Environmental Goods Agreement: How Would US Households Fare?" International Centre for Trade and Sustainable Development, Geneva.

Maskus, K. 2010. "Differentiated Intellectual Property Regimes for Environmental and Climate Technologies," OECD Environment Working Papers 17, OECD Publishing, Paris.

Medvedev, D. 2019. China: Innovation and the New Technology Revolution." Background paper, *Innovative China: New Drivers of Growth*, World Bank, Washington, DC.

Metz, B., O. R. Davidson, J.-W. Martens, S. N. M. van Rooijen, and L. V. W. McGrory, eds. 2000. *Methodological and Technological Issues in Technology Transfer*. A Special Report of IPCC Working Group III. Cambridge: Cambridge University Press for the Intergovernmental Panel on Climate Change.

Monteiro, J. A., and J. P. Trachman. Forthcoming. "Environment-Related Provisions in Preferential Trade Agreements." In *Handbook of Deep Integration Agreements*, edited by A. Mattoo, N. Rocha, and M. Ruta. Washington, DC: World Bank.

REN21 (Renewable Energy Policy Network for the 21st Century). 2018. "Renewables 2018 Global Status Report." REN21, Paris.

Rimmer, M. 2019. "Beyond the Paris Agreement: Intellectual Property, Innovation Policy, and Climate Justice." *Open Access Journal* 8 (1): 1–24.

Sampath, P. G., and P. Roffe. 2012. "Unpacking the International Technology Transfer Debate: Fifty Years and Beyond." ICTSD Working Paper, International Centre for Trade and Sustainable Development, Geneva.

UNCTAD (United Nations Conference on Trade and Development). 2010. *World Investment Report 2010: Investing in a Low-Carbon Economy*. New York and Geneva: United Nations.

UNEP (United Nations Environment Programme). 2017. *The Emissions Gap Report 2017: A UN Environment Synthesis Report*. Nairobi: UNEP.

Yang, Z., P. Slowik, N. Lutsey, and S. Searle. 2016. "Principles for Effective Electric Vehicle Incentive Design." Working Paper, International Council on Clean Transportation, Washington, DC.

Abbreviations

CCS	carbon capture and storage
CDM	Clean Development Mechanism
CO_2	carbon dioxide
CTCN	Climate Technology Centre and Network
EPO	European Patent Office
EV	electric vehicle
FDI	foreign direct investment
GCF	Green Climate Fund
GHG	greenhouse gas
$GtCO_2e$	gigatons of CO_2 emissions
HS	Harmonized Commodity Description and Coding System
IP	intellectual property
IPR	intellectual property rights
LCT	low-carbon technology
LED	light-emitting diode
PV	photovoltaic
R&D	research and development
RE	renewable energy
UNFCCC	United Nations Framework Convention on Climate Change
WTO	World Trade Organization

1 A Framework for Low-Carbon Technology Transfer

INTRODUCTION

Accelerating the development and transfer of low-carbon technologies (LCTs) has been at the core of international climate change negotiations since the 1992 United Nations Framework Convention on Climate Change (UNFCCC). This chapter provides a conceptual framework for understanding the development and diffusion of LCTs, with a focus on the growing importance of technology transfer in the South.[1] The chapter starts by putting the dynamic process of technological change in historical perspective, highlighting how the diffusion of technologies has occurred over many centuries and is now entering a new critical phase of low-carbon transformation. After placing the challenge of low-carbon technological innovation and diffusion in the context of energy transitions, the chapter discusses the distinctive features of LCTs, relative to their carbon-intensive alternatives. Next, it describes the legal basis of LCT under the UNFCCC, and it reviews key findings from the academic literature on the avenues and determinants of LCT transfer and on sources of finance. Finally, the last section provides suggestions on how policy makers can help accelerate the next critical phase of LCT innovation, transfer, and development.

TECHNOLOGICAL INNOVATION AND DIFFUSION IN HISTORICAL CONTEXT

From our earliest ancestors over 3 million years ago to the ongoing journey of *Homo sapiens* that began more than 200,000 years ago, each successive epoch was sustained by core technologies that formed the basis of human and economic development (Basalla 1988). From the early Stone Age to our modern Silicon Age, individual technologies have developed historically through three broad, interactive stages: *invention, innovation,* and *diffusion* (Schumpeter [1934] 2017, 1939). Certain technologies were concocted to meet human needs, whereas others emerged from sheer novelty and gave rise to new uses and desires. Resembling biological processes such as horizontal gene transfer, technological change has always been a cumulative, evolutionary process involving selection, swapping, recombination, and incremental variation (Arthur 2009). Each segment in the chain of technological development—from invention to pilot demonstrations, diffusion, replication, and further improvement—follows a nonlinear, recursive process, whereby each part of the chain interacts endogenously with the other parts (Grubb 2014; Usher [1929] 1954).

Many modern-day technological innovations were made possible by basic technical advances that originated decades or centuries earlier and in many corners of the world, highlighting the collaborative basis of technological change. To take just one example, the remarkable ubiquity of cell phones today would have been impossible without James Clark Maxwell's original discovery of the phenomenon of electromagnetic radiation, through his theory unifying electricity, magnetism, and light in the 1860s. Subsequently, Heinrich Hertz was the first to actualize Maxwell's theoretical discovery by generating, sending, and receiving electromagnetic waves in the late 1880s. That work led to the first radio broadcasts by Oliver J. Lodge and Alexander S. Popov in 1894 and 1995, the first transatlantic transmission of radio signals by Guglielmo Marconi in 1901, the first radio broadcast of music by Reginald A. Fessenden in 1906, and the first vacuum tubes around the same time. The following decades spawned the invention of transistors, integrated circuits, and microprocessors (Smil 2017a, 2017b). Indeed, a decades-long, collaborative chain of cumulative innovation connects the intervening years between Maxwell's discovery and the modern-day microprocessors in products produced by companies such as Apple, Nokia, and Samsung.

The diffusion of technologies has occurred gradually over many centuries, well before the term "technology transfer" entered the parlance of international institutions after the Second World War. Nearly all of our knowledge of the nature of technological change during the preindustrial era is anecdotal, based on archeological evidence and historical interpretation. From the first known use of stone tools approximately 3.3 million years ago by our hominin ancestors in Kenya, to the first known metallurgical advances in copper and iron smelting about 7,000 years ago, our knowledge of early mechanisms of technological dissemination is inherently limited, speculative, and subject to data limitations (Harmand et al. 2015; Schmidt and Avery 1978; Van Noten and Raymaekers 1988).

The Industrial Revolution, which began in Britain in the mid-18th century, marked a profound structural break. The scale of its transformations and the exponential rate of its technological improvements are rivaled perhaps only by the Neolithic Revolution during the Holocene 12,000 years ago, when humankind first developed organized agriculture. The modern industrial era transferred most of the toil and travails of human labor to machines, ushering in multiple, interconnected innovations—such as steam engines and turbines, internal combustion engines, metallurgical advances, Portland cement manufacture, deep oil well drilling, gas turbines, electricity-generating plants, air conditioning, plastics and polymerization, and ammonia synthesis—that spread internationally by railway and steamship (Mumford [1934] 2010; Rosenberg 1982).

Technological differences across countries and firms are some of the key drivers of divergences in total factor productivity, per capita income, and long-run economic growth (Romer 1990; Schumpeter [1934] 2017, 1939; Solow 1956).

During the 19th century, technology transfer from Great Britain and other originating countries became a crucial driver of economic development in continental Europe and the United States (Jeremy 1981; Landes 1969; Rosenberg 1963, 1982). Over the past two centuries, cross-national differences in the adoption rate of new technologies may have accounted for as much as 75 percent of the divergence in per capita incomes between developed and developing economies (Comin and Mestieri 2018). To this day, the ability of developing countries to acquire, configure, and further improve core technologies, and to foster related technical skills and learning among their workforces, remains a key determinant of highly uneven levels of economic development (Bell and Pavitt 1997; De Long and Summers 1991).

Despite the ample developmental gains that accrue from strategic investment in innovation capacities (firm and productivity growth, economic diversification, and so on), many developing countries continue to chronically underinvest in core technologies, research and development (R&D), equipment, skills training, and intellectual property (IP) acquisition (Cirera and Maloney 2017). In some cases, that underinvestment is attributable to weak legal protections of IP, which limit the ability of firms to appropriate the returns from innovation. In other cases, underinvestment may be attributable to organized resistance to technological change, macrofiscal imbalances, risk-averse investors, or short-termism (Mokyr 1994, 2000; Parente and Prescott 1994). Greater investment in strategic public and private R&D, human capital, and complementary infrastructure will be central to moving beyond mere adoption of technologies and acquiring capabilities for further endogenous innovation. Economic history suggests that the process of rising up the technological ladder is often multidecadal and nonlinear, involving collaboration between the executive, the legislature, civil service, universities, and firms to develop regulatory frameworks and long-term industrial strategies capable of activating national innovation systems. Such industrial strategizing was, in different ways, at the heart of the early histories of industrialization in Germany, the United Kingdom, and the United States, and more recently with the "East Asian Miracle" in China, the Republic of Korea, and Japan.

Technology-driven industrialization has transformed the world's wealth—coinciding with a doubling of average and maximum life expectancy globally since the mid-19th century—but at the cost of accelerating climate change and ecological devastation (Oeppen and Vaupel 2002; Riley 2005). As gross world product per capita has increased by an average of 2–3 percent annually since the mid-19th century, so too have global greenhouse gas emissions (Boden, Marland, and Andres 2017; Inklaar et al. 2018; Le Quéré et al. 2018). Left unabated, the sheer scale of global cumulative greenhouse gas emissions will drive accelerating warming that threatens "health, livelihoods, food security, water supply, human security, and economic growth," with the mounting risk that coastal cities could, this century, be inundated by rising sea levels triggered by melting Greenland and Antarctic ice sheets (IPCC 2018). Beyond climate change, human economic activities including intensive agriculture, excessive nitrogen fertilizer use, destruction of tropical forests for food and livestock production, and overfishing are profoundly "reshaping life on Earth," with 1 million species at the brink of extinction (Tollefson 2019).

Meanwhile, per capita energy consumption still varies by more than two orders of magnitude cross-nationally. Low-income countries do not benefit equally from global fossil fuel use, but they are most exposed to the harms of accelerating climate change, which has already increased cross-national inequalities in gross domestic product per capita by about 25 percent compared to a world without global warming (Diffenbaugh and Burke 2019). Despite contributing the least to global cumulative emissions historically, the least developed countries are also the most vulnerable to the extreme weather events, food insecurity, displacement, economic and infrastructure damage, and habitat loss that unmitigated climate change will exacerbate.

THE DIFFUSION OF LCT AS PART OF A LONG HISTORY OF ENERGY TRANSITIONS

Energy transitions at the global scale have throughout history been prolonged, with individual technologies typically requiring a minimum of 50–70 years to move from invention to large-scale adoption and diffusion (Grubler and Wilson 2014; Smil 2010). For certain energy technologies, the innovation stage alone has often extended over a century and the diffusion stage has typically lasted more than 50 years (Fouquet 2010). The definition of "transition" depends critically on one's choice of measure and definition of a threshold, and no single measure adequately captures all the multidimensional processes. Using a typical point of comparison—the point at which the technology's share of total global energy supply crosses the 25 percent threshold—several examples suffice to illustrate the protracted nature of global diffusion. Coal surpassed the 25 percent mark in 1871, more than 500 years after the first commercial coal mines were developed in England. Crude oil surpassed the same mark in 1953, about nine decades after Edwin Drake drilled the first commercial well in Titusville, Pennsylvania, in 1859. Hydroelectricity, natural gas, nuclear power, and other sources such as wind turbines and solar panels have yet to surpass the 25 percent threshold (Sovacool 2016). It is possible, however, that the current transition to a decarbonized global energy system will deliver a far more diversified set of primary energy sources and technologies than has existed in the past, implying that the 25 percent threshold may be less appropriate this century. The most critical factor may instead be the scale and speed at which fossil fuels and related carbon-intensive technologies are phased out rather than the predominance of individual technologies that are to replace them.

In contrast to the gradual pace of historical energy transitions at the global scale, numerous examples of energy transitions have occurred much faster—in under several decades. It is possible for well-designed policies and investments to greatly accelerate deployment of new technologies. Such examples include, among others, the rapid adoption of nuclear power in France and the spread of combined heat and power plants in Denmark from the late 1970s to early 1980s, which were state-led initiatives motivated largely by the oil price shocks and the burgeoning international environmental movement. Other examples include the adoption of air conditioning units in the United States from the late 1940s to 1970—driven simultaneously by urban sprawl, growth in the construction of new homes, marketing of and growing demand for cooling appliances, and innovations in air circulation and heat pumps—and the use of improved cookstoves in China during the 1980s and 1990s, driven by an intensive national program that prioritized indigenous innovation and deployment across hundreds of rural provinces, reduced energy use per capita in rural areas by more than 5 percent annually, and affected half a billion people (Sovacool 2016).

Two historical examples of nonlinear, cross-national technological development—wind turbines and steel manufacture—help to put low-carbon technological "leapfrogging" in historical perspective. The origins of the modern wind turbine hearken back to the first recorded use of the horizontal windmill for irrigating gardens in what are now Afghanistan and the Islamic Republic of Iran (circa 800 CE), although related concepts can be traced further back to Heron of Alexandria (circa 62 CE) and waterwheels used during the prior millennium (Lewis 1993). The windmill concept eventually spread to Europe circa 1100, likely through traders in the Byzantine Empire, whereupon technical efficiency improvements led to vertical windmills and tower mills (Hills 1994; Lewis 1993; Sørensen 1995). Nearly a millennium later, public policies pioneered in Denmark, Germany, and the U.S. state of California, followed by mass production and economies of scale in China, have propelled further wind turbine design improvements and market expansion. In the past two decades alone, cumulative installed wind energy capacity has seen a 25-fold global increase and wind energy patents a 60-fold increase (IRENA 2018). The mean levelized cost of (unsubsidized) wind energy has declined 69 percent to US$42 per megawatt-hour over the past decade, with cost considerations driving wind energy penetration in markets as diverse as Brazil; Taiwan, China; Mexico; South Africa; the United Kingdom; and the U.S. state of Texas (Lazard 2018). The next phase of wind energy development will depend critically on further innovation: improving wind capacity factors, reducing the costs of high-capacity storage solutions, and deploying high-voltage, direct-current transmission lines across long distances (Davis et al. 2018; Huenteler et al. 2018).

The preindustrial origins of iron and steel production provide another instructive example of technology transfer. Iron smelting emerged as far back as the third millennium BCE in Southwest Asia, with the practice appearing to have diffused to Southeast Asia and China, Africa, and eventually Europe (Schmidt and Avery 1978; Van Noten and Raymaekers 1988). From this remote past, modern steelmaking eventually emerged during the Industrial Revolution thanks to several pioneering developments: the replacement of charcoal with coke as fuel in blast furnaces in the 18th century, the invention of the hot blast in Scotland in 1828, Bessemer's steel converter in England in 1856, the Siemens-Martin open-hearth process and electric arc furnaces developed in Germany and France in the late 19th century, and the basic oxygen furnace and continuous casting in the mid-20th century (Hyde 1977; Smil 2016). Today, iron and steel production directly account for approximately 5 percent of global carbon dioxide (CO_2) emissions and 33 percent of industrial emissions, with most production dominated by China, India, and Japan.

About 75 percent of the world's crude steel is produced using coal, iron ore, coke, and limestone to fuel relatively inefficient and CO_2-intensive basic oxygen furnaces. Meanwhile, global steel demand is projected to grow by more than 3 percent per year over the next decade. The next phase of low-carbon steel production will require major innovation and technology transfer, via either hydrogen-based iron smelting in electric arc furnaces or possibly carbon capture and storage technologies. In the absence of those technologies, reducing the sector's emissions will require substituting steel with a new generation of low-carbon materials (Arens et al. 2017; Hanley, Deane, and Gallachóir 2018; Karakaya, Nuur, and Assbring 2018).

Technological diffusion is itself a major driver of further innovation, improved performance, and reduced costs. Many technologies have improved largely in accordance with Wright's law (often described as a "learning curve" or "experience curve"), which postulates that unit costs decline as cumulative output increases (Wright 1936). The negative relationship between cumulative production and unit costs is "one of the best-documented empirical regularities in economics" (Thompson 2012). It is most commonly explained by the idea that technology performance improves as firms learn through accumulated experience, or "learning by doing" (Arrow 1962). The unit costs of solar photovoltaic (PV), for example, have dropped by an average of 10 percent annually since 1990 (Farmer et al. 2019). The remarkable rates of cost reduction were initiated largely by "demand-pull" policies particularly in Germany, Spain, and Japan. These policies incentivized mass production and scale economies most prominently in China, which in turn led to further module efficiency improvements (Kavlak, McNerney, and Trancik 2018).

The costs of individual technologies have, however, improved at vastly different rates. Variation in improvement rates is attributable not only to the volume of cumulative output but also to policy constraints (for example, the failure to price negative pollution externalities) and features intrinsic to particular technologies (Ferioli, Schoots, and van der Zwaan 2009). In contrast to the dramatic cost reductions in solar PV, the real costs of coal, oil, and gas have not come down much over more than a century; and the costs of nuclear power have increased since the 1970s and 1980s, partly because of safety and waste disposal concerns (Farmer and Lafond 2016). Meanwhile, costs for batteries and wind turbines have each improved at an average annual rate of 3.0 percent (Benson and Magee 2014).

Optimal investment in LCT can be understood as a function of the technology's initial conditions (cost competitiveness and accumulated experience), learning rates and uncertainty about future cost, risk aversion, the discount rate, and the level of demand (Way et al. 2019). A potential trade-off exists as well: although diversification of investment can reduce the risks associated with uncertainty about future cost trajectories, specialization can drive increasing returns that drive down unit costs. Strategic investments in quickly improving LCTs are more likely to be amplified by positive feedback (for example, social learning, network, and bandwagon effects), turning investment in further technological capacity into a self-reinforcing phenomenon (Arthur 1989).

Like the Earth's climate system, our sociopolitical, economic, and technological systems have critical thresholds, or "tipping points," beyond which rapid, nonlinear, and large-scale change is possible with strategically targeted interventions (Farmer et al. 2019). Such positive tipping points can be generated not only by investing in the fastest-improving LCTs but also by adopting a sufficiently high and rising economy-wide carbon price, investing in the decarbonization of buildings and transport infrastructure, phasing out carbon-intensive products or production processes that have viable low-carbon substitutes, and, more generally, adopting legally binding and ambitious national legislation to reduce emissions across sectors and change expectations about the future direction of the economy.

DISTINCTIVE FEATURES OF LCTs, RELATIVE TO CARBON-INTENSIVE TECHNOLOGIES

The sheer complexity of technological innovation and diffusion suggests the need for a simplifying framework. If the international transfer of LCTs is to be greatly accelerated within the next several decades, conceptual heuristics may help guide policy makers and governments, entrepreneurs and firms, and investors and financial institutions.

The theoretical literature on technological innovation and transfer is voluminous and has greatly expanded in recent decades. A recent survey identified 96 distinct theories of technological transitions, spanning 22 academic disciplines (Sovacool and Hess 2017). Some theoretical frameworks focus on very specific aspects of technological change (such as sociocultural responses to new technologies). Other frameworks aim to provide a critical, ethics-driven perspective (such as incorporating ideas of distributive justice and normative philosophy). Others, more applicable to the concerns of this report, aim to provide a holistic perspective spanning each stage of technological change—from innovation to diffusion. Much in this literature is applicable to frameworks for understanding LCT transfer, but it is not the purpose of this chapter to extensively review the full range of relevant studies.

Among theories that aim to describe the stages of technological change and to prescribe policies that may accelerate that process, there are two broad schools of thought: the literature on the "economics of innovation" and the more interdisciplinary literature on "innovation systems" (Grubb, McDowall, and Drummond 2017). The former approach is the orthodox perspective in neoclassical economics, and it tends to emphasize the roles of R&D, carbon pricing, market competition, patents, and licenses in promoting LCT transfer (Jaffe and Stavins 1995). From this perspective, the role of the state is primarily to correct market failures and negative externalities. The latter approach, focusing on innovation systems, draws upon further insights from both behavioral sciences and evolutionary economics, and it emphasizes the role of directed regulatory policies and policy sequencing at each stage of the development of a technology. From this perspective, the role of the state is to actively shape the rules of markets and encourage endogenous technological change, to define "mission-oriented" policy rather than merely to respond to market failures (Geels 2002; Grubb, McDowall, and Drummond 2017; Mazzucato 2015, 2016; Metcalfe 1995).

The value and importance of both approaches can be appreciated by first considering the distinctive features of LCTs, particularly from the perspective of governments and firms in developing countries. Table 1.1 describes the main features of LCTs: complexity of production inputs, multiplicity and heterogeneity, high up-front costs, relatively low levels of private R&D investment, competition with incumbent technologies and firms, dependence on basic infrastructure to grow at scale, dependence on natural capital, access to multilateral climate finance, incentives for sharing of IP, and dependence on both market and non-market policy support. Each of these LCT features has important implications for South–South and South–North technology transfer.

Countries with low absorptive capacity will not be able to access LCTs because many (but not all) of these technologies have higher-than-average complexity. For a given LCT, countries or firms will be more likely to develop and leverage a comparative advantage if they already possess the technical

TABLE 1.1 Distinctive features of LCTs

FEATURE	DESCRIPTION
Lower emissions intensity	LCTs are, by definition, less polluting than carbon-intensive technologies. To take the illustrative example of electricity production, life-cycle GHG emissions are highest for coal combustion (675–1,689 gCO_2e/kWh electricity), followed by oil (510–1,170 gCO_2e/kWh), natural gas (290–930 gCO_2e/kWh), biomass, geothermal, hydropower (70 gCO_2e/kWh), nuclear, solar PV (5–217 gCO_2e/kWh), concentrated solar power (7–89 gCO_2e/kWh), and wind energy (7–56 gCO_2e/kWh) (IPCC 2014).
Complexity	The complexity of LCTs is, on average, greater than energy-related technologies in general, when measured by the widely used Economic Complexity Index (Mealy and Teytelboym 2018).
Multiplicity and heterogeneity	LCTs are multifarious and highly heterogeneous, spanning all economic sectors. The total number ranges from about 50 to more than 250 technologies, depending on the definition used (OECD, WTO, and so on). LCTs also have different functions and purposes (such as mitigation, adaptation, and monitoring/measurement). Often governments have highly partial and imperfect information about available technologies, suppliers, and, moreover, their own technology needs. Heterogeneity also means that low-carbon development requires greater-than-usual coordination to exploit complementarities across products and sectors.
High up-front costs	Particularly in energy (but also somewhat in transport, buildings, and industry) sectors, LCTs have high up-front capital costs, low operating costs, and delayed return on investment. Investments therefore usually require longer investment horizons and patient capital. Without access to low-carbon policy support and long-term finance, investments may be biased toward conventional, high-carbon technologies that may have greater short-term return on investment (Jaffe and Stavins 1995).
Competition with powerful incumbent technologies and firms	Technological development is a highly autopoietic process, involving the maintenance and regeneration of the current stock of technologies. Given the high up-front costs and long-term character of the high-carbon capital stock, as well as the survival strategies of incumbent firms invested in maintaining the current capital stock, the diffusion of LCTs is subject to higher-than-usual inertia and competition with incumbents.
Dependence on new infrastructure to grow at scale and on other new technologies	Particularly in developing countries, LCTs may require new investment in infrastructure, from power grids and transmission lines to connect distributed renewable energy generators, to roads to support electric vehicle mobility.
Dependence on natural capital	Countries lacking sufficient wind, sun, or hydro resources are unlikely to see the uptake of renewable energy.
Access to multilateral project finance	LCTs, because they can help tackle both climate and SDG objectives, can leverage growing amounts of multilateral project finance, more so than many other technologies.
Larger knowledge spillovers	Knowledge spillovers from clean technologies are more important than spillovers from dirty technologies (Dechezleprêtre, Ménière, and Mohnen 2017).
Dependence on public policies for diffusion	For the above reasons, large-scale adoption depends on targeted public policies ranging from market-based to nonmarket measures. Such policies may attract greater low-carbon FDI and trade and spur greater private investment domestically.

Note: FDI = foreign direct investment; gCO_2e = grams of carbon dioxide equivalent; GHG = greenhouse gas; kWh = kilowatt-hour; LCT = low-carbon technology; OECD = Organisation for Economic Co-operation and Development; PV = photovoltaic; SDG = Sustainable Development Goal; WTO = World Trade Organization.

knowledge and experience in producing and using closely related technologies requiring similar capabilities (Mealy and Teytelboym 2018). Government and firms may be best advised, therefore, to initially invest in the capabilities that are needed to access "core" technologies. Acquisition of (and specialization in) advanced green technologies on the periphery of the core product space is more likely to occur later in a country's evolutionary process of technological development.

The multiplicity and heterogeneity of LCTs entail that firms and governments in developing economies require a strategic, long-term vision for low-carbon investment and development. LCTs are highly heterogeneous and, like the impacts of climate change, span multiple sectors (energy, industry, transport, buildings, and land use) and may be related to mitigation, adaptation, or environmental monitoring. Moreover, LCTs also have highly heterogeneous costs, rates of improvement, and value added to economic development. Depending on how broadly one defines the range of relevant LCTs, their number may range from about 50 to several hundred (see chapter 2). The primary reason for the considerable range is that a single "green" product can in many cases be used for both environmental and nonenvironmental purposes. For example, manometers—devices that measure pressure levels—can be used to track the efficiency of power plants, but they can also be used to measure blood pressure or in carbon-intensive construction applications. Other technologies, such as photosensitive semiconductor devices like solar PV cells and light-emitting diodes (LEDs), are more straightforwardly low-carbon because they unambiguously are used to reduce energy and carbon intensity. The multiplicity of potential end uses for many green technologies is relevant not only for making progress in eliminating tariffs on low-carbon products but also for understanding the dynamics of innovation and technology transfer.

A critical insight that has emerged from technology-driven assessments and related financing is the importance of scalability, which should inform decisions about which technology investments to prioritize. The multiplicity and diversity of LCT needs present exceptional challenges in relation to the acquisition of finance. Banks and impact investors seek high-impact, scalable projects most likely to produce large returns (whether economic, environmental, or both). The inherently fragmented and compartmentalized nature of many disparate LCTs across sectors, however, often yields limited returns to scale if cross-sectoral complementarities are not simultaneously harnessed. Investments in concentrated solar thermal energy, for example, require complementary investment in grid infrastructure and connections, transmission, and storage to reach full scale. It appears that, for this reason, the accelerated transfer of LCTs may require a more holistic approach, involving coordinated, strategic investments across complementary sectors in each country.

Many technologies that reduce energy intensity or carbon intensity are capital-intensive and long-lived—including, among others, solar PV or concentrated solar power, wind turbines, fuel cells, heat pumps, electric rail, and efficient electricity transmission. Thus, they face political uncertainty regarding future carbon pricing and fossil fuel subsidies. Generally speaking, LCTs require longer investment horizons, less discounting of future benefits, and a more holistic cost–benefit approach accounting for future energy savings, health-related benefits, increased resilience, and avoided ecological damages. These requirements, however, may be less relevant for certain other technologies with significant cost savings—such as when a municipality invests in LEDs rather than incandescent bulbs for streetlights.

Technology costs do change, and at different rates. With the deployment of currently known technologies across multiple sectors, it is technically feasible to achieve net-zero emissions in all essential energy system processes and services (Davis et al. 2018). Significant cost barriers remain, however, and the extraordinary decline of costs in some LCTs has not been associated with comparable cost reductions in others. For example, average costs of solar PV modules worldwide have declined by more than two orders of magnitude since the 1970s—driven by government policy, increased module efficiency, and scale economies (Kavlak, McNerney, and Trancik 2018). In contrast, cost estimates for electrolysis, a promising technology that could store large amounts of surplus intermittent solar energy, have not reached levels compatible with mass deployment (Saba et al. 2018).

Competition with incumbent, high-carbon technologies and firms poses an obstacle to LCT innovation and diffusion cross-nationally, particularly in developing countries. For countries without a domestic fossil fuel industry and heavily reliant on coal, oil, or gas imports, the environmental and fiscal rationales for developing LCT capacities are especially compelling; and governments may face less political inertia during efforts to accelerate the low-carbon transition. In other countries with incumbent fossil fuel firms and an established high-carbon industry, political inertia delaying decarbonization will be greater; governments may pursue "supply-push" policies supporting the development of LCTs as well as "demand-pull" policies supporting the creation of markets with high demand for those technologies. Given the problems of inertia and high-carbon "lock-in" (Seto et al. 2016), it will also be essential in these countries to use carbon pricing, remove fossil fuel subsidies, and establish clear and credible signals that the market for high-carbon energy will diminish over time.

THE LEGAL BASIS FOR LCT TRANSFER UNDER THE UNFCCC

The widespread recognition that unprecedented levels of international technology diffusion—this time of environmentally friendly technologies—must drive the next stage of human and economic development dates to the early 1970s, when concerns about persistent underdevelopment and environmental deterioration hit an inflection point. Around the same time that Leontief (1970) was pioneering the incorporation of environmental pollution externalities within input–output models of the world economy, the United Nations Conference on the Human Environment in 1972 adopted the (legally nonbinding) Stockholm Declaration, urging developed countries to commit far greater finance and resources to tackling chronic socioeconomic and technological underdevelopment internationally (United Nations General Assembly 1972, Principle 12 and Principle 20).

Twenty years after the Stockholm Declaration, the objective of transferring "environmentally sound technologies" to developing countries was formally established in 1992 with the adoption of the UNFCCC and Agenda 21 in Rio de Janeiro. In Agenda 21 (the nonbinding action plan for sustainable development adopted at the Rio Earth Summit), Chapter 34 defines environmentally sound technologies as those that "are less polluting, use all resources in a more sustainable manner, recycle more of their wastes and products, and handle residual wastes in a more acceptable manner than the technologies for which they were substitutes" (United Nations Department of Public Information 1993). The Agenda 21 definition is broad, spanning the gamut of "know-how, procedures, goods and services, and equipment as well as organizational and managerial procedures."

The adoption of the UNFCCC went further, in Article 4.1(c), to establish an explicit obligation for parties to the Convention to "promote and cooperate in the development, application and diffusion, including transfer, of technologies" (United Nations General Assembly 1992). The relevant technologies are defined as the "practices and processes that control, reduce or prevent anthropogenic emissions of greenhouse gases not controlled by the Montreal Protocol in all relevant sectors, including the energy, transport, industry, agriculture, forestry and waste management sectors." Article 4.1(c) places primary emphasis on mitigation technologies, but in recent years the scope of technology transfer discussions in the UNFCCC has expanded to encompass both mitigation and adaptation (Yamin and Depledge 2004). Article 4.5 emphasizes that the goal is not merely to deploy existing technologies from rich countries but also to "support the development and enhancement of endogenous capacities and technologies" of developing countries. The legal-financial basis for carrying out these objectives is described in Article 11, which establishes "a mechanism for the provision of financial resources on a grant or concessional basis, including for the transfer of technology."

The UNFCCC's legal provisions relating to technology transfer institutionalized the paradigm that developed countries would be the primary originators of climate technologies and developing countries the primary recipients (the North–South paradigm). The adoption of the Kyoto Protocol in 1997—including its establishment of the Clean Development Mechanism (CDM)—reinforced the North–South paradigm. Article 10(c) of the Kyoto Protocol recalls the necessity to "take all practicable steps to promote, facilitate and finance" the transfer of technology, particularly to developing countries. Recognizing developing countries' concerns about IP constraints, Article 10(c) notes that not all climate-related technologies are patent-protected and refers specifically to "environmentally sound technologies that are publicly owned or in the public domain." Recognizing the issues of public budgetary constraints and unfavorable regulatory environments in developing countries, Article 10(c) highlights the integral role that private sector investment must play in the international diffusion of technology, asking contracting parties to facilitate "the creation of an enabling environment for the private sector." Furthermore, Article 12 of the Kyoto Protocol established the CDM, under which developed, Annex I countries may accrue "certified emission reduction" credits by financing certified climate change mitigation projects in developing countries, enabling industrialized countries to meet part of their emission abatement targets under the Protocol. International technology transfer was seen as an ancillary benefit of CDM projects, although it was never an explicitly mandated outcome.

The Intergovernmental Panel on Climate Change (IPCC) published its Special Report, *Methodological and Technological Issues in Technology Transfer*, in 2000 (Metz et al. 2000). In the report, the IPCC provided a broad and inclusive definition of technology transfer that has been widely adopted, explicitly or implicitly, by relevant bodies of the UNFCCC: technology transfer is "a broad set of processes covering the flows of know-how, experience and equipment for mitigating and adapting to climate change amongst different stakeholders such as governments, private sector entities, financial institutions, non-governmental organizations (NGOs) and research/education institutions." To maintain consistency with active UNFCCC initiatives, this report also adopts the IPCC's definition but discusses only technologies for mitigating climate change and defines them as "low-carbon technology." Importantly, this definition encompasses not only the physical components or "hardware" of technology—solar panels, wind turbines, lighting units, insulation materials, and so on—but also the "software" (technical know-how and capabilities) and "orgware" (institutional and policy frameworks). The practical implication is that technology transfer requires *system-wide, process-driven* thinking that takes into account the ability of technology providers and third-party organizations to identify impactful projects and suitable partners in host countries; the ability of host governments to create policy, regulatory, and legal frameworks that reduce risks and attract private and public investors; and the ability of host firms to understand, select, adapt, and replicate viable technologies that are suited to domestic circumstances and needs.

After the establishment of a legal and technical architecture for technology transfer under the UNFCCC, a succession of milestones has shaped subsequent efforts in the international arena: the adoption of a technology framework at the seventh session of the Conference of the Parties (COP7) in 2001, which established a project information clearinghouse as well as the Expert Group on Technology Transfer; the Poznan strategic program on technology transfer at COP14 in 2008; the creation of the Technology Mechanism at COP16 in 2010; and the continued recognition of technology transfer objectives in Article 10 of the Paris Agreement. Appendix A lists the various international legal provisions related to technology transfer, which establish the longstanding commitments of parties to the UNFCCC to facilitate and finance mitigation and adaptation-related technology diffusion in developing countries.

For nearly a decade, the UNFCCC has actively sought to synergize the independent activities of the Technology Mechanism and the Financial Mechanism, which together drive technology transfer efforts in the international arena. The Technology Mechanism consists of two branches: The Climate Technology Centre and Network (CTCN, the operational arm), and the Technology Executive Committee (TEC, the policy arm). The Financial Mechanism includes the Green Climate Fund (GCF), Global Environment Facility (GEF),[2] Special Climate Change Fund (SCCF), Least Developed Countries Fund (LDCF), and Adaptation Fund. In practice, integrating these arms and funds has involved translating developing countries' technology requirements into practical and bankable projects and linking the independent technical and financial mechanisms in operational and decision-making processes.

The expansive focus on the hardware, software, and orgware of technology transfer is enshrined in the mandates and activities of these key UN-level initiatives, described in figure 1.1. The two arms of the UNFCCC's Technology Mechanism are among the most important initiatives putting these concepts into practice. The CTCN, for example, has provided (or is currently developing) country-tailored practical solutions and financing for over 137 technology projects in response to individual country requests. CTCN's projects represent the formal execution of the UNFCCC's Technology Mechanism, whereas the TEC's policy-focused research, workshops, and knowledge dissemination represent its epistemic core.

The other two technology-related initiatives listed in figure 1.1—the GEF and the GCF—form part of the Financial Mechanism and belong to a broader set of multilateral climate funds including, among others, the Adaptation Fund, Clean Technology Fund, Forest Investment Program, Global Climate Change Alliance, LDCF, Partnership for Market Readiness, and SCCF. In aggregate, multilateral climate funds provided financing of US$1.9 billion from 2015 to 2016, or just over 3 percent of total public flows of climate finance worldwide

FIGURE 1.1

Timeline of key international developments in LCT transfer

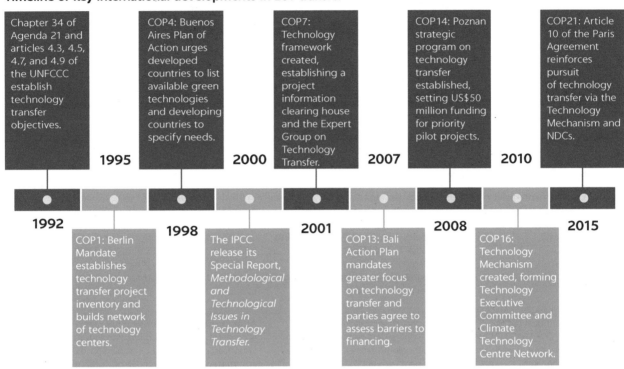

Note: COP = Conference of the Parties; IPCC = Intergovernmental Panel on Climate Change; LCT = low-carbon technology; NDC = Nationally Determined Contribution; UNFCCC = United Nations Framework Convention on Climate Change.

(UNFCCC 2018). The remaining US$56 billion in public climate-related finance came from bilateral government investment and multilateral development banks.

The main achievements of these technology transfer initiatives (described in the third column in table 1.2) provide several key takeaways: (i) the GCF has thus far provided funding commitments and emission reductions on the largest scale; (ii) the CTCN has in a short time pursued the largest number of mitigation and adaptation projects in developing countries facing a diverse set of challenges; and (iii) thus far, however, third-party evaluations of the economic and ecological benefits of these various projects are scant, which leaves some degree of uncertainty about which kinds of technology transfer projects have had the most success (in terms of scale, expertise employed, and terms of technology sharing).

The UNFCCC's track record on technology transfer over the past quarter century has sparked much debate. Early developments under the CDM, for example, were hampered by several issues, such as the additionality of CDM projects; the imbalanced concentration of most technology transfer projects in China and India (such as those under the CDM); the preference for CDM projects in China, involving higher profits from certified emission reductions (CER) for private actors, with far fewer projects transferring renewable energy technologies, delivering substantial CO_2 abatement, and leveraging longer-term benefits from R&D and innovation; a focus on transferring technology

TABLE 1.2 **Select LCT transfer initiatives and their key achievements**

INITIATIVE	MANDATE	ACHIEVEMENTS
Climate Technology Centre and Network (CTCN). Established at COP16 (2010) and formally launched at COP19 (2013), as the operational arm of the Technology Mechanism.	To promote the acceleration of LCT transfer at the request of developing countries. Provides country-tailored technology solutions, capacity building, and advice on policy, legal, and regulatory frameworks by harnessing the expertise of a global network of technology companies and institutions.	In 79 countries, 137 technology projects completed or underway, with US$40 million direct financing (US$670 million anticipated cofinancing). Projects expected to avoid 10.4 million tCO_2e emissions annually. Provided training to 2,500 individuals, with 85 million anticipated beneficiaries.
Technology Executive Committee (TEC). Established at COP16 (2010) as the policy arm of the Technology Mechanism.	To identify and recommend policies that can accelerate the development and transfer of low-carbon, climate-resilient technologies.	Research publications on broad spectrum of tech transfer topics; facilitating knowledge sharing at meetings, at workshops, and on social media.
Global Environment Facility (GEF). Established in 1991 and formally launched in 1992 at the Rio Earth Summit.	Broadly aimed at tackling environmental challenges, but LCT transfer is a cross-cutting theme. Finances pilot technology transfer projects for testing innovative financial mechanisms that are complementary to the work of the CTCN and four Regional Climate Technology Transfer and Financing Centers.	In 1991–2017, US$472.1 million financing to 67 mitigation projects with technology transfer elements (with US$3.2 billion in expected cofinancing); 24 adaption technology projects approved with US$165.9 million committed (US$572.5 million in cofinancing). Projects supported over latest three-year period (2014–17) expected to avoid or sequester 1.9 billion tCO_2e over their lifetimes.
Green Climate Fund (GCF). Established at COP16 (2010) as one of the operational arms of the Financial Mechanism.	To support developing countries in climate mitigation, capacity building, and technology transfer through the financing of projects.	As of October 2019, the GCF has raised the equivalent of US$10.3 billion in pledges from 48 countries, regions, and cities; US$5.1 billion committed financing for 111 projects (with anticipated avoidance of 1.5 billion tCO_2e emissions and enhanced climate resilience for 310 million individuals).

Note: COP = Conference of the Parties; LCT = low-carbon technology; tCO_2e = tons of carbon dioxide equivalent.

"hardware" and relative neglect of "software" and "orgware"; the undifferentiated treatment of highly heterogeneous circumstances and technology needs in developing countries; and unresolved methodological issues in measuring the volume and effectiveness of technology transfer outcomes (Lema and Lema 2013; Phillips, Das, and Newell 2013; Watson et al. 2015; Zhang, Sun, and Huang 2018; Zhang and Yan 2015). Nevertheless, one encouraging result from CDM projects is that most renewable energy diffusion has occurred in countries with the least developed domestic financial markets, enabling deployment in places that otherwise have the most restricted access to financing (Kim and Park 2018).

These concerns have been largely soothed in recent years with the streamlining of technology needs assessments, the mobilization of greater volumes of multilateral climate finance, and country-tailored initiatives under the Technology Mechanism. The ultimate verdict, however, remains to be determined. "While the issue of technology transfer has continued to receive much attention in the international climate policy domain," De Coninck and Sagar (2015) observe, "progress in enhancing our understanding of the various dimensions of technology transfer has been relatively limited." Noting the slow progress made since 1992, some observers have questioned whether the UNFCCC can ultimately deliver on its technology transfer commitments (Glachant and Dechezleprêtre 2016).

AVENUES AND DETERMINANTS OF LCT TRANSFER

LCTs may be transferred between countries and firms through several channels. Those channels include, among others, international trade, foreign direct investment (FDI), patents and licensing, the movement of people across countries, joint international research programs, cooperative agreements, and trade shows. Given the diversity of these channels and given that none of them alone provides unequivocal evidence of the full extent of technology transfer per se, measuring the quantity and quality of technology transfers necessarily involves multiple metrics. Each metric should be prioritized to varying degrees depending on the question, data availability, and data quality. Chapters 2 and 3 in this report undertake a deep analysis of the most important channels for transferring technology—international trade, FDI, and patents.

Previous scholars on technology transfer posit several key drivers of diffusion within countries and leapfrogging across countries: domestic absorptive capacity and technological capabilities (Cirera and Maloney 2017); human capital, skills, and relevant technical know-how (Nelson and Phelps 1966); the size of the market (Keller 2004); greater openness to trade (Keller 2004; Sachs and Warner 1995); geographical proximity to investors and financing (Comin, Dmitriev, and Rossi-Hansberg 2012); and stronger protection of intellectual property rights (IPR) (Dechezleprêtre, Glachant, and Ménière 2013; Dussaux, Dechezleprêtre, and Glachant 2018). Beyond the inverse of these factors, impediments to LCT transfer both within and across countries may include low levels of national income and a larger stock of existing high-carbon capital (refer to chapter 5).

Recognizing the trade-restrictive potential of certain investment measures and local requirements that discriminate against importers, the World Trade Organization (WTO) Agreement on Trade-Related Investment Measures (TRIMs Agreement) regulates trade in goods (but not services) and prohibits any measure inconsistent with the principle of national treatment (Article III of the General Agreement on Tariffs and Trade) and with the prohibition of quantitative import and export restrictions (Article XI). The TRIMs Agreement does not, however, formally cover the issue of international technology transfer via FDI and local content requirements, even though the latter are used frequently. Local content requirements necessarily imply discrimination between imported and domestic goods, and for this reason are inconsistent with the principle of national treatment enshrined in the TRIMs Agreement.

Various WTO agreements provide a legal foundation for balancing the interest in protecting IPR with the interest in enabling the uninhibited diffusion of technologies. IPR are protected and guaranteed under the Agreement on Trade-Related Aspects of Intellectual Property Rights (TRIPs Agreement). Article 7 of the TRIPs Agreement requires that the international regime of IPR protection "should contribute to the promotion of technological innovation and to the transfer and dissemination of technology, to the mutual advantage of producers and users of technological knowledge and in a manner conducive to social and economic welfare." As a counterbalance to Article 7, Article 8 has the purpose of safeguarding the international diffusion of technologies from the abuse of IPR protection in the formulation of national legislation; it safeguards the unimpeded diffusion of technologies against barriers arising from national policies that regulate different aspects of technology transactions, such as restrictive business practices in licensing agreements (Correa 2007). Moreover, Article 66.2 establishes the specific obligation for developed countries to encourage the transfer of technology to least developed countries that are WTO members. To guarantee the regular monitoring of and constant adherence to this provision, the Decision on Implementation of Article 66.2 was adopted by the TRIPs Council in February 2003, resulting in the creation of the WTO Working Group on Trade and Transfer of Technology, to which developed countries must submit detailed annual reports.

Do IPR protection and trade openness support technology transfer?

The question of whether strong IPR regimes and trade openness promote LCT diffusion (particularly in developing countries) remains a matter of contentious dispute. It is an essential area ripe for policy innovation and experimentation, with particularly promising ideas around patent pools and auctioning. Mansfield (1994) provides evidence that strict IPR regimes will have varying effects depending on the nature of the particular technology and industry, because technologies in some industries (such as metals and transportation) often require costly and complex complementary inputs and infrastructure that make it difficult for firms in less developed economies to exploit them. In contrast, other industries (such as chemicals and pharmaceuticals) tend to have products and supply chains that are more easily implementable, with companies more concerned about establishing strict IPR protection. To facilitate technology transfer and investment, firms in developing countries may have a vested interest in securing stronger IPR regimes as the domestic economy diversifies and climbs the technology ladder (Intarakumnerd and Charoenporn 2015).

Regarding the specific effect of IPR on LCT diffusion, the econometric literature finds some evidence of positive impacts. Using green patent data across 96 countries from 1995 to 2006, Dechezleprêtre, Glachant, and Ménière (2013) find that weaker IPR protection and lower openness to trade and FDI are associated with lower rates of LCT diffusion. Using data on trade and FDI between 140 countries from 2006 to 2015, Dussaux, Dechezleprêtre, and Glachant (2018) find that stricter IPR protections in countries outside the Organisation for Economic Co-operation and Development are associated with larger inward FDI by firms producing LCTs but have no significant effect on the imports of low-carbon capital goods. In chapter 3, this report returns to this question and contributes further evidence with a longer time frame and larger set of countries. The chapter concludes that IPR protection has no significant effect on LCT transfer from either high-income or developing countries.

Climate finance for LCT

Climate finance continues to be one of the key issues on how the global community proposes to follow through with the implementation of the Paris Agreement, which aims at mobilizing US$100 billion a year by 2020 from developed countries to developing countries. But what matters is not just the quantity of finance but also the composition and mix of investor types and financing mechanisms because they all influence the direction of LCT innovation and transfer

(Mazzucato and Semieniuk 2018). Lack of knowledge about the risk–return profile of investment in low-emissions technologies remains a key barrier along the entire technology chain, from innovation to diffusion, commercialization, international transfer, and further innovation. This lack of knowledge could lead to a skewed distribution of investment, with some areas overfinanced and others underfinanced.

This chapter does not address the issue of climate finance for LCT in a comprehensive way: this issue is complex and would deserve an entire new study. The chapter does present some insights into the landscape of LCT financing, the sources of finance, and the financing actors that are most likely to fund the different stages of the LCT transfer and innovation cycle. Chapter 5 will provide some answers to the question of how to mobilize larger amounts of finance for LCT transfer and innovation.

Figure 1.2 shows the stages of a typical LCT cycle. The cycle starts in developed countries with innovation—funded by R&D—which is followed by pilots and demonstrations, domestic diffusion, and commercialization. The technology may then be transferred to developing countries; through adoption, diffusion, imitation, and collaborative innovation, these countries may reach the final stage of indigenous innovation. These different stages are associated with financing from different sources and financial actors.

Basic R&D typically requires public financing because of its characteristics of public good. Private markets tend to undersupply R&D because knowledge spillovers prevent firms from fully appropriating the returns to their investments. Moreover, innovation requires long lead times and is highly uncertain. Private investors tend to favor low-risk R&D investments, and private investment in individual high-risk technologies is often driven by just two or three financial actors. Consequently, governments are more likely to provide the capital-intensive, high-risk financing needed to achieve innovations in LCT. Integrating environmental policy targets in technology policy

FIGURE 1.2
Stages of LCT development and deployment

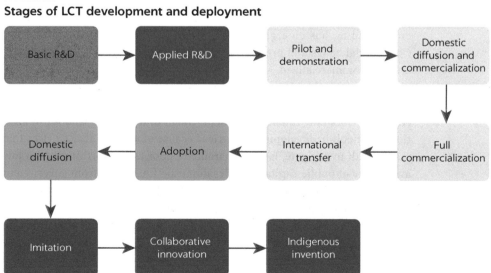

Note: LCT = low-carbon technology; R&D = research and development.

and research programs would help increase technological diversity and redirect funds into LCT research. Furthermore, public–private R&D partnerships could overcome competence lock-ins in fossil fuel–based technologies.

Applied R&D: Development and state banks, state corporations, and even institutional investors typically cover this stage, especially in cases involving large, expensive infrastructure projects. Governments and universities often provide proof-of-concept funds and demonstration support for small firms and start-ups, as do public and private incubators and accelerators.

Pilot and demonstration: Technologies at the pilot and demonstration stage face particular financing challenges that may lead to underinvestment and ultimately to the death of what could have been a promising innovation. Private financiers often refrain from financing these pilots unless public actors mitigate some of the risks. Testing and demonstration may necessitate some form of public support until these technologies can compete with more mature technologies. Missing physical infrastructure (such as power and transport) and scientific infrastructure (such as high-quality universities, research laboratories, and technical institutions dedicated to LCT) also represent significant barriers. Recently, energy crowdfunding platforms are being developed to address the financing gap for the LCT pilot demonstration phase. Policy makers can use fiscal incentives to support LCT in the adoption and diffusion stages, but the short-term nature of these incentives may discourage private investment (Polzin et al. 2015).

Domestic diffusion and commercialization: In this stage, private sector actors take the lead to foster diffusion of the technology, with banks, private equity investors, and internal funds providing financing. Business angels and venture capitalists often invest in start-ups and small innovative firms, whereas large or mature firms deploy internal funds for ongoing commercialization activities. Venture capital has played an important role in the uptake of LCT, especially the boom in solar power production in the late 2000s and 2010s; however, venture capital is often ill-suited to investments in clean energy projects or other forms of LCT deployment that involve long lead times, large sunk costs, or limited commercialization potential. Recently, crowdfunding has emerged as an alternative way to raise seed finance. Commercial banks and project financiers are important when technologies are fully commercialized.

From *international transfer* to *indigenous innovation:* Trade and direct investment have been the major conduits for global technology transfer for centuries. Obtaining financing for deployment of technology and for innovation is difficult in developing countries because of uncertainty and risks that are difficult to mitigate, lack of guarantees, poor creditworthiness, and low availability of public capital. Besides domestic financing—from government and public banks—the most significant public funding sources are development financial institutions (national, multilateral, and bilateral development banks) and international climate funds and aid agencies (often providing limited financing with a concessional or grant component). The CDM of the Kyoto treaty and climate funds under the Financial Mechanism of the UNFCCC have been important funding sources of climate change mitigation technologies. Blended climate finance has been successful in catalyzing private investment by providing funding at concessional terms that compensate for the higher cost of riskier technologies.

CONCLUSIONS

This chapter has presented several findings to guide the next phase of LCT transfer and innovation internationally. First, historical energy transitions at the global scale have often been gradual, protracted processes lasting a minimum of fifty years, but numerous examples of expeditious transitions at the national level provide valuable lessons. Second, the mounting threat of global climate change—as well as the diverse array of economic, social, and ecological benefits of moving toward net-zero emissions—highlight the urgency of accelerating LCT innovation and diffusion both within and across countries. Third, because the cost and performance of many LCTs are rapidly improving, countries that make strategic steps to enhance their absorptive capacity, technological capabilities, and regulatory and legal frameworks could generate positive "tipping points," turning technology-driven development into a self-reinforcing phenomenon (Arthur 1989). Finally, to realize these objectives, it is essential to fundamentally redirect substantial sums of domestic and international finance toward accelerated LCT and to greatly accelerate financing and technical assistance in the developing world.

The chapter has also discussed the international architecture for LCT transfer and innovation. Focused primarily on the North–South diffusion of technologies, the UNFCCC has not yet formulated any comprehensive international regulatory framework governing LCT transfer that addresses the particular challenges and opportunities of emerging South–South transfers. These transfers are likely to accelerate significantly even without a comprehensive international regulatory framework. It is with respect to the poor, least developed countries, however, that the UNFCCC has the greatest role to play in delivering results where markets alone have fallen short. For example, the Green Climate Fund could endeavor to leverage its unique network, institutional capacities, and financial wherewithal to acquire ownership and dissemination rights in patent-protected LCTs for expediting the technology transfer to poor countries through technology donations, aided by voluntary patent pool agreements. In practical terms, poor, least developed countries could lobby for cooperative and differentiated IPR arrangements within the UNFCCC and WTO by following the successful precedent set by the global health sector (see box 1.1).

Analogous international mechanisms could be based on the principle that the large-scale deployment of green technologies is a vital matter of economic security and planetary health. Differentiated legal treatment of patented technologies to promote the accelerated dissemination across poor, least developed countries would arguably have a strong legal basis within the WTO's current legal structures and, moreover, could revamp stalled negotiations around the WTO's Environmental Goods Agreement (refer to chapter 2). Moreover, it was, after all, the poorest countries with the least access to financial markets that attracted a disproportionate share of investment in renewable energy projects under the CDM, highlighting the potential for leveraging UNFCCC initiatives in poor countries (Kim and Park 2018). It was also the least developed, small island nations that lobbied successfully for the inclusion of commitments to pursue efforts to limit global warming to below 1.5°C under the Paris Agreement—a goal that was widely considered unattainable in prior years. Cooperative IPR arrangements such as cross-licensing, patent pooling, technology standards agreements, and other forms of technology sharing could have the greatest, outsized positive impact in the poorest countries with least access to finance.

BOX 1.1

Patents and medicines for all

In response to rising drug prices and patent-related international trade rules that had severely restricted access to life-saving drugs (for example, patented HIV/AIDS medications) in the 1990s, a global political mobilization successfully pressured the international community to deliver the World Trade Organization's Doha Declaration on the Agreement on Trade-Related Aspects of Intellectual Property Rights and Public Health in 2001. The Declaration affirmed that patent rules should be interpreted and implemented to protect public health and to promote access to medicines for all. This resulted in large-scale access to generic versions of patented medications by over 60 low-income and middle-income countries and a dramatic decline in prices (Hoen et al. 2011). Further progress has been made since 2010, when Unitaid established the Medicine Patent Pool (MPP), a mechanism for negotiating voluntary licenses that enable the transfer of high-quality, low-cost HIV, hepatitis C, and tuberculosis medicines in low-income countries. The MPP is expected to generate direct savings of about US$2.3 billion (in net present value) by 2028, with every dollar spent on the MPP generating US$43 in savings in the provision of global public health.

Source: Adapted from Hoen et al. 2011 and Juneja et al. 2017.

Finally, the critical task before policy makers and firms in the South is to attain a solid conceptual grounding that can guide cross-sectoral efforts in implementing a low-carbon development strategy. As will be discussed in chapter 5, a critical first step is to formulate and implement systemic policies such as carbon pricing and the removal of direct or indirect subsidies for polluting activities complemented by demand-pull and technology-push measures as well as adequate funding. In each sector or technological area, governments that successfully align policies covering each of these domains are far more likely to create productive synergies that deliver outsized impact (Grubb 2014). Policy makers and firms can endeavor to use the best available knowledge about the drivers of (and impediments to) LCT diffusion and pursue policy packages that increase the likelihood of garnering productivity spillovers and accelerating low-carbon growth.

NOTES

1. In this report "the gobal South" (or "the South") is broadly defined as all the countries not included in the World Bank definition of high-income countries.
2. Since its formation in 1992, the Global Environment Facility (GEF) has long-running operational experience with financing and facilitating pilot technology transfer projects through four regional initiatives: the Finance and Technology Transfer Centre for Climate Change (FINTECC), Special Climate Change Fund Program for Technology Transfer (SCCF-B), the African Climate Technology Centre (ACTC), the Climate Technology Transfer Mechanisms and Networks in Latin America and the Caribbean (IDB), and the Asia-Pacific Climate Technology Network and Finance Center (CTNFC).

REFERENCES

Arens, M., E. Worrell, W. Eichhammer, A. Hasanbeigi, and Q. Zhang. 2017. "Pathways to a Low-Carbon Iron and Steel Industry in the Medium-Term—The Case of Germany." *Journal of Cleaner Production* 163: 84–98.

Arrow, K. J. 1962. "The Economic Implications of Learning by Doing." *Review of Economic Studies* 29 (3): 155–73.

Arthur, W. B. 1989. "Competing Technologies, Increasing Returns, and Lock-In by Historical Events." *Economic Journal* 99 (394): 116–31.

———. 2009. *The Nature of Technology: What It Is and How It Evolves.* New York: Free Press.

Basalla, G. 1988. *The Evolution of Technology.* Cambridge: Cambridge University Press.

Bell, M., and K. Pavitt. 1997. "Technological Accumulation and Industrial Growth: Contrasts between Developed and Developing Countries." In *Technology, Globalization and Economic Performance,* edited by D. Archibugi and J. Michie, 83–137. Cambridge: Cambridge University Press.

Benson, C. L., and C. L. Magee. 2014. "On Improvement Rates for Renewable Energy Technologies: Solar PV, Wind Turbines, Capacitors, and Batteries." *Renewable Energy* 68: 745–51.

Boden, T. A., G. Marland, and R. J. Andres. 2017. "Global, Regional, and National Fossil-Fuel CO_2 Emissions." Carbon Dioxide Information Analysis Center, Oak Ridge National Laboratory, U.S. Department of Energy, Oak Ridge, TN.

Cirera, X., and W. Maloney. 2017. *The Innovation Paradox: Developing-Country Capabilities and the Unrealized Promise of Technological Catch-Up.* Washington, DC: World Bank.

Comin, D., M. Dimitriev, and E. Rossi-Hansberg. 2012. "Heavy Technology: The Process of Technological Diffusion over Time and Space." Vox, November 26. https://voxeu.org/article/heavy-technology-process-technological-diffusion-over-time-and-space.

Comin, D., and M. Mestieri. 2018. "If Technology Has Arrived Everywhere, Why Has Income Diverged?" *American Economic Journal: Macroeconomics* 10 (3): 137–78.

Correa, C. M. 2007. *Trade Related Aspects of Intellectual Property Rights: A Commentary on the TRIPS Agreement.* Oxford: Oxford University Press.

Davis, S. J., N. S. Lewis, M. Shaner, S. Aggarwal, D. Arent, I. L. Azevedo, S. M. Benson, T. Bradley, J. Brouwer, Y.-M. Chiang, C. T. M. Clack, A. Cohen, S. Doig, J. Edmonds, P. Fennell, C. B. Field, B. Hannegan, B.-M. Hodge, M. I. Hoffert, E. Ingersoll, P. Jaramillo, K. S. Lackner, K. J. Mach, M. Mastrandrea, J. Ogden, P. F. Peterson, D. L. Sanchez, D. Sperling, J. Stagner, J. E. Trancik, C.-J. Yang, and K. Caldeira. 2018. "Net-Zero Emissions Energy Systems." *Science* 360 (6396): eaas9793.

Dechezleprêtre, A., M. Glachant, and Y. Ménière. 2013. "What Drives the International Transfer of Climate Change Mitigation Technologies? Empirical Evidence from Patent Data." *Environmental and Resource Economics* 54 (2): 161–78.

Dechezleprêtre A., Y. Ménière, and M. Mohnen, 2017. "International Patent Families: From Application Strategies to Statistical Indicators." *Scientometrics* 111 (2): 793–828.

De Coninck, H., and A. Sagar. 2015. "Making Sense of Policy for Climate Technology Development and Transfer." *Climate Policy* 15 (1): 1–11.

De Long, J. B., and L. H. Summers. 1991. "Equipment Investment and Economic Growth." *Quarterly Journal of Economics* 106 (2): 445–502.

Diffenbaugh, N. S., and M. Burke. 2019. "Global Warming Has Increased Global Economic Inequality." *Proceedings of the National Academy of Sciences* 116 (20): 9808–13.

Dussaux, D., A. Dechezleprêtre, and M. Glachant. 2018. "Intellectual Property Rights Protection and the International Transfer of Low-Carbon Technologies." Working Paper 288, January, Grantham Research Center for Climate Change and the Environment.

Farmer, J. D., C. Hepburn, M. C. Ives, T. Hale, T. Wetzer, P. Mealy, R. Rafaty, S. Srivastav, and R. Way. 2019. "Sensitive Intervention Points in the Post-Carbon Transition." *Science* 364 (6436): 132–34.

Farmer, J. D., and F. Lafond. 2016. "How Predictable Is Technological Progress?" *Research Policy* 45 (3): 647–65.

Ferioli, F., K. Schoots, and B. C. C. van der Zwaan. 2009. "Use and Limitations of Learning Curves for Energy Technology Policy: A Component-Learning Hypothesis." *Energy Policy* 37 (7): 2525–35.

Fouquet, R. 2010. "The Slow Search for Solutions: Lessons from Historical Energy Transitions by Sector and Service." *Energy Policy* 38 (11): 6586–96.

Geels, F. W. 2002. "Technological Transitions as Evolutionary Reconfiguration Processes: A Multi-level Perspective and a Case-Study." *Research Policy* 31 (8–9): 1257–74.

Glachant, M., and A. Dechezleprêtre. 2016. "What Role for Climate Negotiations on Technology Transfer?" *Climate Policy* 17 (8): 962–81.

Grubb, M. 2014. *Planetary Economics: Energy, Climate Change and the Three Domains of Sustainable Development*. Oxon, U.K., and New York: Routledge.

Grubb, M., W. McDowall, and P. Drummond. 2017. "On Order and Complexity in Innovations Systems: Conceptual Frameworks for Policy Mixes in Sustainability Transitions." *Energy Research and Social Science* 33: 21–34.

Grubler, A., and C. Wilson, eds. 2014. *Energy Technology Innovation: Learning from Historical Successes and Failures*. New York and Laxenburg: Cambridge University Press and International Institute for Applied Systems Analysis.

Hanley, E. S., J. P. Deane, and B.Ó. Gallachóir. 2018. "The Role of Hydrogen in Low Carbon Energy Futures—A Review of Existing Perspectives." *Renewable and Sustainable Energy Reviews* 82 (Part 3): 3027–45.

Harmand, S., J. E. Lewis, C. S. Feibel, C. J. Lepre, S. Prat, A. Lenoble, X. Boës, R. L. Quinn, M. Brenet, A. Arroyo, N. Taylor, S. Clément, G. Daver, J.-P. Brugal, L. Leakey, R. A. Mortlock, J. D. Wright, S. Lokorodi, C. Kirwa, D. V. Kent, and H. Roche. 2015. "3.3-Million-Year-Old Stone Tools from Lomekwi 3, West Turkana, Kenya." *Nature* 521: 310–15.

Hills, R. L. 1994. *Power from Wind: A History of Windmill Technology*. Cambridge: Cambridge University Press.

Hoen, E. T., J. Berger, A. Calmy, and S. Moon. 2011. "Driving a Decade of Change: HIV/AIDS, Patents and Access to Medicines for All." *Journal of the International AIDS Society* 14 (1): 15.

Huenteler, J., T. Tang, G. Chan, and L. D. Anadon. 2018. "Why Is China's Wind Power Generation Not Living Up to Its Potential?" *Environmental Research Letters* 13 (4): 044001.

Hyde, C. K. 1977. *Technological Change and the British Iron Industry, 1700–1870*. Princeton, NJ: Princeton University Press.

Inklaar, R., H. de Jong, J. Bolt, and J. L. van Zanden. 2018. "Rebasing 'Maddison': New Income Comparisons and the Shape of Long-Run Economic Development." GGDC Research Memorandum GD-174, Groningen Growth and Development Centre, University of Groningen.

Intarakumnerd, P., and P. Charoenporn. 2015. "Impact of Stronger Patent Regimes on Technology Transfer: The Case Study of Thai Automotive Industry." *Research Policy* 44 (7): 1314–26.

IPCC (Intergovernmental Panel on Climate Change). 2014. *Climate Change 2014: Mitigation of Climate Change*. Contribution of Working Group III to the Fifth Assessment Report of the Intergovernmental Panel on Climate Change. Cambridge and New York: Cambridge University Press.

———. 2018. *Global Warming of 1.5°C*. Geneva: IPCC.

IRENA (International Renewable Energy Agency). 2018. *Renewable Capacity Statistics 2018*. Abu Dhabi, United Arab Emirates: IRENA.

Jaffe, A. B., and R. N. Stavins. 1995. "Dynamic Incentives of Environmental Regulations: The Effects of Alternative Policy Instruments on Technology Diffusion." *Journal of Environmental Economics and Management* 29 (3): S43–S63.

Jeremy, D. J. 1981. *Transatlantic Industrial Revolution: The Diffusion of Textile Technologies between Britain and America, 1790–1830s*. Cambridge, MA: MIT Press.

Juneja, S., A. Gupta, S. Moon, and S. Resch. 2017. "Projected Savings through Public Health Voluntary Licences of HIV Drugs Negotiated by the Medicines Patent Pool (MPP)." *PloS One* 12 (5): e0177770.

Karakaya, E., C. Nuur, and L. Assbring. 2018. "Potential Transitions in the Iron and Steel Industry in Sweden: Towards a Hydrogen-Based Future?" *Journal of Cleaner Production* 195: 651–63.

Kavlak, G., J. McNerney, and J. E. Trancik. 2018. "Evaluating the Causes of Cost Reduction in Photovoltaic Modules." *Energy Policy* 123: 700–10.

Keller, W. 2004. "International Technology Diffusion." *Journal of Economic Literature* 42 (3):752–82.

Kim, J., and K. Park. 2018. "Effect of the Clean Development Mechanism on the Deployment of Renewable Energy: Less Developed vs. Well-Developed Financial Markets." *Energy Economics* 75 (C): 1–13.

Landes, D. S. 1969. *The Unbound Prometheus: Technological Change and Industrial Development in Western Europe from 1750 to the Present*. Cambridge: Cambridge University Press.

Lazard. 2018. "Lazard's Levelized Cost of Energy Analysis—Version 12.0." Lazard, New York.

Lema, A., and R. Lema. 2013. "Technology Transfer in the Clean Development Mechanism: Insights from Wind Power." *Global Environmental Change* 23 (1): 301–13.

Leontief, W. 1970. "Environmental Repercussions and the Economic Structure: An Input–Output Approach." *The Review of Economics and Statistics* 52 (3): 262–71.

Le Quéré, C., R. M. Andrew, P. Friedlingstein, S. Sitch, J. Hauck, J. Pongratz, P. A. Pickers, J. I. Korsbakken, G. P. Peters, J. G. Canadell, A. Arneth, V. K. Arora, L. Barbero, A. Bastos, L. Bopp, F. Chevallier, L. P. Chini, P. Ciais, S. C. Doney, T. Gkritzalis, D. S. Goll, I. Harris, V. Haverd, F. M. Hoffman, M. Hoppema, R. A. Houghton, G. Hurtt, T. Ilyina, A. K. Jain, T. Johannessen, C. D. Jones, E. Kato, R. F. Keeling, K. Klein Goldewijk, P. Landschützer, N. Lefèvre, S. Lienert, Z. Liu, D. Lombardozzi, N. Metzl, D. R. Munro, J. E. M. S. Nabel, S. Nakaoka, C. Neill, A. Olsen, T. Ono, P. Patra, A. Peregon, W. Peters, P. Peylin, B. Pfeil, D. Pierrot, B. Poulter, G. Rehder, L. Resplandy, E. Robertson, M. Rocher, C. Rödenbeck, U. Schuster, J. Schwinger, R. Séférian, I. Skjelvan, T. Steinhoff, A. Sutton, P. P. Tans, H. Tian, B. Tilbrook, F. N. Tubiello, I. T. van der Laan-Luijkx, G. R. van der Werf, N. Viovy, A. P. Walker, A. J. Wiltshire, R. Wright, S. Zaehle, and B. Zheng. 2018. "Global Carbon Budget 2018." *Earth System Science Data* 10 (4): 2141–94.

Lewis, M. J. T. 1993. "The Greeks and the Early Windmill." In *History of Technology*, edited by G. Hollister-Short and F. A. J. L. James, 141–89. London: Bloomsbury Academic.

Mansfield, E. 1994. "Intellectual Property Protection, Foreign Direct Investment, and Technology Transfer." International Finance Corporation Discussion Paper 19, World Bank, Washington, DC.

Mazzucato, M. 2015. *The Entrepreneurial State: Debunking Public vs. Private Sector Myths*. New York: Public Affairs.

——. 2016. "From Market Fixing to Market-Creating: A New Framework for Innovation Policy." *Industry and Innovation* 23 (2): 140–56.

Mazzucato, M., and G. Semieniuk. 2018. "Financing Renewable Energy: Who Is Financing What and Why It Matters." *Technological Forecasting and Social Change* 127: 8–22. https://eprints .soas.ac.uk/24245/.

Mealy, P., and A. Teytelboym. 2018. "Economic Complexity and the Green Economy." INET Oxford Working Paper 2018-03, Institute for New Economic Thinking at the Oxford Martin School, University of Oxford, Oxford.

Metcalfe, J. S. 1995. "Technology Systems and Technology Policy in an Evolutionary Framework." *Cambridge Journal of Economics* 19 (1): 25–46.

Metz, B., O. R. Davidson, J.-W. Martens, S. N. M. van Rooijen, and L. V. W. McGrory, eds. 2000. *Methodological and Technological Issues in Technology Transfer*. A Special Report of IPCC Working Group III. Cambridge: Cambridge University Press for the Intergovernmental Panel on Climate Change.

Mokyr, J. 1994. "Cardwell's Law and the Political Economy of Technological Progress." *Research Policy* 23 (5): 561–74.

——. 2000. "Innovation and Its Enemies: The Economic and Political Roots of Technological Inertia." In *A Not-So-Dismal Science: A Broader View of Economics*, edited by M. Olson and S. Kähkönen, 61–91. Oxford: Oxford University Press.

Mumford, L. (1934) 2010. *Technics and Civilization*. Chicago: University of Chicago Press.

Nelson, R. R., and E. S. Phelps. 1966. "Investment in Humans, Technological Diffusion, and Economic Growth." *American Economic Review* 56 (1/2): 69–75.

Oeppen, J., and J. W. Vaupel. 2002. "Broken Limits to Life Expectancy." *Science* 296 (5570): 1029–31.

Parente, S. L., and E. C. Prescott. 1994. "Barriers to Technology Adoption and Development." *Journal of Political Economy* 102 (2): 298–321.

Phillips, J., K. Das, and P. Newell. 2013. "Governance and Technology Transfer in the Clean Development Mechanism in India." *Global Environmental Change* 23 (6): 1594–1604.

Polzin, F., M. Migendt, F. A. Täube, and P. von Flotow. 2015. "Public Policy Influence on Renewable Energy Investments—A Panel Data Study across OECD Countries." *Energy Policy* 80 (May): 98–111.

Riley, J. C. 2005. "Estimates of Regional and Global Life Expectancy, 1800–2001." *Population and Development Review 31* (3): 537–43.

Romer, P. M. 1990. "Endogenous Technological Change." *Journal of Political Economy* 98 (5, Part 2): S71–102.

Rosenberg, N. 1963. "Technological Change in the Machine Tool Industry, 1840–1910." *Journal of Economic History* 23 (4): 414–43.

——. 1982. *Inside the Black Box: Technology and Economics.* Cambridge: Cambridge University Press.

Saba, S. M., M. Müller, M. Robinius, and D. Stolten. 2018. "The Investment Costs of Electrolysis—A Comparison of Cost Studies from the Past 30 Years." *International Journal of Hydrogen Energy* 43 (3): 1209–23.

Sachs, J. D., and A. M. Warner. 1995. "Natural Resource Abundance and Economic Growth." NBER Working Paper 5398, National Bureau of Economic Research, Cambridge, MA.

Schmidt, P., and D. H. Avery. 1978. "Complex Iron Smelting and Prehistoric Culture in Tanzania." *Science* 201 (4361): 1085–89.

Schumpeter, J. A. (1934) 2017. *Theory of Economic Development.* Oxon, U.K.: Routledge.

——. 1939. *Business Cycles: A Theoretical, Historical, and Statistical Analysis of the Capitalist Process.* New York: McGraw-Hill.

Seto, K. C., S. J. Davis, R. B. Mitchell, E. C. Stokes, G. Unruh, and D. Ürge-Vorsatz. 2016. "Carbon Lock-In: Types, Causes, and Policy Implications." *Annual Review of Environment and Resources* 41: 425–52.

Smil, V. 2010. *Energy Transitions: History, Requirements, Prospects.* Santa Barbara, CA: Praeger.

——. 2016. *Still the Iron Age: Iron and Steel in the Modern World.* Oxford, U.K.: Butterworth-Heinemann.

——. 2017a. "Thank Maxwell for Cellphones." *IEEE Spectrum* 54 (3): 24.

——. 2017b. *Energy and Civilization: A History.* Cambridge, MA: MIT Press.

Solow, R. M. 1956. "A Contribution to the Theory of Economic Growth." *Quarterly Journal of Economics* 70 (1): 65–94.

Sørensen, B. 1995. "History of, and Recent Progress in, Wind-Energy Utilization." *Annual Review of Energy and the Environment* 20 (1): 387–424.

Sovacool, B. K. 2016. "How Long Will It Take? Conceptualizing the Temporal Dynamics of Energy Transitions." *Energy Research and Social Science* 13: 202–15.

Sovacool, B. K., and D. J. Hess. 2017. "Ordering Theories: Typologies and Conceptual Frameworks for Sociotechnical Change." *Social Studies of Science* 47 (5): 703–50.

Thompson, P. 2012. "The Relationship between Unit Cost and Cumulative Quantity and the Evidence for Organizational Learning-by-Doing." *Journal of Economic Perspective* 26 (3): 203–24.

Tollefson, J. 2019. "Humans Are Driving One Million Species to Extinction." *Nature*, May 6. https://www.nature.com/articles/d41586-019-01448-4.

UNFCCC (United Nations Framework Convention on Climate Change). 2018. "2018 Biennial Assessment and Overview of Climate Finance Flows: Technical Report." UNFCCC Standing Committee on Finance, Bonn.

United Nations Department of Public Information. 1993. "Agenda 21: Programme of Action for Sustainable Development; Rio Declaration on Environment and Development; Statement of Forest Principles." The Final Text of Agreements Negotiated by Governments at the United

Nations Conference on Environment and Development (UNCED), 3–14 June 1992, Rio de Janeiro, Brazil. United Nations Department of Public Information, New York.

United Nations General Assembly. 1972. "Declaration of the United Nations Conference on the Human Environment." U.N. Doc. A/Conf.48/14/Rev.1(1973); 11 ILM 1416 (1972), Stockholm.

———. 1992. "United Nations Framework Convention on Climate Change." New York: United Nations.

Usher, A. P. (1929) 1954. *A History of Mechanical Inventions*. Cambridge, MA: Harvard University Press.

Van Noten, F., and J. Raymaekers. 1988. "Early Iron Smelting in Central Africa." *Scientific American* 258 (6): 104–11.

Watson, J., R. Byrne, D. Ockwell, and M. Stua. 2015. "Lessons from China: Building Technological Capabilities for Low Carbon Technology Transfer and Development." *Climatic Change* 131 (3): 387–99.

Way, R., F. Lafond, F. Lillo, V. Panchenko, and J. D. Farmer. 2019. "Wright Meets Markowitz: How Standard Portfolio Theory Changes when Assets Are Technologies Following Experience Curves." *Journal of Economic Dynamics and Control* 101: 211–38.

Wright, T. P. 1936. "Factors Affecting the Cost of Airplanes." *Journal of the Aeronautical Sciences* 3 (4): 122–28.

Yamin, F., and J. Depledge. 2004. *The International Climate Change Regime: A Guide to Rules, Institutions and Procedures*. Cambridge: Cambridge University Press.

Zhang, C., and J. Yan. 2015. "CDM's Influence on Technology Transfers: A Study of the Implemented Clean Development Mechanism Projects in China." *Applied Energy* 158 (15): 355–65.

Zhang, Y.-J., Y.-F. Sun, and J. Huang. 2018. "Energy Efficiency, Carbon Emission Performance, and Technology Gaps: Evidence from CDM Project Investment." *Energy Policy* 115: 119–30.

2 Trade and Foreign Direct Investment as Channels of Low-Carbon Technology Transfer

INTRODUCTION

International trade and foreign direct investment (FDI) are two of the most important channels for the international diffusion and transfer of technology. Firms that engage in international trade tend to be larger, more productive, and more technologically advanced than firms operating solely in a domestic market (Claessens and Schmulker 2007; Helpman, Melitz, and Yeaple 2004; Keller and Yeaple 2009). Whereas trade offers the ability to quickly move technology embedded within physical products, FDI offers the potential to transfer physical products and the knowledge, skills, and processes to produce or operate them.

The extent to which trade and FDI do transfer technology and knowledge is difficult to disentangle. Commonly cited studies from the late 1990s and early 2000s find little evidence of significant knowledge and productivity spillovers from FDI and trade (Gorg and Greenaway 2004; Gorg and Strobl 2001; Meyer 2004). The explosive growth of global value chains (GVCs) from the late 1990s onward dramatically altered these dynamics, with the academic and economic literature later finding more consensus on the positive relationship and higher potential for welfare gains delivered through trade and FDI.

This chapter begins with an assessment of international trade and FDI as channels for increasing the transfer of low-carbon technologies (LCTs). Next, the chapter provides empirical evidence on the extent to which the traditional North–South technology transfer paradigm is still valid or is shifting to more complex modes (Chen 2018; Kirchherr and Urban 2018; Urban 2018). Specific focus is given to the role of emerging economies—especially China, whose impact on these shifting patterns of LCT trade and FDI is unmatched. This analysis aims to provide further empirical support for evidence-based polices that can more effectively foster the transfer of LCTs.

CHANNELS FOR TECHNOLOGY TRANSFER

Technology can be transferred through multiple transmission channels that can be categorized into seven types:

1. Importation of intermediate and capital goods through international trade
2. Movement of capital and knowledge through inward and outward FDI, including joint ventures
3. Movement of people through migration or through business, travel, and educational purposes
4. Licensing for the use of foreign technologies (for example, patents, copyrights)[1]
5. Collaboration on international research
6. Integration into GVCs, benefitting from knowledge and technology transfer between buyers and suppliers
7. Diffusion of codified and disembodied knowledge through the Internet and other media (Fu, Pietrobelli, and Soete 2011)

This chapter focuses on the first two such channels: LCT transfer through international trade and through FDI. Patents are discussed in depth in chapter 3. Additional channels for the transfer of LCT are recognized but not examined explicitly in this chapter.

International trade and FDI can introduce goods and services that are less polluting and more energy-efficient compared to those currently available on a domestic market, can foster spillovers of environmental good practice to domestic firms, and, in exceptional cases, can lead to technology leapfrogging (Gallagher and Zarsky 2007). But they can also bring heavily polluting "brown" technologies. Whether and how trade and investment create pollution havens by entering markets with lower environmental standards and resulting in increases in carbon dioxide (CO_2) emissions remains an open debate.[2] Measuring the extent and the impact of brown technology transfers is a critical area for investigation but is beyond the scope of this chapter.

Unlike other forms of technology transfer, trade moves a physical product with embedded technology between locations relatively quickly. Even the world's largest cargo can be transported around the globe in just a matter of weeks. By leveraging global markets to tap into the larger stock of knowledge from cumulative research and development (R&D) activities in the North, countries in the South can import a variety of intermediate products and capital equipment they could otherwise not afford or produce domestically (Coe, Helpman and Hoffmaister 1997; Grossman and Helpman 1991; van Pottelsberghe de la Potterie and Lichtenburg 2001).

Importing low-carbon capital goods (machinery) has traditionally been considered the most robust channel of technology transfer via trade because it increases productivity and the likelihood of generating positive environmental and innovative externalities (Navaretti and Tarr 2000). Further analyses suggest that importing intermediate goods can be equally impactful (Taglioni and Winkler 2016). In light of the urgent need to scale up deployment of LCTs across all countries, including those with limited technological capacity, trade offers the quickest mechanism for delivering and deploying LCTs.

Technology transfers through FDI are often considered more knowledge-intensive than those through trade because of the longer-term and deeper engagement in the receiving country (Dechezleprêtre, Glachant, and Ménière 2013). Assessments on which types of firms benefit from FDI spillovers tend to find that small firms with low productivity can often benefit the most (Keller and Yeaple 2009).

Increasingly, research finds that FDI-receiving countries benefit strongly from direct and indirect knowledge spillovers between foreign and domestic firms (Bitzer and Kerekes 2008; Dechezleprêtre, Glachant, and Ménière 2013; Newman et al. 2015). Multinational firms that invest around the world tend to share certain characteristics: they are technologically advanced and operate at higher international standards, including using management systems that monitor and actively seek to reduce environmental impacts. In the case of high-tech sectors—where many LCTs would be considered—FDI spillovers are found to have even more impact (Keller and Yeaple 2009).

Furthermore, FDI is a crucial source of financing for the deployment of LCTs (Buchner, Brown, and Corfee-Morlot 2011; Golub, Kaufmann, and Yeres 2011). FDI into renewable energy (RE) is most often invested to develop downstream power production facilities and other infrastructure assets, rather than into the manufacturing processes that could lead to more knowledge and skills spillovers in the domestic economy. In addition, FDI can crowd out domestic companies, push lower-productivity firms into bankruptcy, and lead to the capture by foreign firms of monopoly rents in underdeveloped sectors.

MEASURING TRADE AND FDI

The trade analysis in this chapter is based on trade data obtained from the United Nations International Trade Statistics Database (UN COMTRADE), using the Harmonized Commodity Description and Coding System (HS).[3] At the most granular six-digit level recognized by the World Trade Organization (WTO), very few subheadings contain products that are exclusively low-carbon or are used only in the production of environmentally friendly LCT. Most products are lumped together with similar products that can be considered "dual use"—meaning they may or may not be climate-friendly. This chapter relies also on trade values because the units and prices reported to UN COMTRADE vary by country and by product, complicating direct comparisons through available data.

The falling cost of production of many LCT products means that nominal and real value of trade flows may differ substantially. Manufacturing prices of many LCTs in the early 1990s were vastly higher than they are today. Increasing economies of scale through deployment and accelerated technological progress have helped to create a virtuous circle of falling costs. According to the International Renewable Energy Agency (IRENA), solar photovoltaic (PV) module prices have fallen 80 percent over the past decade, and wind turbine prices have been reduced between 30 and 40 percent.[4] Therefore, it is likely that trade figures overestimate the flow of technology in the 1990s and early 2000s and underestimate the amount of technology transfer happening today.

FIGURE 2.1

Global levelized cost of energy from utility-scale renewable power generation technologies, 2010–17

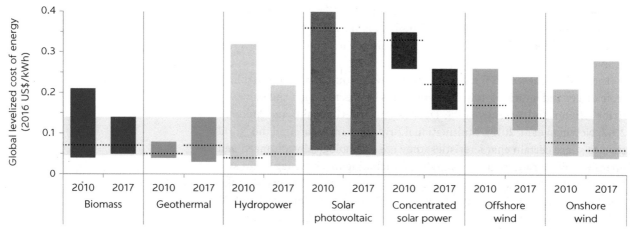

Source: Adapted from IRENA Renewable Energy Cost Database, https://www.irena.org/Statistics/View-Data-by-Topic/Costs/LCOE-2010-2017.
Note: The dashed lines are the global weighted average levelized cost of energy value for plants commissioned each year. Cost of capital is 7.5 percent for Organisation for Economic Co-operation and Development (OECD) countries and China and 10 percent for the rest of the world. The gray band represents the fossil fuel–fired power generation cost range. kWh = kilowatt-hour.

The dashed lines in figure 2.1 show the global weighted average of the levelized cost of energy (LCOE)[5] for plants commissioned in 2010 and 2017. This average has fallen dramatically for solar PV and concentrated solar power (CSP) and to a lesser extent for on- and offshore wind, according to IRENA.

FDI—to the extent that the data are available and reliable—is at best a proxy for technology transfer. FDI data are notoriously unreliable because many announced investments take years to come fully online—if they do at all. This makes accurately tracking the transfer of funds and technologies complicated.[6] Occasionally, the motivation of a firm is quite clear when the investment is a one-off, asset-seeking acquisition—such as the very well-noted acquisition of German wind engineering firm Vensys by China's Goldwind in 2008—but this clarity is quite rare.

This chapter uses the most accurate available FDI data by focusing on investment in RE. Other low-carbon FDI—in agriculture, mining, forestry, and construction—are not assessed. Calculating investment in these other sectors would require a case-by-case assessment and access to firm's private data (Golub, Kaufmann and Yeres 2011).

Identifying traded LCT

Determining which products to include in an analysis of LCT is a challenge. This difficulty is perhaps best evidenced by the collapse of the WTO Environmental Goods Agreement (EGA) negotiations in late 2016 when negotiators could not agree on competing lists (de Melo and Solleder 2019; ICTSD 2016). Although consensus has not been reached on a list of environmentally friendly goods, this chapter draws on three well-established and well-recognized lists, each produced by a different type of stakeholder: an international organization (the World Bank), the multilateral Asia-Pacific Economic Cooperation (APEC) forum, and academia.[7] Each list varies in scope but provides a representative and manageable sample of traded climate change mitigation technology products—backed by a degree of consensus on their environmental friendliness—for deeper analysis.[8] Box 2.1 gives a brief overview of the lists adopted for this report. After eliminating duplications, the combination of all the products in those three lists results in a new list comprising 107 traded LCTs.[9] That list is provided in appendix B.

Each list described in box 2.1 contains a different mix of capital, intermediate, and consumption goods, as defined by Broad Economic Categories[10] (table 2.1). The mix of technological sophistication of the goods on each list also differs, pointing to the fact that technology transfer is not exclusively high-tech (table 2.2). The World Bank Group list actually includes eight low-technology products, and the Glachant, Dussaux, and Dechezleprêtre list includes five natural resource–based products used as inputs to more sophisticated LCTs. Notably, all three lists exclude lithium (HS 282520) and lithium batteries (HS 850650), which have become commonly used in the manufacturing of electric vehicles and many other energy storage systems. Lithium's absence highlights another challenge of codifying LCT lists—technological change.

The following section uses gross trade data from the UN COMTRADE database to quantify LCT trade between countries and to explore the importing and exporting patterns of emerging economies to determine the direction of North and South trade flows. We recall that, for the purposes of this report, the World Bank's income group classifications are used to define the "North" as high-income countries and the "South" as all economies not classified as high income. Special attention is paid to emerging economies—including Brazil, China, India, Mexico, the Republic of Korea, and South Africa—and their relative success or lack thereof in absorbing LCT and developing their own LCT sectors.

BOX 2.1

Lists of climate change–related technologies

Asia-Pacific Economic Cooperation List of Environmental Goods (APEC54): Asia-Pacific Economic Cooperation (APEC) members endorsed this list in 2012, pledging to reduce applied tariff rates on these products to 5 percent or less by the end of 2015. The agreement was intended to signal commitment to pursuing green growth objectives, addressing climate change, and securing sustainable economic development. The list contains many dual-use products, and member states were allowed to exercise "ex-outs" to avoid tariff reduction commitments on goods they deemed of national interest.

World Bank Group Climate-Friendly and Clean-Energy Technologies List (WBG43): The World Bank's *International Trade and Climate Change: Economic, Legal, and Institutional Perspectives* (World Bank 2008) report identified 43 traded "climate-friendly and clean-energy technologies." The report discussed the need for liberalizing trade in clean energy technologies, while at the same time flagging the issue of carbon leakage in developing countries. At that time, the authors found that the complete zeroing of tariffs on these 43 goods would lead to a 7 percent increase in the volume of trade.

Glachant, Dussaux, and Dechezleprêtre List of Climate Change–Related Technologies (GDD30): Glachant, Dussaux, and Dechezleprêtre have authored many peer-reviewed publications on the international diffusion and transfer of low-carbon technologies. Their analysis is based upon a list of 30 low-carbon technologies, including various types of renewable energy technologies, energy storage, electric and hybrid vehicles, and other products related to energy efficiency in construction and heavy industries.

TABLE 2.1 **Decomposition of traded products by broad economic category**

	NUMBER OF TRADED PRODUCTS		
BROAD ECONOMIC CATEGORY	WBG43	APEC54	GDD30
Capital goods	**22**	**20**	**14**
Capital goods[a]	22	20	13
Transport equipment, industrial	—	—	1
Intermediate goods	**19**	**34**	**15**
Industrial supplies not elsewhere specified, processed	8	1	7
Parts and accessories	11	33	8
Consumption goods	**2**	**0**	**0**
Durable	1	—	—
Nondurable	1	—	—
Other	—	—	1[b]

Note: APEC54 = Asia-Pacific Economic Cooperation List of Environmental Goods; GDD30 = Glachant, Dussaux, and Dechezleprêtre List of Climate Change–Related Technologies; WBG43 = World Bank Group Climate-Friendly and Clean-Energy Technologies List; — = not available.
a. Except for transport equipment.
b. Passenger motorcars.

TABLE 2.2 **Technological classification of exports**

	NUMBER OF TRADED PRODUCTS		
	WBG43	APEC54	GDD30
High technology	14	27	18
Medium technology	20	26	7
Low technology	8	0	0
Resource based	1	1	5

Source: Calculations based on Lall 2000.
Note: APEC54 = Asia-Pacific Economic Cooperation List of Environmental Goods; GDD30 = Glachant, Dussaux, and Dechezleprêtre List of Climate Change–Related Technologies; WBG43 = World Bank Group Climate-Friendly and Clean-Energy Technologies List.

TRADE AS A CHANNEL OF LCT TRANSFER

Global trade of these 107 LCTs has plateaued since 2011, a potentially worrying sign for climate change mitigation. Exports have risen nearly 20-fold—from US$43.6 billion in 1990 to an estimated US$809.9 billion in 2017 (figure 2.2). Despite strong year-on-year export growth in the early 1990s and 2000s, LCT trade has actually failed to grow in value terms in three of the past six years. Bilateral trade volumes have fluctuated by product and country pair, with no clear pattern of continued decline or growth. If one uses installed capacity of RE as an indicator of LCT trade volumes, the steady rise in installed capacity would suggest more production, and potentially trade, of these products albeit at lower prices. This increase, however, would include only a subset of the 107 LCT products.

FIGURE 2.2

Total value of LCT exports, 1990–2017

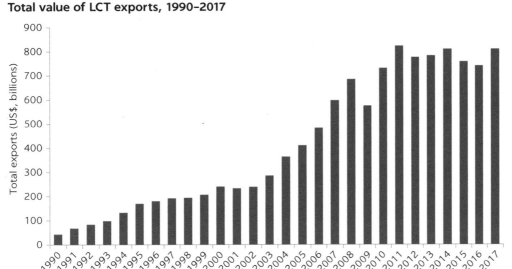

Source: World Bank World Integrated Trade Solution (database), https://wits.worldbank.org, using the 1988/92 Harmonized Commodity Description and Coding System classification.
Note: LCT = low-carbon technology.

FIGURE 2.3

LCT export growth versus growth of all exports, excluding LCT, 1990–2016

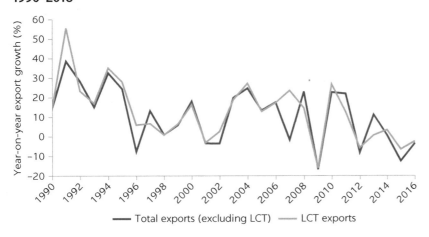

Source: World Bank World Integrated Trade Solution (database), https://wits.worldbank.org, using the 1988/92 Harmonized Commodity Description and Coding System classification.
Note: LCT = low-carbon technology.

The slowdown in year-on-year growth in trade values is slightly less worrying considering the general slowdown in global trade. Figure 2.3 illustrates how the year-on-year growth of LCT exports has tracked that of total exports relatively closely, indicating that LCT trade is not immune to macroeconomic conditions. On the positive side, however, LCT exports have been growing at a compound annual growth rate of 11.1 percent, outpacing that

FIGURE 2.4

APEC54, WBG43, and GDD30 total exports, by value, 1990–2017

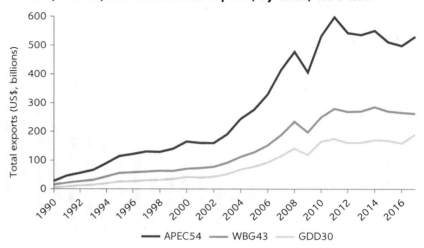

Source: World Bank World Integrated Trade Solution (database), https://wits.worldbank.org.
Note: APEC54 = Asia-Pacific Economic Cooperation List of Environmental Goods;
GDD30 = Glachant, Dussaux, and Dechezleprêtre List of Climate Change–Related
Technologies; WBG43 = World Bank Group Climate-Friendly and Clean-Energy
Technologies List.

of total exports (9.7 percent) and merchandise exports (6.0 percent) from 1990 to 2016, and faster (4.2 percent) than the broader universe of high-technology exports (3.4 percent) since tracking of these exports began in 2000. In addition, available 2017 trade data already show a year-on-year increase of 11.4 percent in total value of exports, even though not all countries have yet reported.

Each of the three LCT lists (APEC54, GDD30, and WBG43) has shown a similar trend of strong export growth before tapering off in 2011 (figure 2.4). Despite the differences in the number of products included in the lists, their varying composition along final use, and the diversity in technological sophistication, export flows for each list mirror each other quite closely. The 107 LCTs identified for this chapter accounted for a 4.3 percent share of global exports in 2016, up from 3.1 percent in 1990.[11]

Trade of LCT by income group

This section decomposes total trade of LCT by income group, matching trade data to the income classifications each year or over a time period. Roughly one-third of countries are classified as high income in 2019 (see table B.3 in appendix B). The number of high-income countries has more than doubled since 1992, the year climate change was drawn into the public spotlight during the Rio Earth Summit. Since that time, the number of low-income and lower-middle-income countries has shrunk by over one-third. When interpreting trade flows by income group, it is important to recognize that the total number of countries in each group has shifted year on year, with the number of high-income and upper-middle-income countries growing and the number of low-income and lower-middle-income countries shrinking. Box 2.2 highlights the reclassification of important emerging economies featured in this analysis.

Income group classification changes, select countries

Brazil   Brazil had been considered an upper-middle-income country since 1989, before falling into lower-middle-income status from 2002 to 2005. It has been upper-middle income since 2006.

China   China has been classified as an upper-middle-income country since 2010. From 1987 to 1996, it had been considered low income. That changed briefly, in 1997, when it was classified as lower-middle income, before being reclassified as low income again for one more year in 1998. From 1999 to 2009, China was classified as lower-middle income.

India   India achieved lower-middle-income status in 2007 and remains classified as such.

Korea, Rep. of   Korea graduated into high-income status in 1995, fell back into upper-middle-income status after the Asian Financial Crisis in 1997, before regaining high-income status again in 2001. Korea has been included in the subset of countries for further analysis because it was not a high-income country in 1990, and because it has become a relatively successful exporter of low-carbon technologies.

Mexico   Mexico was classified as upper-middle income in 1990 and remains so.

South Africa   South Africa was classified as upper-middle income in 1988, fluctuated between that and lower-middle-income status a number of times in the late 1990s and early 2000s, before reaching upper-middle-income status again in 2004, where it has remained.

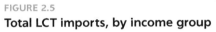

FIGURE 2.5

Total LCT imports, by income group

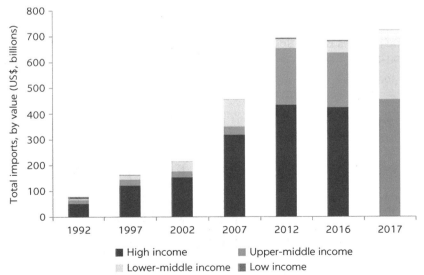

Source: World Bank World Integrated Trade Solution (database), https://wits.worldbank.org.
Note: Data for 2017 are estimated. LCT = low-carbon technology.

Imports of LCT by income groups

The ratio of imports by countries in the North and South has narrowed slightly since the early 1990s, taking into account the shifting composition of countries within each income group over time (figure 2.5). Higher income per capita is strongly correlated with higher imports of LCT, supporting Kuznets's hypothesis of higher demand for environmental quality as income per capita increases (Pueyo and Linares 2012). Indeed, when one holds the 1992 income group classification constant (figure 2.6), LCT imports have risen sharply among lower-income countries, especially as those countries have graduated into higher-income classifications. In 1992, for instance, only 23 of 125 low-income and lower-middle-income countries were importing LCT products. By 2016, nearly two-thirds (53 of 84) of countries still classified as low income or lower-middle income were importing LCT (figure 2.7).

FIGURE 2.6

Share of total LCT imports, by income group

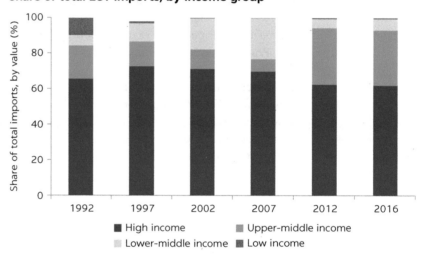

Source: World Bank World Integrated Trade Solution (database), https://wits.worldbank.org.
Note: LCT = low-carbon technology.

FIGURE 2.7

Total imports by the South, 1992 income group classification, 1992–2016

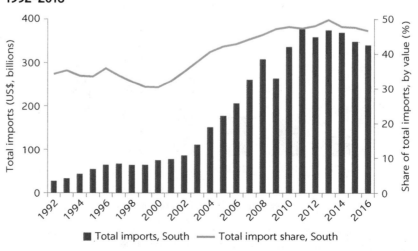

Source: World Bank World Integrated Trade Solution (database), https://wits.worldbank.org.

TABLE 2.3 **Top-10 LCT importers, by value, 2016**

ECONOMY	TOTAL IMPORTS (US$, BILLIONS)	SHARE OF GLOBAL IMPORTS (%)
All economies	*685.4*	*100*
China	108.8	15.9
United States	90.6	13.2
Germany	47.3	6.9
Mexico	24.4	3.6
Hong Kong SAR, China	22.5	3.3
Japan	22.0	3.2
Korea, Rep.	21.5	3.1
Canada	20.5	3.0
United Kingdom	19.8	2.9
France	18.8	2.7

Source: World Bank World Integrated Trade Solution (database), https://wits.worldbank.org.
Note: LCT = low-carbon technology.

TABLE 2.4 **Top-10 South LCT importers, by value, 2016**

COUNTRY	TOTAL IMPORTS (US$, BILLIONS)	SHARE OF SOUTH IMPORTS (%)
All South economies	*260.6*	*100*
China	108.8	41.8
Mexico	24.4	9.4
Russian Federation	13.7	5.3
India	13.2	5.1
Turkey	12.5	4.8
Thailand	10.0	3.8
Malaysia	9.5	3.6
Vietnam	9.3	3.6
Brazil	7.2	2.7
Indonesia	5.9	2.3

Source: World Bank World Integrated Trade Solution (database), https://wits.worldbank.org.
Note: LCT = low-carbon technology.

China is now the world's top importer of these 107 LCT products (15.9 percent), ranking ahead of the United States (13.2 percent) and Germany (6.9 percent) in 2016 (table 2.3). The share of imports among these top three markets has been fairly consistent over the past decade, with the United States slightly narrowing the margin with China since 2014. China accounts for more than 40 percent of all LCT products imported by developing countries. In 2017, China imported more than US$1 billion of 23 separate goods, up from 19 in 2016. Mexico was the second-largest market for LCTs in 2016. No other developing countries rank in the global top 10. The third-largest importer among countries not classified as high income was the Russian Federation, which had previously been classified as high income from 2012 to 2014.[12] Turkey, Thailand, and Vietnam, which have enjoyed relatively strong economic growth over the past 20 years, have also emerged as growing markets for LCT (table 2.4 and table B.5 in appendix B).

Exports by income groups

Developing countries' share of global LCT exports by value has grown considerably since the early 2000s, primarily driven by China's rapidly growing competitiveness in LCT-related export sectors (figure 2.8). With the exception of China, LCT technology and knowledge remains concentrated in developed economies—although this includes recently developed high-income economies such as the Republic of Korea and Taiwan, China.[13] Together, high-income economies accounted for 72.8 percent of total LCT exports by value in 2016, nearly triple the share of upper-middle-income economies (25.1 percent) (figure 2.9).

FIGURE 2.8

Total LCT exports, by income group

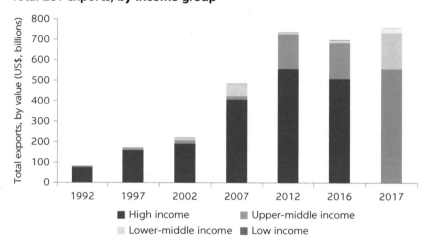

Source: World Bank World Integrated Trade Solution (database), https://wits.worldbank.org.
Note: Data for 2017 are estimated. LCT = low-carbon technology.

FIGURE 2.9

Share of total LCT exports, by income group

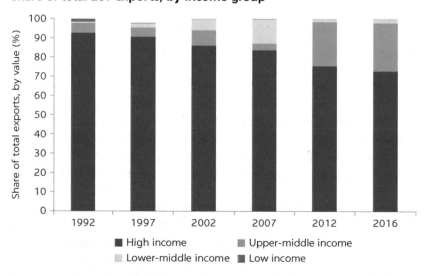

Source: World Bank World Integrated Trade Solution (database), https://wits.worldbank.org.
Note: LCT = low-carbon technology.

TABLE 2.5 **Top-10 global exporters of LCT, 2016**

ECONOMY	TOTAL EXPORTS (US$, BILLIONS)	SHARE OF GLOBAL EXPORTS (%)
All economies	*698.5*	*100.0*
China	117.6	16.8
Germany	87.5	12.5
United States	77.1	11.0
Japan	51.3	7.3
Korea, Rep.	45.0	6.4
Italy	23.8	3.4
Hong Kong SAR, China	20.8	3.0
Taiwan, China	20.1	2.9
United Kingdom	19.7	2.8
Singapore	19.3	2.8

Source: World Bank World Integrated Trade Solution (database), https://wits.worldbank.org.
Note: LCT = low-carbon technology.

TABLE 2.6 **Top-10 South exporters of LCT, by value, 2016**

ECONOMY	TOTAL EXPORTS (US$, BILLIONS)	SHARE OF SOUTH EXPORTS (%)
All South economies	*189.9*	*100*
China	117.6	61.9
Mexico	18.7	9.9
Malaysia	11.6	6.1
Thailand	8.4	4.5
India	5.0	2.6
Vietnam	4.8	2.6
Romania	4.0	2.1
Turkey	2.9	1.5
Brazil	2.7	1.4
South Africa	2.4	1.3

Source: World Bank World Integrated Trade Solution (database), https://wits.worldbank.org.
Note: LCT = low-carbon technology.

China was the world's top exporter of the 107 LCTs in 2016, accounting for 16.8 percent of total exports (table 2.5). In terms of exports to each income group, China is the top exporter of LCT to each of the income categories besides its own (table 2.6 and table 2.7). It ranks fourth in terms of total exports to upper-middle-income economies, in part because China itself is the largest importer of LCT in that group. Mexico was the second-largest exporter among developing economies, with 2.7 percent of global market share, followed by Malaysia, Thailand, India, and Vietnam. Notably, 8 of the 10 top developing economy importers of LCT are also among the top-10 exporters of LCT, suggesting that there is not only demand for low-carbon products but also the capabilities to produce LCT for other markets.

Low-income countries play very little role in LCT markets, either as buyers or sellers, and are less active in LCT trade than they are in trade of all

TABLE 2.7 **Top-five exporters to each income group, 2016**

DESTINATION MARKET	TOP-FIVE ORIGIN MARKETS (IN ORDER)
High-income countries	China, Germany, United States, Japan, Mexico
Upper-middle-income countries	United States, Republic of Korea, Germany, China, Japan
Lower-middle-income countries	China, Republic of Korea, Germany, Japan, United States
Low-income countries	China, United Arab Emirates, India, United States, South Africa

Source: World Bank World Integrated Trade Solution (database), https://wits.worldbank.org.

TABLE 2.8 **Share of total trade and of LCT trade, by income group, 2015–16**

INCOME CLASSIFICATION	SHARE OF TOTAL EXPORTS, 2015–16 (%)	SHARE OF TOTAL LCT EXPORTS, 2015–16 (%)	SHARE OF TOTAL IMPORTS, 2015–16 (%)	SHARE OF TOTAL LCT IMPORTS, 2015–16 (%)
High income	67.5	73.0	69.4	61.9
Upper-middle income	26.7	25.2	22.6	31.6
Lower-middle income	5.6	1.9	7.4	6.2
Low income	0.2	0.01	0.6	0.3

Source: World Bank World Integrated Trade Solution (database), https://wits.worldbank.org.
Note: LCT = low-carbon technology.

goods (table 2.8). In 2015–16, the distribution of LCT imports and exports by income group was not dramatically divergent from the distribution of trade of all goods among income groups (table 2.8). High-income countries are slightly larger exporters of LCT, and upper-middle-income countries are slightly larger importers of LCT.

Low-income countries and lower-middle-income countries together accounted for just 2 percent of exports of the 107 products in 2015–16, 1.9 percent and 0.01 percent, respectively. This finding should not be misconstrued as meaning that low-income countries are completely absent from low-carbon industries. Some of these countries play an important role in upstream segments of the supply chain. For example, the manufacture of a crystalline silicon solar PV module requires silica and silver as raw materials, the latter of which is produced primarily in Bolivia, Mexico, and Peru. These raw materials are then traded to be processed into polysilicon, silver paste, and glass and traded again before finally being assembled to create crystalline silicon PV wafers and cells (CEMAC 2017). These upstream activities are rarely included on lists of environmentally friendly production.

South–South trade

Patterns of LCT trade need to be considered within the context of South–South trade to determine if they are shifting (table 2.9). Overall, global trade as a percentage of gross domestic product has yet to regain the momentum it had before the 2008–09 financial crisis, showing weaker than expected performance again in 2018.[14] In 2016, South–South trade accounted for 11.2 percent of total global trade. Growth has slowed in emerging markets and developing economies, although developing countries' trade with China has shown resilience (see UNCTAD 2018; World Bank 2019). Before 2016, South–South trade had been

TABLE 2.9 **Direction of trade for total exports versus LCT exports, by value, 1992, 2002, and 2016**

DIRECTION OF TRADE	1992		2002		2016	
	ALL PRODUCTS (%)	LCT PRODUCTS (%)	ALL PRODUCTS (%)	LCT PRODUCTS (%)	ALL PRODUCTS (%)	LCT PRODUCTS (%)
North–North	58.8	61.4	61.1	61.5	47.1	45.4
North–South	18.6	26.7	18.0	24.6	19.7	27.3
South–North	17.4	5.2	15.9	10.7	21.7	18.1
South–South	5.0	2.0	5.0	2.5	11.2	9.0

Source: World Bank World Integrated Trade Solution (database), https://wits.worldbank.org.
Note: LCT = low-carbon technology.

rising steadily since the early 1990s, outpacing the growth rate of total world trade (measured in either imports or exports).

In 2016, South–South trade accounted for 9.0 percent of all LCT exports, but for 11.2 percent of total global exports. The share of North–South trade, the traditional direction of technology transfer from more to less advanced countries, is noticeably higher for LCT products than for total goods. China, the Republic of Korea, the United States, Japan, and Germany are the top-five exporters of LCT to the global South. China is the top destination market of each exporter, with the exception of the United States, which exports more LCTs to Mexico, with China as its second-largest LCT export destination.

The share of South–North and South–South trade has risen steadily since the early 1990s, which suggests growing capabilities in the South. Meanwhile, the share of North–North trade has fallen sharply since the early 2000s, likely because of increased domestic production and offset by imports from China and the global South. North–South trade has risen significantly and now represents about a quarter of all LCT trade.

Although South–North LCT trade flows have grown, only a few countries are participating in this phenomenon to any significant degree. China accounted for 56.1 percent of the total value of LCT exports from South to North in 2016. Mexico had the second-largest share of South–North exports, accounting for 13.6 percent. Brazil, India, and South Africa account for much smaller shares of South–North exports, providing a combined 4.3 percent of exports to high-income countries.

Removing China as an importer and exporter from the dataset, we find that both South–North and South–South trade have still been increasing (figure 2.10). Since 2002, the share of exports from South to North has increased 40.2 percent, and the share of trade between developing countries has more than doubled (figure 2.11). These gains are relatively small in terms of total value, but they are encouraging.

Trade of select developing countries

As evident through the trade analysis, emerging economies play an important role in the transfer of LCTs. This section focuses on six countries—Brazil, China, India, Korea, Mexico, and South Africa—selected on the basis of their current and future importance in the production, trade, and deployment of LCTs. As centers of production and critical hubs in regional and global value chains, these countries are positioned for continued economic growth. But growing

FIGURE 2.10

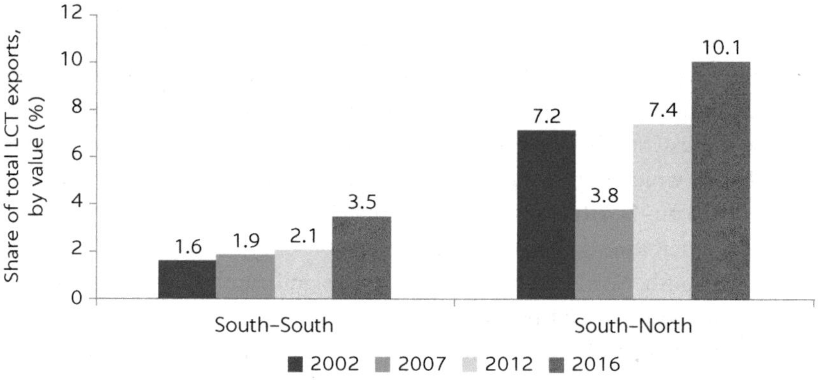

Share of total LCT exports, by value and income group, without China

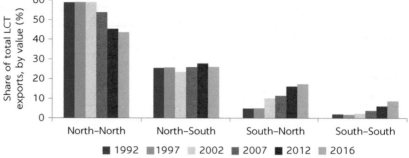

Source: World Bank World Integrated Trade Solution (database), https://wits.worldbank.org.
Note: LCT = low-carbon technology.

FIGURE 2.11

Share of total South–South and South–North LCT exports, by value, without China

Source: World Bank World Integrated Trade Solution (database), https://wits.worldbank.org.
Note: LCT = low-carbon technology.

sustainably will increasingly hinge on producing more with less, reducing the carbon intensity of production, and mitigating environmental impacts.

These six countries, in particular, have an important role to play not only in absorbing the LCTs necessary to speed their own transitions to low-carbon economies but also in transferring these technologies to low-income and lower-middle-income neighbors. China and Korea have already become quite successful in attracting and absorbing new technologies, using this success as a lever to rapidly drive indigenous innovation. Others have had varying degrees of success, integrating into some GVCs (for example, Brazil, Mexico, and South Africa in the automotive GVC) but remaining outliers in many other LCT industries.

China first diverged from its peers in the early 2000s, beginning to increase its imports before also becoming, a few years later, a major exporter of LCT (figure 2.12 and figure 2.13). Each country began by importing more LCTs than it exported, suggesting these technologies were first introduced and absorbed before indigenous innovation processes set in. South Africa was the first of these

FIGURE 2.12

Total LCT imports, select countries, 1992–2016

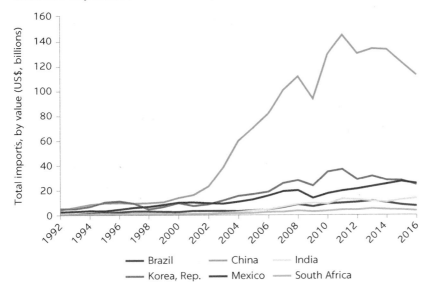

Source: World Bank World Integrated Trade Solution (database), https://wits.worldbank.org.
Note: LCT = low-carbon technology.

FIGURE 2.13

Total LCT exports, select countries, 1992–2016

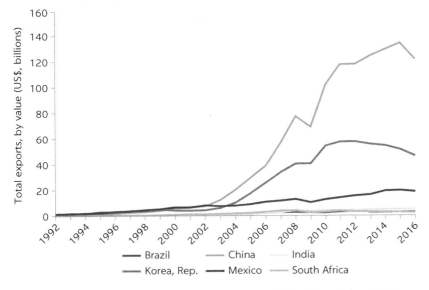

Source: World Bank World Integrated Trade Solution (database), https://wits.worldbank.org.
Note: LCT = low-carbon technology.

countries to become a net LCT exporter in 2000 but reverted to being a net importer in 2009. Korean LCT exports overtook imports in 2005.

Among its peers, China is the largest exporter of LCT (figure 2.13). Mexico's market share grew in the 1990s, but it shrank from the 2000s onward. Brazil, India, and South Africa have not been able to keep pace with their peers; however, India's exports have been growing since 2012, diverging from Brazil and South Africa, whose LCT export industries have stagnated.

TABLE 2.10 Top import origin markets and export destinations for LCTs, by value and share, select economies

	TOP-FIVE LCT IMPORT ORIGIN MARKETS (SHARE OF TOTAL, %), 2015–16
Brazil	United States (20.1), China (17.9), Germany (13.0), Republic of Korea (6.3), Italy (6.0)
China	Republic of Korea (19.8), Japan (17.5), Taiwan, China (15.7), Germany (8.2), United States (7.7)
India	China (38.4), Germany (10.4), United States (9.8), Japan (6.6), Republic of Korea (4.5)
Korea, Rep.	China (26.6), Japan (19.2), United States (14.9), Germany (8.9), Norway (3.0)
Mexico	United States (39.7), China (17.9), Japan (9.0), Republic of Korea (7.6), Germany (5.7)
South Africa	China (21.9), Germany (18.2), United States (9.8), Italy (6.4), United Kingdom (4.5)
	TOP-FIVE LCT EXPORT DESTINATION MARKETS (SHARE OF TOTAL, %), 2015–16
Brazil	United States (17.6), China (13.4), Argentina (12.3), Indonesia (5.9), Germany (5.1)
China	Hong Kong SAR, China (19.3), United States (12.9), Japan (7.7), Republic of Korea (4.9), India (4.2)
India	United States (11.6), United Arab Emirates (7.0), United Kingdom (4.3), Saudi Arabia (4.1), Bangladesh (3.0)
Korea, Rep.	China (46.5), United States (8.5), Vietnam (5.8), Mexico (3.9), Japan (3.4)
Mexico	United States (89.3), Canada (1.2), China (0.8), Brazil (0.7), Netherlands (0.6)
South Africa	Germany (28.2), United States (15.5), United Kingdom (5.6), Spain (5.4), Namibia (3.7)

Source: World Bank World Integrated Trade Solution (database), https://wits.worldbank.org.
Note: LCT = low-carbon technology.

Table 2.10 shows the top import origins and export destinations for Brazil, China, India, Korea, Mexico, and South Africa. Similar to the network structure of GVCs in other sectors, most LCT trade centers around the hubs of China, Germany, and the United States. The largest shares of imports tend to come from the geographically closest hub, with the exception of South Africa, which imports more from China despite its being at a further distance than Europe. A similar pattern is observed for top export destinations, along with the introduction of regional markets as important export destinations. These trade patterns suggest complex, interrelated trade relationships, where technology transfer is an inherent dimension of the business ecosystem.

Of the total US$404.9 billion of LCT products exported by the selected countries to all partners in 2017, only 0.5 percent of the total was exported to low-income countries and about 30 percent to the North. China accounted for the largest value of LCT exports to low-income and lower-middle-income countries, followed by Korea and India. Interestingly, of the 34 destination countries for Indian LCT exports in 2017, 27 were in Sub-Saharan Africa. For South Africa, essentially all LCT exports to low-income countries in 2017 went to partners in Sub-Saharan Africa—led by Mozambique, the Democratic Republic of Congo, and Zimbabwe. These trends emphasize the role of global as well as regional value chains.

Product-level analysis

Reflecting the bilateral trade relationships, the most commonly traded individual LCT products are also part of complex, interrelated trade networks. For both imports and exports of the 107 LCT products identified in this chapter, 4 of the top-5 traded products are the same. These 4 products accounted for over 30 percent in 2017. Perhaps unsurprisingly, the same 4 products were also in the top-5 imports and exports of the six countries selected for analysis.[15]

Untangling which countries import or export which LCT requires firm-level analysis methodologies. For instance, China's top import in 2017 (optical devices, appliances, and instruments) was also its top export. China's and Korea's top-five LCT exports accounted for over half of their LCT exports in 2017, whereas Mexico's top-five products accounted for just slightly less than half of its export basket. India is the only country to import more from developing countries—primarily China and other upper-middle-income countries—than it does from developed countries, which could signify that it is not importing the most advanced technology but rather more suitable or affordable technologies from its developing peers.

Clear dependencies are also evident in the trade data. By far India's top import in 2017 was solar PV/LEDs from China. Mexico specializes in exporting electric control panels, essentially all of which went to the United States. As evident in table 2.10, Mexico is primarily a supplier to the United States and is yet to advance into neighboring regional markets, with only 4.2 percent of its total LCT exports by value destined for developing countries in 2017.

FDI AS A CHANNEL OF LCT TRANSFER

FDI into LCT is a critical channel for technology transfer to developing countries seeking to grow domestic industries, produce lower-carbon products, and put themselves on a path toward sustainable economic growth. UNCTAD (2010) defines "low-carbon foreign investment" as the transfer of technologies, practices, or products by multinational firms to host countries—through equity and nonequity forms of participation—such that the firm's operations, products, and services generate significantly lower greenhouse gas emissions than would otherwise prevail in the industry under business-as-usual circumstances. UNCTAD also considers the acquisition of LCTs, processes, and products as low-carbon foreign investment.

FDI data are not as systematically captured as trade data, and thus leave much to be desired in terms of coverage and accuracy. The simplest, most accurate way to measure FDI into LCT is to focus on RE investments. However, even within this more narrowly defined sector, data coverage is limited, especially for developing countries. Often, it is not national governments or even national state-owned utilities but rather cities, community energy projects, and large corporations that invest in RE (Motyka, Slaughter, and Amon 2018). Table 2.11 captures some of the general determinants of FDI as well as how climate change–specific factors may influence FDI into these sectors.

Comparing data on RE investment is complicated by the lack of available public information and differing measurement methodologies. One of the most reputable sources for information on investment is the *Renewables Global Status Report* (GSR), published since 2005. The 2018 edition reports on investment in RE through a wide set of financing vehicles (for example, asset finance, venture capital, and capital markets), in both domestic and foreign markets. The most recent GSR reported that domestic and foreign investment in "renewable power and fuels"[16] totaled US$279.8 billion in 2017 (REN21 2018). BloombergNEF, found that global "clean energy"[17] investment—covering a broader number of industries and products—totaled US$332.1 billion in 2018, the fifth year in a row in which investment exceeded US$300 billion (BloombergNEF 2019). RE is now the third-largest sector in the world for

TABLE 2.11 Motives and determinants of FDI in LCT sectors

FDI MOTIVE	ECONOMIC DETERMINANTS	CLIMATE CHANGE-SPECIFIC FACTORS
Market-seeking	• Market size • Per capita income • Market growth • Access to regional/global markets	• Rapid growth in LCT sectors (for example, because of green industrial policies) • Strong public procurement of LCT • Energy policy (for example, rapid deployment of renewable energy) • Clear government policy signals for climate action (for example, ambitious Nationally Determined Contributions, National Adaptation Programs of Action)
Natural resource-seeking	• Access to raw materials	• Natural endowments (for example, high solar irradiance, accessible geothermal energy)
Efficiency-seeking	• Different comparative advantages (for example, labor costs) • Incentive policies (for example, subsidies, tax rebates, concessionary loans) • Trade policies (for example, preferential market access, export promotion incentives)	• Access to energy-efficient infrastructure, renewable energy, or both • Access to environmental supporting services • Agglomeration effects (for example, clusters, special economic zones) • Network effects
Strategic asset-seeking	• Access to new competitive advantages • Availability of and access to skilled labor • Strategic infrastructure	• Access to low-carbon market/technology knowledge • Access to local R&D ecosystem (for example, knowledge, financing) • Agglomeration effects • Network effects • Brand building, reputational benefits

Source: Calculations based on UNCTAD 2010.
Note: FDI = foreign direct investment; LCT = low-carbon technology; R&D = research and development.

greenfield investment, although it still trails investment in the coal, oil, and gas sectors (Shehadi 2019).

Cementing its leadership in the green economy, China set a new record for its RE investment, providing 45 percent of total global investment in RE—counting its domestic expenditure and FDI—in 2017 (REN21 2018). India was credited for 4 percent and Brazil for 2 percent of global RE investment. Investment into developing countries accounted for a record 63 percent of global investment in RE in 2017 (US$177 billion).

Asset-seeking investment is the most intuitive type of investment related to technology transfer, headlined by mergers and acquisitions. Rarely does a firm from a developing country acquire a business (and its technology) from a developed country. On average, more than 90 percent of mergers and acquisitions are executed by firms headquartered in the European Union and the United States. China, and to an even lesser extent Brazil and India, has occasionally sought to purchase technology outright through this type of asset-seeking investment, but this has been less frequent and on a much smaller scale.

Efficiency-seeking and market-seeking FDI can lead to technology transfer within domestic manufacturing sectors. In general, when a firm is considering investing in a developing country, its executives are most concerned with political stability and a business-friendly regulatory environment (Kusek and Silva 2018). Investment determinants, however, vary by sector, by motivation, and by firm size. In RE, for instance, an investor may seek a specific natural phenomenon, such as geothermal features or high solar irradiance.

The following section draws on RE FDI data from the *Financial Times' fDi Markets* database, one of the few databases to specifically classify investment into RE sector. This database tracks information[18] on capital investment and direct jobs created associated with global outward FDI, covering the years

2003 to 2018.[19] The *fDi Markets* database is one of the largest on FDI, although coverage of deals in developing countries is believed to be lacking in comparison to information on FDI from and between developed countries. In addition, *fDi Markets* does not differentiate between public, private, and semiprivate investors, meaning that its data also include investment from state-owned enterprises. One should also take into account that these investments may have a lag in delivery and development, and some deals may never come to fruition. The database defines the RE sector as encompassing all investment into the following subsectors: (i) biomass power, (ii) geothermal electric power, (iii) hydroelectric power, (iv) marine electric power, (v) other electric power generation (alternative/renewable energy), (vi) solar electric power, and (vii) wind electric power.

In 2018, foreign investors put US$82.5 billion into RE sectors, according to *fDi Markets*, which brings total investment into RE to US$795.2 billion through 3,790 investment deals from 2003 to 2018 (table 2.12). FDI grew quite steadily until the 2008–09 financial crisis but has been volatile since.

In 2018, one-third of investment into RE came from the South. This ratio has grown steadily, in large part because of China, which accounted for 29.1 percent of all outward FDI into RE in 2018. From 2003 to 2018, countries from the global South were responsible for 16.7 percent of outward FDI investment into RE by value, and 12.2 percent of the number of investments.[20]

Roughly half of all FDI into RE recorded by *fDi Markets* has been invested into the global South. Investment into the South dipped following the 2008–09 financial crisis, but it has since recovered and has remained fairly stable at just above 50 percent of all FDI recorded. Electricity production was the primary purpose for roughly 85 percent of total RE investment. About half of this

TABLE 2.12 **FDI into renewable energy, by year, 2003–18**

YEAR	NUMBER OF PROJECTS	CAPITAL INVESTMENT (US$, BILLIONS)	ESTIMATED NUMBER OF JOBS CREATED
2003	40	7.5	5,036
2004	25	5.1	1,263
2005	56	8.8	3,038
2006	141	24.4	15,973
2007	251	42.2	17,546
2008	385	88.6	30,247
2009	321	77.3	28,275
2010	266	47.3	15,759
2011	337	64.7	23,596
2012	221	47.1	21,915
2013	317	67.8	23,328
2014	199	43.9	23,404
2015	308	79.0	21,735
2016	304	68.1	17,382
2017	255	41.0	13,157
2018	364	82.5	18,740
Total	**3,790**	**795.2**	**280,394**

Source: Calculations based on fDi Markets https://www.fdiintelligence.com/fdi-markets.

investment went into developing countries, emphasizing the significant role FDI plays as a source of financing for RE deployment in these countries.

FDI into RE manufacturing is much less common. Since 2003, it has accounted for just 10.7 percent of total recorded RE FDI flows. Roughly 85 percent of that total came from high-income countries, with two-thirds flowing into developing countries—suggesting efficiency-seeking motives. Almost all of that went into greenfield investment. Most projects went into countries that were lower-middle income or have since graduated to upper-middle income. The poorest countries have attracted almost no investment, especially from their fellow neighbors in the South.

China overtook Germany to become the top investor in RE in 2018. Sinohydro, a subsidiary of the wholly state-owned Power Construction Corporation of China (PowerChina), accounted for nearly three-quarters of the 2018 sum—with a single investment into hydroelectric power in Indonesia totaling US$17.8 billion dollars.[21] This single investment was enough to vault PowerChina into the top-five investing firms since 2003.

The top sources of outward investment have been mostly advanced economies (table 2.13) and China. Among developing countries, the second-largest total sum of investment came from India, which ranked 17th, followed by Malaysia (18th) and Thailand (20th).

FDI from developing countries tends to reflect their comparative advantages in certain technologies. For example, China invests more than one-third of its total FDI in hydroelectric power and an almost equal amount into solar electric power. Also well-known for hydro, Brazil has put more than one-third of its outward FDI into hydroelectric power since 2003, followed by investment in biomass power generation. Almost half of reported outward FDI from India is going into wind power and only 24.6 into solar, despite the country's well-known expertise in solar systems.

South–South investment flows

South–South investment flows totaled US$99.9 billion between 2003 and 2018,[22] accounting for 14.1 percent of the total sum of investment. Most South–South

TABLE 2.13 **Total outward RE FDI, by country, 2018**

COUNTRY	NUMBER OF PROJECTS	TOTAL INVESTMENT (US$, BILLIONS)
Total	**364**	**82.4**
China	33	24.0
Germany	45	11.7
Spain	40	8.1
Japan	10	4.6
France	25	4.0
Italy	32	3.7
Canada	21	3.6
United States	21	2.8
Thailand	12	2.7
Denmark	13	1.9

Source: Calculations based on fDi Markets, https://www.fdiintelligence.com/fdi-markets.
Note: RE FDI = renewable energy foreign direct investment.

investments into RE have gone into large hydropower projects (table 2.14) because many developing countries—including most notably China—have expertise in these technologies.

China is the largest source country for FDI into RE in lower-middle-income countries and the second-largest source of FDI into RE in low-income countries, after the United States.

During 2003–18, Indonesia received more than one-fourth of all South–South FDI. Of that, three-fourths went into hydroelectric power—all of which came from China. The remainder consisted mostly of investment into biomass power and geothermal electric power.

According to *fDi Markets,* India received the largest amount of FDI (table 2.15). Brazil and Mexico were the second- and third-leading destinations. Only 13.2 percent of the total investment across these three countries went into manufacturing, most of it going into electricity production. These three countries are not strong exporters of LCT, suggesting that the investment they have received has not led to transformative technology transfer. Interestingly, China does not appear to have been an attractive market for FDI into RE sectors over this time period.

Role of multinational firms in FDI

A single multinational firm can often have an outsized impact on investment trends, evidenced by the fact that the top-five investing firms account for 12.8 percent of total FDI (table 2.16). These firms also account for a large share

TABLE 2.14 **Total South–South RE investment, by subsector, 2003–18**

SUBSECTOR	TOTAL INVESTMENT, (US$, BILLION)	SHARE OF TOTAL INVESTMENT (%)
Total	**99.9**	**100.0**
Hydroelectric power	39.8	39.8
Solar electric power	23.6	23.7
Wind electric power	15.2	15.3
Biomass power	14.5	14.5
Geothermal electric power	3.7	3.7
Other	3.1	3.1

Source: Calculations based on fDi Markets, https://www.fdiintelligence.com/fdi-markets.
Note: RE = renewable energy.

TABLE 2.15 **Total RE FDI, top source economies and subsectors, select economies, 2003–18**

ECONOMY	INVESTMENT (US$, BILLIONS)	TOP-THREE SOURCE ECONOMIES	TOP-THREE SUBSECTORS
India	29.9	China, United States, United Kingdom	Solar, wind, other
Brazil	27.5	United States, Spain, France	Biomass, wind, solar
Mexico	26.2	Spain, United States, Italy	Solar, wind, hydro
South Africa	14.3	Italy, Ireland, Saudi Arabia	Solar, wind, biomass
China	14.2	United States; Canada; Hong Kong SAR, China	Wind, solar, biomass
Korea, Republic	4.2	Germany, United States, Japan	Biomass, solar, other

Source: Calculations based on fDi Markets, https://www.fdiintelligence.com/fdi-markets.
Note: RE FDI = renewable energy foreign direct investment.

TABLE 2.16 Top foreign direct investors, 2003–18

PARENT COMPANY	NUMBER OF PROJECTS	SUM OF INVESTMENT (US$, BILLIONS)	SHARE OF TOTAL INVESTMENT (%)	PROJECT TYPE (NUMBER OF)		
				NEW	CO-LOCATION	EXPANSION
Grand total	**3,790**	**795.2**	**100.0**	**3,538**	**89**	**163**
Iberdrola (Spain)	88	28.0	3.5	79	2	7
Enel[a] (Italy)	153	27.5	3.4	137	7	9
Power Construction Corporation of China (PowerChina)	2	17.9	2.3	2	0	0
Électricité de France (EDF)	75	14.7	1.9	70	0	5
Energias de Portugal (EDP)	36	14.1	1.8	35	0	1

Source: Calculations based on fDi Markets, https://www.fdiintelligence.com/fdi-markets.
a. Includes subsidiary Enel Green Power.

of total investment from their country. Iberdrola, the world's top investor in RE, accounts for 27.0 percent of all RE investment that has come out of Spain since 2003. Enel accounts for 59.5 percent of all outward RE FDI from Italy, and Energias de Portugal accounts for 78.3 percent of outward RE FDI from Portugal.

The degree to which these top firms invest in the global South varies, but investment into low-income countries is very low. After ChinaPower, Enel has invested the most money into the South, more than 50 percent of its total recorded FDI, whereas Électricité de France and Energias de Portugal have invested more heavily in the North. These firms' FDI into RE in low-income countries has been minimal. Électricité de France has invested US$619 million into low-income countries to lead the group, followed by Energias de Portugal.

MOVEMENT OF PEOPLE AS A CHANNEL OF LCT TRANSFER

Although this chapter has focused on trade and FDI, intranational and international movement of people is critical for knowledge and technology transfer. The former cannot happen without the latter—trade and investment are conducted by businesspeople moving around the world seeking opportunity. Noting that technology is best explained and demonstrated in person, Hovhannisyan and Keller (2015) show that a 10 percent increase in short-term, cross-border labor movement (that is, business travel) leads to a modest but significant 0.2 percent increase in patenting in the destination country.

Beyond business travel, movement of people can transfer knowledge and skills in multiple ways including, among others, nationals studying or working abroad and later applying new knowledge gained after returning to their home country, temporary relocation and even emigration of foreign professionals into a country, labor turnover of highly skilled workers from multinational firms to domestic firms (Golub, Kaufmann, and Yeres 2011; Hoekman, Maskus, and Saggi 2004). Assessing the literature on emigration, recent World Bank (2018) analysis finds that a large part of what makes high-skilled workers more productive is the work environment in the destination country: if they had not left their home countries, these workers may never have been so productive or developed higher skills.

Freedom to travel between countries is primarily determined by one's passport and the various visa processes and policies, including restrictions, of destination countries. The Henley Passport Index, based in part on International Air

Transport Association data, provides a rigorous measure of travel freedom spanning the past 14 years. When looking at the selected countries of focus in this chapter, China and Korea both show marked improvement in the ease of travel since 2006, whereas traveling as a national from India, Mexico, and South Africa has become more difficult (table 2.17). The more restricted it is for someone to travel, the higher the transaction costs for studying and working abroad, and the more difficult it is to enter a country, the less likely it is that a country will attract global talent.

International education mobility

The number of individuals studying abroad continues to soar, having risen from 2.1 million students in 2001 to more than 5 million in 2018.[23] Students coming from East Asia and the Pacific region have been a major driving force, but the Institute for International Education, in partnership with the OECD and the United Nations Educational, Scientific, and Cultural Organization, has found outward mobility of students increasing across all regions (figure 2.14). Long the

TABLE 2.17 **Henley Passport Index ranking, select countries**

COUNTRY	2006	2019
Brazil	20th (tie)	17th (tie)
China	78th (tie)	67th (tie)
India	71st (tie)	80th
Korea, Rep.	11th (tie)	1st (tie)
Mexico	21st (tie)	24th
South Africa	37th	51st (tie)

Source: Henley Passport Index, https://www.henleypassportindex.com/passport.

FIGURE 2.14

Outbound international education mobility, by region, 2007 versus 2017

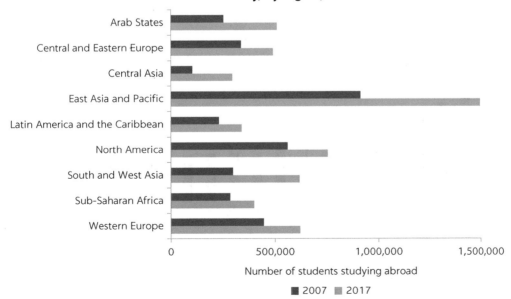

Source: Institute of International Education's Project Atlas, https://www.iie.org/Research-and-Insights/Project-Atlas/.

primary destination for international students, the United States now accounts for slightly less than a quarter of the world's international students. The U.S. share has been declining as other countries have instituted policies to attract foreign students and to retain them in their local labor force once they have completed their studies (Institute of International Education 2018). China, the most successful developing country to have instituted such policies, attracted 10 percent of all inbound international students in 2018, up from less than 2 percent in 2001, tying it with the United Kingdom as the second-most popular destination for international students. In an effort to retain some of these students, the Chinese government has put in place policies to ease the process of attaining residency after studying for foreigners choosing to work in strategic sectors, including engineering research centers, high-tech companies, and foreign-funded R&D centers (in June 2016).

Making it easier for students and professionals to visit and relocate to a country can provide a significant boost to knowledge, technology transfer, and innovation. Available evidence shows immigrants play an outsized role in inventing (figure 2.15) and are disproportionately employed in science, technology, engineering, and mathematics (STEM) fields, often as inventors and innovators (World Bank 2018).

The primary challenge for developing countries is to facilitate temporary movement abroad and to encourage those who leave to return and apply their knowledge in the local economy (Hoekman, Maskus, and Saggi 2004). Failing to attract nationals to return can result in brain drain. Emigration of high-skilled workers, in particular, can reduce income levels by 6 percent in origin countries with per capita income levels below US$3,000 (World Bank 2018). Remittances sent back home help to defray the cost, but they do not fully compensate for the loss.

FIGURE 2.15

Share of immigrants among inventors in OECD countries

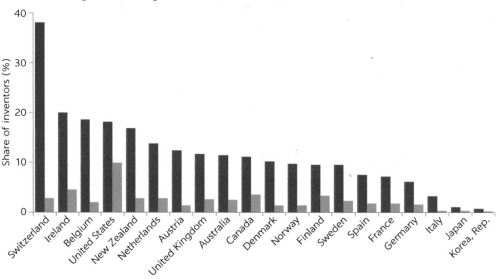

■ Share of inventors who are immigrants ■ Share of inventors from developing countries

Source: World Bank 2018.
Note: Immigrants identified via patents filed under the Patent Cooperation Treaty. OECD = Organisation for Economic Co-operation and Development.

Developing country governments can help to foster knowledge and technology transfer by implementing policies and incentives that effectively facilitate the free movement of students and labor. Diaspora engagement programs, for example, can help to connect diaspora investors and entrepreneurs with investment opportunities in their home countries. Incentive policies to encourage the return of a country's high-skilled diaspora have demonstrated return on investment (World Bank 2018). The Malaysian Returning Expert Program, which provides tax breaks to successful emigrants who return to Malaysia, is a notable example. Return migration has increased, and the program has roughly paid for itself as the return migrants pay taxes—even at lower rates.

ABSORPTIVE CAPACITY AS A DETERMINANT OF LCT TRANSFER

The degree to which workers, local firms, and domestic industries benefit from LCT knowledge spillovers and technology transfers through trade and FDI ultimately depends on the absorptive capacity of domestic actors. Absorptive capacity refers to the "ability to identify, assimilate, and exploit knowledge" (Cohen and Levinthal 1990). Developing absorptive capacity in LCT sectors is not unlike doing so in other high-technology sectors. Countries with established manufacturing industries in sectors such as aircraft, steel, and glass have been shown to have a competitive advantage in developing solar and wind manufacturing (Huberty and Zachmann 2011; Jha 2017). At the firm level, absorptive capacity is often associated with the number of workers with tertiary education, managerial skills and management systems, use of modern technologies, firm size, proximity to other firms in the same sector, and whether or not the firm exports—to name but a few factors. When a firm has absorptive capacity, it can then strengthen and develop technical capabilities, which, in turn, can support indigenous technology development and innovation.

Much of the recent literature on absorptive capacity has focused on spillovers from FDI and participation in GVCs. A large study of over 25,000 firms in 78 different low- to middle-income countries found that, for low-productivity firms, national policies to support education, trade openness, and openness in financial markets were significant mediating factors of FDI spillovers, with the importance of these conditions diminishing as firms became more productive (Farole and Winkler 2012).

FDI spillovers tend to depend on the degree of interaction between buyers and suppliers (for example, the share of outputs going to a single buyer) and the length of the trading relationship (Winkler 2013). A study on how China has built technological capabilities in LCT sectors finds that advances in capabilities were more often achieved via bottom-up market relationships between Chinese and foreign firms, facilitating knowledge flows and learning, rather than top-down efforts to foster indigenous R&D (Watson et al. 2015). Studies on market-seeking FDI—measured by the share of a foreign firm's output sold domestically— demonstrate that, when foreign firms source more intermediate inputs from local suppliers, especially from low- and medium-productivity firms, spillovers tend to be higher (Farole and Winkler 2012). Although interesting, these ex post assessments leave much to be desired in identifying policies and strategic pathways for developing absorptive capacities in specific infant industries, such as LCT.

Advances in data collection have allowed for deeper exploration of the determinants of absorptive capacity, capabilities, and their role in the economic geography of innovation—allowing for more predictive analysis. This emerging field assumes that innovation and diversification occur as part of a cumulative process of building capabilities and are therefore path dependent. It follows that innovation and diversification are more likely to occur in regions, and sectors within those regions, that demonstrate existing capabilities in related technologies (Boschma and Frenken 2011; Hidalgo et al. 2007). One recent study on "eco-technologies" in the European Union finds this hypothesis to hold, with regions with an existing knowledge base in related technologies being more likely to enter into and more likely to develop patents in LCT (van den Berge and Weterings 2018). The empirical findings of this branch of study are improving with better-quality data, offering important insights into the relatedness of products and the likelihood of developing industries in specific regions. These initial studies confirm that one-size-fits-all policies are unlikely to be effective in fostering the development of new green sectors. Chapter 5 further explores these issues.

CONCLUSIONS

This chapter has described some of the shifts in the landscape of international LCT trade and investment, highlighting their importance as channels of LCT transfer and know-how. Given data limitations, the analysis of these flows suggests that the traditional North–South technology transfer paradigm is still predominant but that South–South and South–North technology transfers are becoming increasingly relevant within LCT sectors. This shift has been driven by China's rapid development of capabilities in LCT sectors and a small cohort of emerging economies that have leveraged factor endowments, existing capabilities, and links to global trade hubs to carve out global market share and become attractive investment destinations.

In order to make more informed, evidence-based decisions, policy makers will need better and more data, and data analysis, to deepen their understanding of LCT products, value chains, and investment flows. Updated and improved multiregional input-output tables could help to deliver more accurate insight into the multiple components involved in LCT manufacturing. These tables could also help countries to find consensus on products that could be included in bilateral or multilateral preferential trade agreements. Policy makers also need to understand how much investment is being channeled to meet low-carbon commitments. Improved data collection and classification of investment into environmentally friendly activities and industries would be beneficial.

Many of the policies or reforms needed to promote LCT transfer through trade and investment are the same as those necessary for all products and sectors: stable macroeconomic conditions, access to finance, a good investment climate, preferential market access, connectivity, and so on. For a start, policy coherence—clear climate commitments and actions to demonstrate follow-through on those commitments—can signal to the private sector that the government is serious about low-carbon development and thus help to attract investment. Depending on a country's fiscal and institutional capacity, such actions could include sector-specific support policies to boost productivity and competitiveness in green industries, and technical regulations on products that can be imported and sold in the domestic market. The feasibility of implementing such policies and the likelihood of effectiveness will depend on the country context. A more complete discussion of policies can be found in chapter 5.

The following multilateral, bilateral, and regional initiatives and policies can provide further impetus for LCT trade and investment.

Multilateral cooperation for trade liberalization. Governments that support climate action need to push for progress at reducing tariff and nontariff barriers to trade in LCTs at the multilateral level. None of the WTO agreements requires signatories to take specific actions to prevent negative environmental externalities or requires them to put in place environmental protection measures. This must change. At the very least, the Environmental Goods Agreement (EGA) negotiations should be revived. Since July 2014, 46 WTO members have been negotiating the EGA as a means to remove barriers to trade in goods that have positive environmental or climate change impacts.[24] Because the EGA is a plurilateral trade agreement, all WTO members would enjoy most-favored-nation tariff rates for environmental goods once it is ratified. EGA negotiations were suspended in December 2016 when the parties failed to reach a consensus on outstanding issues after China submitted a new list of products at a late stage in the process (European Parliament 2019). The EGA faces a number of negotiation challenges. First, the current version of the EGA covers only tariffs for certain environmental goods, and nontariff barriers and trade in services are excluded. Second, the parties have not yet agreed upon a common list of the goods covered. Third, the parties have not agreed on the extent of the tariff reductions, and a few countries have raised concerns about the potential elimination of tariffs on certain sensitive goods. Extensive negotiations will be necessary to resolve these issues.

Meanwhile, unilateral tariff reductions could offer an immediate dollar-value incentive to increase trade. Econometric assessments suggest that, if tariffs on LCT were liberalized, the largest increases in imports of LCT would be for lower-income countries (de Melo and Solleder 2018). But governments from these countries have been reluctant to further liberalize, expressing concern over trade balances and the detrimental impact on domestic firms. Multiple studies have shown, however, that these countries would benefit from large increases in welfare gains—such as access to lower-cost, clean energy—which would also disproportionately benefit low-income households. Other sticking points also need to be addressed multilaterally, including how best to apply the WTO Agreement on Trade-Related Aspects of Intellectual Property Rights (TRIPS) in a way that removes impediments to technology transfer and actually encourages and incentivizes transfer of LCTs to developing countries. A balance will need to be struck on these issues, across parties, with mechanisms to address distributional impacts.

Services market liberalization. Much of this chapter focused on trade in goods, but many of these goods were destined for use in services sectors. More can be done at the multilateral level to clarify existing WTO commitments and bilateral level to develop new commitments and guidelines on energy markets and services. Many countries are just now putting in place legal frameworks for third-party access to energy facilities, permit and licensing policies for captive RE systems, competition safeguards, and regulatory transparency. Although many of these issues focus on the domestic market, recent trends toward privatization and energy market liberalization, in light of the need to rapidly transition away from fossil fuels, have created new opportunities for fundamentally different approaches to energy systems and regulation.

Regional integration and bilateral trade agreements with stronger environmental provisions. Trade liberalization and environmental protection can be mutually supportive. As the number and regulatory coverage of preferential trade agreements has soared over the past three decades, so too has the number of environmental provisions contained in these agreements (Monteiro and Trachman, forthcoming). Agreements negotiated between developed countries, and between developed and developing countries, tend to include the highest number of such provisions. Committing to a clear path of sequenced reforms to support environmental objectives can boost economic and welfare gains. Analysis of the impact of environmental provisions has shown that their inclusion has been correlated with increased trade flows (Berger et al. 2020). Even in cases where developing countries sign agreements with more developed partners, the former's exporters have been shown to benefit from the inclusion of environmental provisions (Berger et al. 2018). These agreements have also helped to drive bilateral and multilateral cooperation on issues such as private product standards and environmental subsidies.

NOTES

1. Licensing contracts vary according to the form and size of the payment for which the licensee is responsible (fixed fees versus royalties), the degree of exclusivity (single licensee versus patent pools), and the division of rents across the parties involved (Gallini and Wright 1990). In principle, evidence related to licensing and observational data on royalty fees would be the most robust metric indicating that technology transfer has occurred; however, product-specific data on licensing fees are very limited or not publicly available. Nevertheless, as Dussaux, Dechezleprêtre, and Glachant (2018) point out, the omission of licensing data from empirical analyses of technology transfer is not necessarily a major issue, because in recent years licensing fees represent a very small portion of global gross domestic product.

2. See Zhang and Zhou (2016) for a discussion on the impact of FDI in China, where the authors find evidence that FDI has contributed to a reduction in CO_2 emissions.

3. Products are classified by a unique HS number, increasing in detail by incremental numbers of digits (that is, two-digit, four-digit, and six-digit). For more information on the United Nations International Trade Statistics Database (UN Comtrade), see https://comtrade.un.org/.

4. For more information, see the International Renewable Energy Agency's (IRENA) web page on "Costs" at https://www.irena.org/costs.

5. The LCOE is the net present value of the unit cost of electrical energy over the lifetime of a generating asset. It allows the comparison of different technologies (for example, wind, solar, and natural gas) of unequal life spans, project sizes, capital costs, risks, returns, and capacities.

6. Firms produce goods and provide services that may vary widely in the degree of potential climate impact. Missing information on production processes or specific outputs makes it difficult to determine if LCT is the most significant part of an investment or a business. In many cases, technology transfer is difficult to quantify; it occurs less explicitly and more implicitly through indirect knowledge spillovers, such as those generated through reverse engineering or the circulation of skilled labor. All factors vary by industry.

7. The list of 54 environmental goods established by the Asia-Pacific Economic Cooperation (APEC) forum is arguably the most well-known, because it is the only list agreed and acted upon by governments around the world. The last list presented for negotiation of the WTO EGA comprised 411 products at the HS six-digit level (de Melo and Solleder 2018). These 411 products were drawn from nationally constructed lists and other previous iterations produced by the OECD, academia, and other organizations. The OECD defined

a list of 334 Environmentally Preferable Products (EPPs) in the context of the Doha Round of Negotiations, which was then reduced to an EPP-Core list of 107 products (Zugravu-Soilita 2016). The OECD later compiled a new Combined List of Environmental Goods (CLEG), totaling 248 products (Garsous 2019). See de Melo and Solleder (2018), Garsous (2019), or Steenblik (2005) for further discussion on green goods lists.

8. Interestingly, only four products appear on all three lists, highlighting again the wide variation in defining what is or is not an LCT (see appendix B).

9. Only 106 of these products are under HS1988/1992 classification: 850230. Before 1996, wind turbines [850231–Electric generating sets; wind-powered (excluding those with spark-ignition or compression-ignition internal combustion piston engines) and 850239–Electric generating sets (excluding those with spark-ignition or compression-ignition internal combustion piston engines) other than wind powered] were classified under 850230–Electric generating sets, etc.

10. The Broad Economic Category classification is intended to categorize trade statistics into aggregated classes or types of goods according to their final use. See https://unstats.un.org/unsd/trade/classifications/bec.asp.

11. Note that 2016 is the latest year with the most available data for low-income countries. At the time of writing, those yet to report 2017 trade data include some relatively important developing economies—notably Bangladesh, Cambodia, Ethiopia, Thailand, and the United Arab Emirates.

12. From the perspective of climate change, Russia seems an unlikely champion. More than one-third (34.9 percent) of its LCT imports were "Machinery; for liquefying air or gas, not used for domestic purposes" (HS 841960), which is, again, included only on the APEC list of environmental goods. The debate over whether or not products related to natural gas belong on an environmental list is not taken up in this chapter.

13. The large increase in exports from upper-middle-income countries in figure 2.8 and figure 2.9 is attributable to China's reclassification to upper-middle-income status in 2010. China now accounts for roughly three-quarters of all exports from upper-middle-income countries. Table B.6 in annex B illustrates the outsized role China has played within its income group in 2016.

14. Data from the World Bank's online tool: https://data.worldbank.org/indicator/NE.TRD.GNFS.ZS?end=2017&start=1992.

15. The products are the following: (i) HS 901380—Optical devices, appliances and instruments; not elsewhere classified in heading no. 9013 (including liquid crystal devices); these products can be used in producing heliostats for solar power systems; (ii) HS 854140—Electrical apparatus; photosensitive, including PV cells, light-emitting diodes (LEDs); these products are used in the production of solar cells and modules; (iii) HS 853710—Boards, panels, consoles, desks, and other bases; these products can be used in producing electronic control equipment for wind energy systems. This category is likely to include dual-use products and (iv) HS 847989—Machines and mechanical appliances; this is a catch-all classification for machinery not elsewhere classified, which can refer to, in some instances, equipment for prevention of air pollution, noise treatment, water contamination prevention, or machines for squeezing radioactive waste (Vossenaar 2014). This category is likely to include dual-use products.

16. The GSR uses investment data from BloombergNEF, which includes all biomass, geothermal, and wind power projects of more than 1 megawatt (MW); all hydropower projects of between 1 MW and 50 MW; all solar power projects, with those less than 1 MW estimated separately; all ocean energy projects; and all biofuel projects with an annual production capacity of 1 million liters or more.

17. "Clean energy" is defined in BloombergNEF as renewables above certain generation scale parameters, as well as "energy smart technologies" such as electric vehicles and energy storage.

18. This information is tracked through (i) *Financial Times* newswires and internal information sources, (ii) media sources, including all of the world's top business sources, (iii) project data received from over 2,000 industry organizations and investment agencies, and (iv) data purchased from market research and publication companies. Each project identified is cross-referenced against multiple sources, with primary focus on direct company sources. See https://www.fdimarkets.com/faqs/.

19. This information is not always released by companies. In such cases, *fDi Markets* uses a proprietary econometric model to estimate the investment and job creation figures.

This chapter includes these estimates, relying on *fDi Markets* as one of the world's most trusted sources of FDI data, in order to sketch a very rough estimate of FDI flows.

20. Calculated keeping the World Bank's 2003 country income classification constant.

21. This investment is not listed in the company's portfolio on its website.

22. Using the World Bank Group's 2003 income group country classifications. Note that these figures change depending on the year chosen for income group classifications. Considering the desire to trace transformation over time, these tables were compiled using the 2003 income group classification, matching the earliest available data from *fDi Markets*.

23. Data from the Institute of International Education's *Project Atlas*, https://www.iie.org /Research-and-Insights/Project-Atlas/.

24. These 46 economies include European Union countries and Australia; Canada; China; Costa Rica; Hong Kong SAR, China; Iceland; Israel; Japan; Republic of Korea; New Zealand; Norway; Switzerland; Singapore; Taiwan, China; Turkey; and the United States (European Commission 2016).

REFERENCES

Berger, A, C Brandi, J. F. Morin, and J. Schwab, 2020. "The Trade Effects of Environmental Provisions in Preferential Trade Agreements. In *International Trade, Investment, and the Sustainable Development Goals*, edited by C. Beverelli, J. Kurtz, and D. Raess. Cambridge: Cambridge University Press.

Bitzer, J., and M. Kerekes. 2008. "Does Foreign Direct Investment Transfer Technology across Borders? New Evidence." *Economic Letters* 100 (3): 355–58.

BloombergNEF. 2019. "Clean Energy Investment Trends, 2018." BloombergNEF, New York.

Boschma, R., and K. Frenken. 2011. "Technological Relatedness and Regional Branching." In *Beyond Territory. Dynamic Geographies of Knowledge Creation, Diffusion and Innovation*, edited by H. Bathelt, M. P. Feldman, and D. F. Kogler, 64–81. London: Routledge.

Buchner, B., J. Brown, and J. Corfee-Morlot. 2011. "Monitoring and Tracking Long-Term Finance to Support Climate Action." OECD/IEA Climate Change Expert Group Papers 2011/03, OECD Publishing, Paris.

CEMAC (Clean Energy Manufacturing Analysis Center). 2017. "Benchmarks of Global Clean Energy Manufacturing." CEMAC, Washington, DC.

Chen, Y. 2018. "Comparing North–South Technology Transfer and South–South Technology Transfer: The Technology Transfer Impact of Ethiopian Wind Farms." *Energy Policy* 116 (May): 1–9.

Claessens, S., and S. L. Schmukler. 2007. "International Financial Integration through Equity Markets: Which Firms from Which Countries Go Global?" Policy Research Working Paper 4146, World Bank, Washington, DC.

Coe, D. T., E. Helpman, and A. W. Hoffmaister. 1997. "North–South R&D Spillovers." *Economic Journal* 107: 134–49.

Cohen, W. M., and D. Levinthal. 1990. "Absorptive Ccapacity: A New Perspective on Learning and Innovation." *Administrative Science Quarterly* 35 (1): 128-152.

Dechezleprêtre A., M. Glachant, and Y. Ménière. 2013. "What Drives the International Transfer of Climate Change Mitigation Technologies? Empirical Evidence from Patent Data." *Environmental and Resources Economics* 54 (2): 161–78.

De Melo, J., and J.-M. Solleder. 2018. "Barriers to Trade in Environmental Goods: How Important They Are and What Should Developing Countries Expect from Their Removal." FERDI Working Paper P235, Fondation pour les Études et Recherches sur le Développement International. https://www.researchgate.net/publication/328744244_.

———. 2019. "What's Wrong with the WTO's Environmental Goods Agreement: A Developing Country Perspective." *Vox*, March 13. https://voxeu.org/article/what-s-wrong-wto-s -environmental-goods-agreement.

Dussaux D., A. Dechezleprêtre, and M. Glachant. 2018. "Intellectual Property Rights Protection and the International Transfer of Low-Carbon Technologies." Working Paper 288, January, Grantham Research Center for Climate Change and the Environment.

European Commission. 2016. "The Environmental Goods Agreement (EGA): Liberalising Trade in Environmental Goods and Services." European Commission, Brussels. http://trade.ec.europa.eu/doclib/press/index.cfm?id=1116.

European Parliament. 2019. "Plurilateral Environmental Goods Agreement (EGA): Multilateral and Plurilateral Trade Agreements within and outside the WTO Framework." Legislative Train 11.2019, European Parliament. http://www.europarl.europa.eu/legislative-train/api/stages/report/current/theme/a-balanced-and-progressive-trade-policy-to-harness-globalisation/file/environmental-goods-agreement-(ega).

Farole, T., and D. Winkler. 2012. "Foreign Firm Characteristics, Absorptive Capacity and the Institutional Framework: The Role of Mediating Factors for FDI Spillovers in Low- and Middle-Income Countries." Policy Research Working Paper 6265, World Bank, Washington, DC.

Fu, X., C. Pietrobelli, and L. Soete. 2011. "The Role of Foreign Technology and Indigenous Innovation in the Emerging Economies: Technological Change and Catching Up." *World Development* 39 (7): 1204–12.

Gallagher, K. P., and L. Zarsky. 2007. *The Enclave Economy: Foreign Investment and Sustainable Development in Mexico's Silicon Valley.* Cambridge, MA: MIT Press.

Gallini, N. T. and B. D. Wright. 1990. "Technology Transfer under Asymmetric Information." *Rand Journal of Economics* 21 (1): 147–60.

Golub, S. S., C. Kaufmann, and P. Yeres. 2011. "Defining and Measuring Green FDI: An Exploratory Review of Existing Work and Evidence." OECD Working Papers on International Investment, OECD Publishing, Paris.

Gorg, H., and D. Greenaway. 2004. "Much Ado about Nothing? Do Domestic Firms Really Benefit from Foreign Direct Investment?" *World Bank Research Observer* 19 (2): 171–97.

Gorg, H., and E. Strobl. 2001. "Multinational Companies and Productivity Spillovers: A Meta-Analysis." *Economic Journal* 111 (475): 723–39.

Grossman, G. M., and E. Helpman. 1991. "Trade, Knowledge Spillovers, and Growth." *European Economic Review* 35 (2–3): 517–26.

Helpman, E., M. Melitz, and S. R. Yeaple. 2004. "Export versus FDI with Heterogeneous Firms." *American Economic Review* 94 (1): 300–16.

Hidalgo, C. A., B. Klinger, A.-L. Barabasi, and R. Hausmann. 2007. "The Product Space Conditions the Development of Nations." *Science* 317 (5837): 482–87.

Hoekman, B., K. E. Maskus, and K. Saggi. 2004. "Transfer of Technology to Developing Countries: Unilateral and Multilateral Policy Options." Policy Research Working Paper 3332, World Bank, Washington, DC.

Hovhannisyan, N., and W. Keller. 2015. "International Business Travel: An Engine of Innovation?" *Journal of Economic Growth* 20 (1): 75–104.

Huberty, M., and G. Zachmann. 2011. "Green Exports and the Global Product Space: Prospects for EU Industrial Policy." Bruegel Working Paper 2011/07, Bruegel, Brussels.

ICTSD (International Centre for Trade and Sustainable Development). 2016. "Ministerial Talks to Clinch Environmental Goods Agreement Hit Stumbling Block." *Bridges* 20 (42): 1–4.

Institute of International Education. 2018. "A World on the Move: Trends in Global Student Mobility, Issue 2." Institute of International Education, New York.

Jha, V. 2017. *Building Supply Chain Efficiency in Solar and Wind Energy: Trade and Other Policy Considerations.* Geneva: International Centre for Trade and Sustainable Development.

Keller, W., and S. Yeaple. 2009. "Multinational Enterprises, International Trade, and Productivity Growth: Firm-Level Evidence from the United States." *Review of Economics and Statistics* 91 (4): 821–31.

Kirchherr, J., and F. Urban. 2018. "Technology Transfer and Cooperation for Low Carbon Energy Technology: Analysing 30 Years of Scholarship and Proposing a Research Agenda." *Energy Policy* 119 (2018): 600–09.

Kusek, P., and A. Silva. 2018. "What Investors Want: Perceptions and Experiences of Multinational Corporations in Developing Countries." Policy Research Working Paper 8386, World Bank, Washington, DC.

Lall, S. 2000. "The Technological Structure and Performance of Developing Country Manufactured Exports, 1985–98." *Oxford Development Studies* 28(3): 337–69.

Meyer, K. E. 2004. "Perspectives on Multinational Enterprises in Emerging Economies." *Journal of International Business Studies* 35 (4): 259–76.

Monteiro, J. A., and J. P. Trachman. Forthcoming. "Environment-Related Provisions in Preferential Trade Agreements." In *Handbook of Deep Integration Agreements*, edited by A. Mattoo, N. Rocha, and M. Ruta. Washington, DC: World Bank Group.

Motyka, M., A. Slaughter, and C. Amon. 2018. "Global Renewable Energy Trends." Deloitte Insights, September 13.

Navaretti, G. B., and D. G. Tarr. 2000. "International Knowledge Flows and Economic Performance: A Review of the Evidence." *World Bank Economic Review* 14 (1): 1–15.

Newman, C., J. Rand, T. Talbot, and F. Tarp. 2015. "Technology Transfers, Foreign Investment and Productivity Spillovers." *European Economic Review* 76 (May): 168–87.

Pueyo, A., and P. Linares. 2012. "Renewable Technology Transfer to Developing Countries: One Size Does Not Fit All." IDS Working Paper Volume 2012 (412), Institute of Development Studies, Brighton, U.K.

REN21 (Renewable Energy Policy Network for the 21st Century). 2018. "Renewables 2018 Global Status Report." REN21, Paris.

Shehadi, S. 2019. "fDi Renewable Energy Investments of the Year 2019—the winners." *fDi Intelligence*, March 11.

Taglioni, D., and D. Winkler. 2016. *Making Global Value Chains Work for Development*. Trade and Development Series. Washington, DC: World Bank.

UNCTAD (United Nations Conference on Trade and Development). 2010. *World Investment Report 2010: Investing in a Low-Carbon Economy*. New York and Geneva: United Nations.

———. 2018. *Key Statistics and Trends in International Trade 2017: International Trade Rebounds*. Geneva: UNCTAD.

Urban, F. 2018. "China's Rise: Challenging the North–South Technology Transfer Paradigm for Climate Change Mitigation and Low Carbon Energy." *Energy Policy* 113 (February): 320–30.

van den Berge, M., and A. Weterings. 2018. "Relatedness in Eco-Technological Development in European Regions." Paper presented at the DRUID Society Conference, CBS, Copenhagen, June 16–18.

van Pottelsberghe de la Potterie, B., and F. Lichtenburg. 2001. "Does Foreign Direct Investment Transfer Technology across Borders?" *Review of Economics and Statistics* 83 (3): 490–97.

Vossenaar, R. 2014. "Identifying Products with Climate and Development Benefits for an Environmental Goods Agreement." ICTSD Issue Paper 9, International Centre for Trade and Sustainable Development, Geneva.

Watson, J., R. Byrne, D. Ockwell, and M. Stua. 2015. "Lessons from China: Building Technological Capabilities for Low Carbon Technology Transfer and Development." *Climatic Change* 131 (3): 387–99.

Winkler, D. 2013. "Potential and Actual FDI Spillovers in Global Value Chains: The Role of Foreign Investor Characteristics, Absorptive Capacity and Transmission Channels." Policy Research Working Paper 6424, World Bank, Washington, DC.

World Bank. 2008. *International Trade and Climate Change: Economic, Legal, and Institutional Perspectives*. Washington, DC: World Bank.

———. 2018. *Moving for Prosperity: Global Migration and Labor Markets*. Policy Research Report. Washington, DC: World Bank.

———. 2019. *Global Economic Prospects, January 2019: Darkening Skies*. Washington, DC: World Bank.

Zhang, C., and X. Zhou. 2016. "Does Foreign Direct Investment Lead to Lower CO_2 Emissions? Evidence from a Regional Analysis in China." *Renewable and Sustainable Energy Reviews* 58 (May): 943–51.

3 Using Patents to Measure the International Transfer of Low-Carbon Technologies and Its Determinants

INTRODUCTION

As discussed in chapter 1, accelerating the transfer of low-carbon technologies (LCTs) is crucial to limit global warming to 1.5°C above preindustrial levels. This chapter uses data on cross-border patent transfers to examine current trends in the dissemination of LCTs and explores options for accelerating the uptake of these technologies, especially in developing countries.

A patent gives an exclusive right to an inventor to use and sell the invention for a certain number of years. By limiting competition and creating a temporary monopoly rent, patents not only help innovators reap rewards but also provide incentives for others to invest in new innovations. Patents are a common measure of innovation: applying for a patent is a costly process, and inventors do it only for innovations they expect to exploit and benefit from. Not all patents have the same quality, however, which makes cross-country comparisons informative but challenging. Firms that export capital goods and invest in foreign countries use patents to protect their intellectual property (see Dechezleprêtre et al. 2011; Dechezleprêtre, Glachant, and Ménière 2013; de la Tour, Glachant, and Ménière 2011; Eaton and Kortum 1999; Glachant et al. 2013; Maskus 2004). Thus, patents are also a measure of technology transfer because they give the right to commercially exploit the invention in the country where the patent is filed and because patentable technologies must be both novel to the local context and susceptible to industrial application.[1]

Using patent-transfer data from the PATSTAT database maintained by the European Patent Office (EPO),[2] the first part of the chapter describes current trends in LCT innovation and transfer, and discusses the factors that encourage or impede the diffusion of LCTs in developing countries. Unlike the datasets used in previous studies, which focused on renewable energy, low-carbon buildings, and cleaner vehicle technologies, the PATSTAT data cover all types of LCT, including energy-efficient manufacturing technologies, which cannot be measured using current trade data or foreign direct investment (FDI) data.

The second part of the chapter constructs an econometric model using a dataset of 75 countries observed from 2006 to 2015 to measure the impact of different factors on patent transfers. These factors include local capacity for technological absorption, environmental policies, intellectual property rights (IPR) protections, FDI restrictions, tariffs, nontariff barriers, and market size. The methodology consists in estimating a gravity model of patent transfer with exporter-year fixed effects and country-pair fixed effects. The final section concludes the chapter.

MEASURING LCT WITH PATENT DATA

Measuring technology transfer with patent data offers critical advantages. Patents contain important contextual information—such as the patent holder's country of residence, the year the technology was invented, and the countries in which the technology was patented—as well as detailed technical information, which allows the patented technologies to be organized into highly specific categories. Moreover, the EPO's PATSTAT database is comprehensive, allowing for the identification of patent transfers for any given technology between any pair of countries, whereas the available data on cross-country investment are extremely limited (Dussaux, Dechezleprêtre, and Glachant 2018).

Although analyzing patents offers many important methodological advantages, three caveats should be noted. First, although many transferred technologies are patented (Guellec and van Pottelsberghe de la Potterie 2001), some firms may instead rely on industrial secrecy—as well as other, more complex tools—to shield their intellectual property from imitation. Technologies that are transferred but not protected by a local patent will not appear in the dataset. Some firms may use a combination of industrial secrecy and patents to safeguard proprietary technologies; in these cases, local patents will still indicate that technology transfer is occurring, but they will not fully describe that technology. Second, stronger IPR protections could prompt inventors to switch from secrecy to patent protection, which would result in a larger number of patent transfers without affecting the total amount of technology transferred (Cohen, Nelson, and Walsh 2000). By contrast, Dussaux, Dechezleprêtre, and Glachant (2018) use data on international trade and FDI, which are not subject to the potential substitution between patented and unpatented technologies.[3] Finally, some patents are purely strategic, barring the use of certain technologies by competitors even when those technologies are not used by the firm that holds the patent. The inclusion of strategic patents in the dataset could therefore cause the analysis to overestimate the degree of technology transfer actually occurring. The significant monetary and administrative costs involved in the patent-filing process mitigate this risk, however, and empirical evidence shows that technologies are patented in an average of just two countries each (Dechezleprêtre et al. 2011).[4]

DATA SOURCES AND ACCOUNTING METHODOLOGY FOR LCT

The EPO created the PATSTAT database in 2006. PATSTAT is organized according to the Cooperative Patent Classification (CPC) scheme, which was jointly developed by the EPO and the U.S. Patent and Trademark Office (USPTO).[5] The CPC includes a specific category of patents defined as "Technologies or applications for mitigation or adaptation against climate change." These technologies are identified by CPC codes beginning with Y02. The analysis presented in this chapter focuses on mitigation and excludes adaptation technologies. It covers the seven following LCT fields:

1. **Buildings**. Y02B—"Climate change mitigation technologies related to buildings, e.g. housing, house appliances or related end-user applications."
2. **Carbon capture and storage (CCS)**. Y02C—"Capture, storage, sequestration or disposal of greenhouse gases."
3. **Information and communication**. Y02D—"Climate change mitigation technologies in information and communication technologies, i.e. information and communication technologies aiming at the reduction of their own energy use."
4. **Energy**. Y02E—"Reduction of greenhouse gas emissions related to energy generation, transmission or distribution."
5. **Manufacturing**. Y02P—"Climate change mitigation technologies in the production or processing of goods."
6. **Transportation**. Y02T—"Climate change mitigation technologies related to transportation."
7. **Wastewater treatment and management**. Y02W—"Climate change mitigation technologies related to wastewater treatment or waste management."

The dataset covers over 800,000 patents filed between 1990 and 2015[6] under the seven LCT fields listed above. The largest number of patented technologies is in the energy, manufacturing, and transportation sectors, which is consistent with the weight of those sectors in total greenhouse gas (GHG) emissions. CCS, a recent and more limited field, accounts for the fewest patented technologies. About one-fourth of all patented LCTs are defined as "high-value technologies," which have been patented in at least two patent offices. The ratio of high-value technologies to total technologies is broadly consistent across fields (table 3.1).

When a new technology is patented, the patent holder has one year in which to file patent applications in foreign countries. This period is known as the priority year, because the current patent holder can claim priority over other applicants. Patents on the same technology filed in multiple countries form a

TABLE 3.1 **Patented technologies, by field, 1990–2015**

COOPERATIVE PATENT CLASSIFICATION (CPC) CODE	FIELD	PATENTED TECHNOLOGIES (THOUSANDS OF PATENTS)	HIGH-VALUE TECHNOLOGIES (THOUSANDS OF PATENTS)
Y02 excl. Y02A	All low-carbon technologies	834	220
Y02B	Buildings	90	27
Y02C	Carbon capture and storage	7	3
Y02D	Information and communication	47	19
Y02E	Energy	270	65
Y02P	Manufacturing	209	48
Y02T	Transportation	182	70
Y02W	Wastewater treatment and management	107	15

Source: Calculations based on the PATSTAT database.
Note: High-value technologies are defined as those that have been patented in at least two patent offices.

patent family, but each patent family has only one priority patent. Restricting the analysis to priority patents helps ensure that each technology is counted only once. When a technology originally patented in country A is subsequently patented in country B, this is regarded as a technology transfer from country A to country B. Country A is defined as the inventor country and country B as the recipient country. Several studies in the literature use this approach (Dechezleprêtre et al. 2011; Dechezleprêtre, Glachant, and Ménière 2013; de la Tour, Glachant, and Ménière 2011; Eaton and Kortum 1996, 1999; Glachant et al. 2013; Maskus 2004).

Differences in the requirements for filing a patent across countries create heterogeneity in patent quality. The analysis in this chapter mitigates qualitative differences by focusing on high-value technologies (see table 3.1),[7]—that is, patents filed in at least two countries tend to have greater economic value than do patents filed in a single country (Guellec and van Pottelsberghe de la Potterie 2001; Harhoff, Scherer, and Vopel 2003).

Although all other emerging economies are represented in PATSTAT, India is not included. To date, the Indian patent office has declined to make its data available publicly and free of charge. Consequently, PATSTAT includes Indian patents that have been transferred to other countries, but not foreign patents that have been transferred to India. To prevent this disparity from distorting the analysis, India is explicitly excluded from the dataset for this report.[8]

THE TRANSFER OF LCTs

Between 1990 and 2015, the annual growth rate of LCTs averaged about 8 percent per year, roughly double the growth rate for all technologies, but it fell significantly between 2012 and 2015 (figure 3.1). This slowdown has been documented by other studies (for example, Dechezleprêtre 2017) and is not a

FIGURE 3.1

Global growth of inventions in LCTs and all technologies, 1990–2015

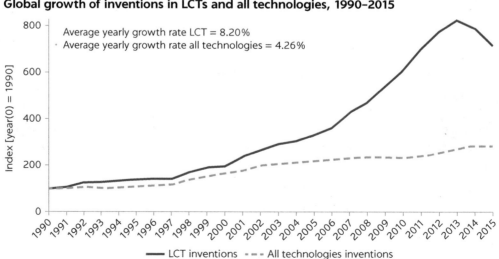

Average yearly growth rate LCT = 8.20%
Average yearly growth rate all technologies = 4.26%

—— LCT inventions – – – All technologies inventions

Source: Calculations based on PATSTAT data.
Note: The index is a normalized to 100 measure of patented inventions. The Y variable equals 100 * (number of patented inventions / number of patented inventions in year 1990). Low-carbon technology (LCT) includes only mitigation technology.

measurement error. Two factors drove the decline in the LCT growth rate observed between 2012 and 2015. First, innovation in LCT is influenced by the price of crude oil, which plunged during the period, making renewable energy less competitive against fossil fuels and weakening fuel-efficiency incentives. Second, public investment in renewable energy research and development peaked in 2009 and declined thereafter.[9] The global financial crisis put government budgets under pressure, shifting public funds away from research and development (R&D) toward recovery packages.

Between 1990–2000 and 2005–15, the total number of LCT innovations increased by 316 percent. Although the number of innovations increased across all LCT fields, some fields grew more quickly than others (figure 3.2). LCT innovations in information and communication technology (ICT) grew most rapidly, whereas LCT innovations in water management increased by only 39 percent. The energy, transportation, and manufacturing sectors accounted for the largest share of LCT innovations over the period.

LCT innovations are concentrated in high-income economies. Just five economies accounted for 73 percent of all LCTs invented between 2010 and 2015 (figure 3.3). Japan produced the largest share, followed by the United States, Germany, the Republic of Korea, and China. This order remains broadly similar across technological fields. France was one of the top-five innovators in transportation and CCS technologies, and Taiwan, China, was in the top five for ICT.

High-income countries produced at least 80 percent of LCT innovations in all technological fields. Lower-middle-income and low-income countries produced almost no LCT innovations during the period (figure 3.4).[10] This imbalance highlights the urgent need to accelerate international LCT transfer to lower-income countries.

China is a global leader in LCT innovation. Between 2010 and 2015, China produced 8 percent of the world's LCT innovations, far more than any other developing country (table 3.2). China produced more than 15 times as many

FIGURE 3.2

Growth of LCTs, by field, 1990–2000 and 2005–15

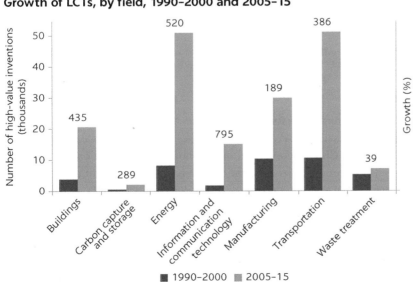

Source: Calculations based on PATSTAT data.

FIGURE 3.3

Top-five innovators in LCT, 2010–15

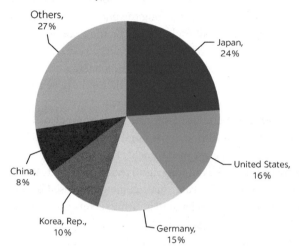

Source: Calculations based on PATSTAT (database), https://www.epo.org/index.html.

FIGURE 3.4

Innovations in LCT across income groups, 2010–15

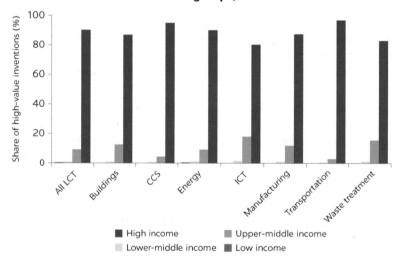

Source: Calculations based on PATSTAT (database), https://www.epo.org/index.html.
Note: CCS = carbon capture and storage; ICT = information and communication technology; LCT = low-carbon technology.

LCT innovations as the Russian Federation (0.5 percent), more than 25 times as many as Brazil (0.3 percent), and 77 times as many as Mexico (0.1 percent). Importantly, China's contribution to global LCT innovation significantly exceeds its economic size. The ratio between China's share of patented innovations and its share in global gross domestic product (GDP) is about 70:100. By contrast, Russia's ratio is about 20:100, Brazil's is about 9:100, and Mexico's is less than 6:100. Together, Brazil, China, Russia, and South Africa contribute about 10 percent to global LCT innovation, but South Africa is not among the top-10 climate change mitigation innovators in the developing world.

Despite its leadership in LCT innovation, according to Medvedev (2019), China submits only a small percentage of its LCTs to overseas patenting offices. Moreover, the citation rate for China's renewable energy technologies patents is

TABLE 3.2 **The top-10 inventors of LCT among developing countries, 2010–15**

COUNTRY	SHARE OF LCT INNOVATIONS (%)	SHARE OF GLOBAL GDP (%)
China	8.0	11.1
Russian Federation	0.5	2.4
Brazil	0.3	3.4
Mexico	0.1	1.7
Malaysia	0.1	0.4
Turkey	0.1	1.4
Ukraine	0.1	0.2
Thailand	< 0.1	0.5
Romania	< 0.1	0.3
Bulgaria	< 0.1	0.1

Source: Calculations based on PATSTAT data.
Note: Data for India are not available. LCT = low-carbon technology.

very low when compared to patents received by firms from Germany, Japan, and the United States.[11] Low patent quality may indicate that firms attempt to use patents to create barriers to entry for competitors, blocking freedom. Medvedev (2019) also report that both foreign and local firms in China complain about IPR breaches, the difficulty of enforcing claims, and gaps in regulations.

LCT transfer to developing countries

The transfer of LCT to developing countries is crucial for two reasons. First, acquiring any new technology, LCT included, tends to have highly positive implications for productivity growth and the achievement of development objectives. For example, renewable energy technologies can play a critical role in the electrification of remote areas. Second, LCT transfer can decrease the cost of decarbonization in developing countries, which are currently projected to produce the bulk of carbon emissions over the next several decades (EIA 2016).

The PATSTAT data show negligible levels of LCT transfer to low-income countries. Between 2010 and 2015 roughly 71 percent of all patent transfers occurred between high-income countries, 23 percent were transfers from high-income to middle-income countries, and 4 percent were transfers from middle-income to high-income countries. Transfers between middle-income countries accounted for just 1 percent of the total, and almost no patents were transferred to or from low-income countries. Developing countries' share in LCT patent transfers has increased over time, however: previously—between 1990 and 1995—a full 91 percent of LCT patent transfers occurred between high-income countries.

The shares of LCT patents received by Germany, Japan, and Korea significantly exceed their shares of global carbon emissions, whereas those received by China and Russia are lower than their contributions to global carbon emissions (figure 3.5 and table C.1 in appendix C). The United States accounts for 18 percent of global carbon emissions and receives 18 percent of LCT patents. By contrast, China and Russia account for 36 and 6 percent of global carbon emissions, respectively, whereas they receive just 25.4 and 1.6 percent, respectively, of global LCT patents transfers.[12] Given China's enormous carbon output, accelerating LCT transfer to China will be vital to meet global climate targets.[13]

FIGURE 3.5

Share of LCT patents received and carbon emissions, select countries, 2010–15

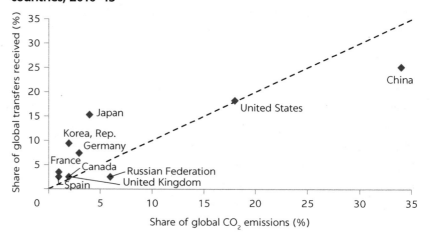

Source: Calculations based on PATSTAT data and World Bank data.
Note: Patents invented and filed in the same country are excluded. Only the top-10 low-carbon technology (LCT) recipients are included for clarity. CO_2 = carbon dioxide.

FIGURE 3.6

Share of LCT patents received and carbon emissions, select developing countries, 2010–15

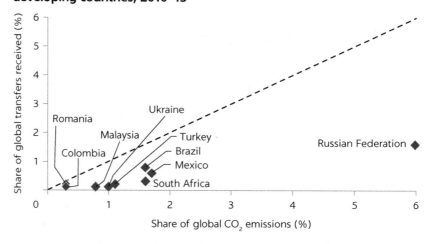

Source: Calculations based on PATSTAT data and World Bank data.
Note: For clarity, the figure shows the top-10 low-carbon technology (LCT) recipients, excluding China. CO_2 = carbon dioxide.

Other countries in the sample—Brazil, Malaysia, Mexico, South Africa, Turkey, and Ukraine—receive a lower share of LCT patent transfers relative to their significantly larger share of global carbon emissions. These countries should be considered priorities for accelerating LCT transfer (figure 3.6). By contrast, Colombia and Romania produce a share of carbon emissions that only modestly exceeds their share of LCT patent transfers.

The roles of China and Russia in LCT transfer

China and Russia specialize in different types of LCTs. Chinese LCT inventions focus on the energy sector (29 percent), ICT (20 percent), manufacturing

(19 percent), and buildings (18 percent) (figure 3.7a). Meanwhile, most foreign LCT patents registered in China focus on the energy sector (31 percent), transportation (29 percent), and manufacturing (19 percent) (figure 3.7b). Russia's LCT inventions are heavily concentrated in the energy and manufacturing sectors. Almost half of Russia's LCT innovations have applications in the energy sector, and over one-quarter have applications in the manufacturing sector (figure 3.8a). By contrast, the distribution of foreign LCT patent is more balanced (figure 3.8b). Like China, Russia receives a much larger share of LCT patents for transportation (31 percent) than it produces locally (11 percent).

FIGURE 3.7

China's invention and importation of LCTs, 2010–15

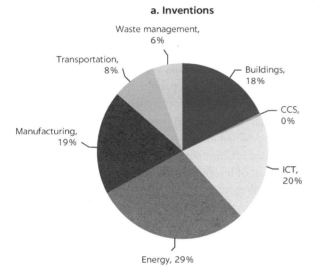
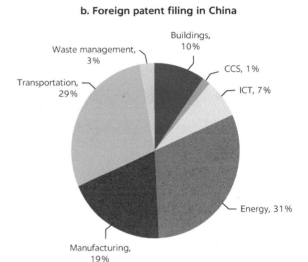

Source: Calculations based on PATSTAT data.
Note: CCS = carbon capture and storage; ICT = information and communication technology.

FIGURE 3.8

The Russian Federation's invention and importation of LCTs, 2010–15

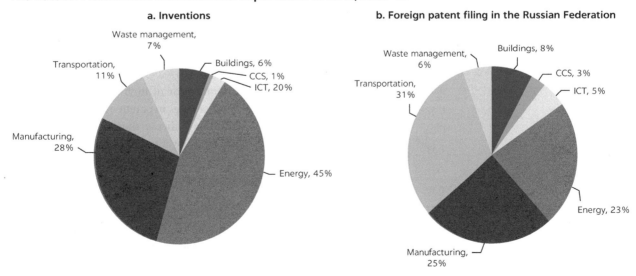

Source: Calculations based on PATSTAT data.
Note: CCS = carbon capture and storage; ICT = information and communication technology.

Between 2010 and 2015, 93 percent of outbound Chinese LCT patent transfers were to high-income economies. Major recipients of Chinese LCT patents included the United States (31 percent), Japan (11 percent), and Korea (9 percent). Among developing countries, the only significant recipients of Chinese LCT patents were Russia (2 percent), South Africa (1.1 percent), and Brazil (1 percent) (figure C.1 in appendix C).

High-income economies also accounted for most of Russia's outbound LCT patents, with the largest share going to the United States (18 percent). China received the second-largest share of Russian LCT patents (16 percent), followed by Ukraine (3 percent), Brazil (1.7 percent), and South Africa (0.8 percent), which pushed the total share of developing countries to 23 percent of Russia's total outbound LCT patents. Like China, Russia files about 10 percent of its LCT patents in Japan and Korea (figure C.2 in appendix C).

High-income economies account for the vast majority of inbound LCT patents filed in both China and Russia. Between 2010 and 2015, firms from high-income economies filed more than 94 percent of inbound LCT patents in China and Russia (see figures C.3 and C.4 in appendix C). The United States alone accounted for 24 percent of the foreign LCT patents filed in both countries; however, the distribution of inbound LCT patents from other economies varied substantially. For example, Japan represented 31 percent of LCT patents filed in China but just 11 percent of those filed in Russia, whereas Germany accounted for 11 percent of LCT patents filed in China but 18 percent of those filed in Russia. Distance is a major determinant of international trade and FDI, the two main channels of international technology transfer, and the heterogeneity in inbound patents is consistent with the geographical distance separating the different countries, as well as their relative size.

The role of India in LCT transfer

As discussed earlier, India has been excluded from our analysis because of its absence from the PATSTAT database. Despite that absence, India's contribution to LCT transfer, and global carbon emissions, is too important to ignore. This section uses data from the WIPO's Patentscope dataset, which includes India. To identify LCTs in Patentscope, the analysis uses IPC codes selected by Dechezleprêtre, Glachant, and Ménière (2013) covering four technological fields: transportation, energy production, energy use, and methane capture. The number of patent families is used to proxy the number of LCT innovations, and an indicator of high-value innovations is used to account for differences in patent quality.[14]

The Patentscope data indicate that India accounts for 0.52 percent of total LCT innovations, making it the developing world's second-largest LCT innovator after China. India's share of global LCT patents is much smaller than that of China (1.51 percent), but significantly larger than those of South Africa (0.22 percent), Turkey (0.13 percent), and Russia (0.11 percent) (table 3.3). Importantly, the Patentscope data produce a ranking of LCT innovators in the developing world that is very similar to the ranking produced by the PATSTAT data (refer to table 3.2). The shares of the countries differ, however, because PATSTAT encompasses a wider range of LCT fields.

TABLE 3.3 **The top-10 LCT inventors among developing countries, according to Patentscope data, 2010–15**

COUNTRY	SHARE OF GLOBAL LCT PATENTS (%)
China	1.51
India	0.52
South Africa	0.22
Turkey	0.13
Russian Federation	0.11
Brazil	0.10
Malaysia	0.07
Thailand	0.04
Belarus	0.04
Tunisia	0.02

Source: Calculations based on Patentscope data.
Note: LCT = low-carbon technology.

Like PATSTAT, the Patentscope data indicate that the share of carbon emissions among developing countries exceeds their share of patent transfers. This disparity is especially wide in India and Russia, which contribute 6 percent and 5.3 percent to global carbon emissions, respectively, but which receive just 1 percent and 0.2 percent of all LCT patent transfers. These findings indicate considerable scope to accelerate LCT transfer to India and Russia.

DRIVERS OF LCT INNOVATION AND TRANSFER

Drivers of innovation in LCTs

Changes in relative prices greatly influence LCT innovation.[15] High fossil fuel prices tend to increase demand for LCT substitutes, and this dynamic prevails whether the increase in fossil fuel prices is caused by policy decisions (for example, carbon taxes) or market conditions. Some firms that rely on fossil fuel–based technologies will switch to LCT alternatives, whereas others will invest in new LCT innovations. Because these decisions involve long-term changes in the structure of production, the anticipated trajectory of relative prices plays a critical role in determining their impact on LCT innovation and uptake (see Newell, Jaffe, and Stavins 1999 and Popp 2002 for empirical evidence).

Long-term trends in relative prices have especially important implications for innovation. Like other technologies, R&D in LCT often entails lengthy lead times, high levels of risk, and large sunk costs (Scherer, Harhoff, and Kukies 2000). In addition to a favorable projection of the future financial viability of LCT innovations, the availability of financing can have a major impact on R&D, especially among small and credit-constrained firms (Jaffe, Newell, and Stavins 2003). Governments often help this process by introducing incentives such as R&D tax credits and subsidies to encourage innovation.

IPR protections affect both innovation and technology transfer. Without sufficient protection, a firm's innovations can be appropriated by competitors, allowing them to reap the benefits of the innovation without incurring the R&D costs necessary to create it. IPR protections can internalize the benefits of R&D investment by granting a patent holder exclusive rights to commercialize an innovation for a defined period, usually 20 years. While encouraging investment in R&D, however, patents also give market power to the patent holder, which, in turn, can limit the diffusion of new technologies and slow international technology transfer.

The intensity of product market competition also influences innovation. Theoretical analysis (for example, Aghion et al. 2005) has shown that the relation between product market competition and innovation is not linear. At low levels of competition, an increase in intensity can induce firms to innovate in order to pull away from their close competitors. At high levels of competition, an increase in intensity can reduce innovation by weakening incentives for lagging firms to catch up to technological leaders. The latter effect is also more likely to prevail in "unleveled" industries, where few firms are in close competition with one another.

Innovation in LCT is inhibited both by the presence of positive externalities on the supply side and by negative externalities on the demand side. The challenge of internalizing the benefits of new technology is not unique to LCT;

however, LCT innovations must also compete with technologies that generate negative externalities. For example, a coal-fired power plant may give rise to serious environmental costs that are not reflected in the price of the electricity it generates. Unless these costs can be internalized through regulation, carbon-intensive technologies will enjoy an unfair advantage over LCTs (Jaffe, Newell, and Stavins 2005).

Empirical evidence shows that environmental regulations can induce innovation in LCT (see also Brunel 2019; Johnstone and Labonne 2006; Lanoie et al. 2011). Pollution-abatement expenditures also have been shown to encourage investment in LCT innovation (Brunnermeier and Cohen 2003; Jaffe and Palmer 1997; Lanjouw and Mody 1996). Some studies suggest that, although regulation plays an important role in LCT innovation, it is not the most important driver (Calel and Dechezleprêtre 2016; Popp, Hafner, and Johnstone 2011). Other studies have shown that environmental policies affect the emergence of high-quality LCT innovations only, whereas competition encourages the creation of low-quality LCT innovations (Nesta, Vona, and Nicolli 2014).

Theoretical drivers of technology transfers

International trade and FDI are the most important channels for technology transfer.[16] Consequently, the factors that affect trade and FDI also affect the transfer of LCT, as measured by cross-border patent filing. The scope and scale of trade and FDI in LCTs reflect the characteristics of both the importing and exporting countries, though importing country characteristics are generally more important. The following drivers of technology transfer have been identified:

- **Restrictive trade and FDI policies unequivocally discourage technology transfer** (figures C.7 and C.8 in appendix C). Tariff and nontariff barriers inhibit imports of capital goods and the technologies they embody. Meanwhile, restrictions on FDI can discourage foreign firms from transferring productive technology to the domestic economy.
- **The effect of local capacity on technological absorption is ambiguous, because it entails two countervailing dynamics.** An adequate degree of local technological capacity is necessary to exploit the transferred technology; however, a very high degree of local technological capacity can increase the risk of imitation, potentially deterring foreign patent holders from transferring their technologies. Strong IPR protections can mitigate this risk, but only partially.
- **National environmental policies also entail two opposing effects on LCT transfer.** On the one hand, robust environmental protections can promote innovation and technology transfer by increasing domestic demand for LCT. On the other hand, environmental policies can also increase public investment in innovation, which may crowd out private investment and deter technology transfer. Because the stock of LCTs likely captures the former effect,[17] the empirical model used in this analysis likely underestimates the positive impact of environmental policies on LCT innovation and technology transfer.
- **Similarly, IPR protections have a theoretically ambiguous effect on LCT innovation and technology transfer.** Robust IPR protections can encourage technology transfer (this is the so-called market expansion effect)

by reassuring patent holders that their technology will be protected from imitation. Those protections can also enhance the market power of patent holders, creating monopolistic price distortions that limit the volume of sales and disadvantage local competitors. Consequently, the net impact of strong IPR protections on technology transfer is unclear (Maskus 2000).

The methodology for estimating the determinants of LCT transfer

The effects of national policies and other country characteristics on LCT transfer are estimated using the following gravity model:

$$TRANSFER_{ijkt} = \exp(\alpha_{1k} Ink_{jkt} + \alpha_{2k} POL_{jt} + \alpha_{3k} X_{jt} + \alpha_{4k} FTA_{ijt} + \mu_{ikt} + u_{ijkt}) \quad (3.1)$$

$TRANSFER_{ijkt}$ represents the number of patents in technology k filed in country j by inventors located in country i. Because this analysis focuses on technology transfer to developing countries, the recipient country j is restricted to developing countries. Ink_{jkt} is the log of the discounted stock of patented inventions in technology k in country j and serves as a proxy for country j's absorptive capacities that are specific to technology k.[18] POL_{jkt} is a vector that includes the stringency of IPR protections, the strictness of climate regulations, the level of FDI restrictions, the level of tariff barriers, and the level of nontariff barriers. X_{jt} is a vector of control variables that includes the flexibility of business, labor, and credits regulations; the income level of the recipient country measured by logged GDP per capita; and the size of its economy measured by logged population. μ_{ikt} represents the exporter-year fixed effects. It captures all the characteristics of the country of the inventors that affect the transfer of LCT patents at any time. For instance, it controls for the amount of knowledge in technology k of the inventors located in country i. FTA_{ijt} is a dummy variable equal to 1 if country i and country j are in a free trade agreement. This analysis estimates three versions of the model (box 3.1).

Data used in the empirical analysis

Cross-border patent transfer
Data on cross-border patent filing and patented inventions come from PATSTAT. As described earlier in the section titled "Data Sources and Accounting Methodology for LCT," LCT patent filings are identified using the Y02 code of the CPC maintained by the EPO. Model (3.1) is estimated for eight technological fields: all LCT; buildings; CCS; ICT; energy generation, transmission, and distribution; manufacturing; transportation; and waste management. The data underpinning each potential determinant of LCT transfer are described in the following subsections.

Local capacity for technological absorption and innovation
Local technological capacity is divided into two categories. The first category covers generic absorptive capacity, which allows for the exploitation of all kinds of technologies. The second covers specific absorptive capacities related to a given technological field. The number of researchers, R&D expenditure as a share of GDP, and enrollment in tertiary education can be used as proxies for generic absorptive capacities. Unfortunately, these data are unavailable for

BOX 3.1

Model specifications and estimation strategy

μ_{ikt} equals $\sum_i \alpha_{ikt} E_{it}$ where E_{it} is a dummy variable equal to 1 when the exporting country is country i at year t. α_{ikt} is the parameter specific to exporter i for technology k at year t. A high value of α_{ikt} means that patent filing from country i in technology k to any country was high, all other things being equal.

The three estimated versions of model (3.1) vary in u_{ijkt}:

Model	u_{ijkt}
A	$\beta_k D_{ij} + v_{ijkt}$
B	$\beta_k D_{ij} + \rho_{ik} + \omega_{ijkt}$
C	$\delta_{ijk} + \varepsilon_{ijkt}$

Specification A adds a vector of gravity variables D_{ij} that includes the distance between the two countries and whether they share a border, have a common official language, or have a colonial tie. These variables are usual in gravity estimation and capture an important part of the variation in the transfer. Trade and foreign direct investment are inversely proportional to distance, and their magnitudes are greater between countries that speak a common language. These variables should similarly influence patents, which are another measure of technology transfer.

Specification B augments specification A with importer-year fixed effects ρ_{ik} that capture characteristics of the importing country that do not vary over time. Such characteristics include the degree of political

stability, the nature of the political regime, and the degree of remoteness between the importer j and other importing countries. Specification B is superior to specification A because InK_{jkt} and POL_{jt} can be correlated with ρ_{ik}, which are omitted in specification A.

Specification C includes country-pair fixed effects δ_{ijk}, which capture time-invariant characteristics that influence cross-border patent filing from country i to country j. Such characteristics include the gravity variables D_{ij} and other omitted variables, such as the existence of a trade war between country i and country j. Specification C is superior to both specification A and specification B because ε_{ijkt} contains fewer omitted variables than v_{ijkt} and ω_{ijkt}.

Because the dependent variable $TRANSFER_{ijkt}$ is a count variable, model (3.1) is estimated using the Pseudo Poisson Maximum Likelihood estimator (Silva and Tenreyro 2006) to minimize the estimation bias and avoid truncating country pairs with 0 transfers. Robust standard errors are clustered at the country level.

Although the analysis accounts for many factors affecting the patents transfer, it is possible that there are omitted variables in the error terms. Because of the use of exporter-year fixed effects, country-pair fixed effects, and a large number of controls, not much scope exists to mitigate further endogeneity issues.

Finally, there is no evidence for multicollinearity in the empirical estimation because the correlation coefficients between all regressors do not go above 0.5 or below –0.5 (table C.10 in the appendix C).

a large number of countries, and including generic absorptive capacities in the model would severely truncate the estimation sample and lead to estimation bias. By contrast, specific absorptive capacities can be proxied by the discounted stock of patented innovations in a given field, and PATSTAT encompasses nearly all patented innovations.

Intellectual property rights

IPR protections are measured using the IPR indicator in the Executive Opinion Survey (EOS) produced by the World Economic Forum (WEF). The EOS asks a representative sample of leading business executives in each economy to quantify, on a scale of 1 to 7, the strength of IPR protections.[19] The random sampling follows a dual-stratification procedure based on the size of the company and the sector of activity, which ensures that both large and small firms representing the various economic sectors of the economy are captured in the final country-level score.[20] The 2011 EOS covered 142 economies accounting for 98 percent of global GDP, with an average of 98 respondents per country. As expected, IPR protections are strongly correlated with GDP per capita and with the patent protection index commonly used in the literature (Park and Lippoldt 2008).

The enforcement of IPR protections is measured using the WEF's IPR Index and the Fraser Institute's Legal Systems Index. This approach, which follows that of previous studies (Dussaux, Dechezleprêtre, and Glachant 2018; Maskus and Yang 2013), assumes that a weak legal system necessarily implies weak IPR protections, regardless of the formal stringency of a country's IPR laws. The Legal Systems Index is extracted from the Fraser Institute's annual reports on global economic freedom (Gwartney, Lawson, and Hall 2014). It is a composite index ranging from 0 to 10 that includes indicators of the legal enforcement of contracts, judicial independence, the impartiality of courts, and the integrity of the legal system. The IPR Index value is multiplied by the Legal Systems Index value, and the product is rescaled from 0 to 10.

Environmental policies

Data on the relative stringency of environmental policies come from Yale University's Environmental Performance Index (EPI).[21] The EPI ranks 180 economies on 24 performance indicators across 10 dimensions of environmental integrity: air quality, water quality, lead exposure, biodiversity, tree-cover loss, fisheries, climate and energy, air pollution, wastewater treatment, and sustainable nitrogen management in agriculture. The EPI score is a weighted average of the indicators in these 10 areas, with the largest weights accorded to air quality and climate and energy. Rescaling the EPI to a maximum of 10 enables comparisons with the estimated coefficients of the different explanatory variables. EPI scores are positively correlated with constant GDP per capita at 75 percent. Finland, Iceland, and New Zealand have the highest EPI scores, whereas China, the Arab Republic of Egypt, and Turkey have the lowest (see figure C.5. of appendix C).

Foreign direct investment

The relative restrictiveness of FDI policy is proxied by the "controls on the movement of capital and people" indicator from the Fraser Institute's 2015 Economic Freedom of the World report (Gwartney, Lawson, and Hall 2015). This indicator has three components: restrictions on foreign ownership and investment, capital controls, and the freedom of foreigners to visit. The first component is based on the WEF's Global Competitiveness Report (WEF 2018).[22] The second comes from the International Monetary Fund's annual report on exchange arrangements and exchange restrictions, which includes information on up to 13 types of international capital controls (IMF 2018a). The 0–10 rating is the percentage of capital controls not imposed as a share of the total number of capital controls listed, multiplied by 10. The third component measures visa requirements for foreign visitors using data from Lawson and Lemke (2012). China is the most restrictive economy in the sample, followed by Saudi Arabia, Ukraine, and the United States (see figure C.6 in appendix C). FDI controls in China, the United States, and Russia are, respectively, 93 percent, 64 percent, and 37 percent higher than the sample average.

Trade policies

The restrictiveness of trade policies reflects the impact of both tariffs and nontariff barriers to trade. The indicator for tariffs comes from the Fraser Institute's 2015 Economic Freedom of the World report. Tariffs are measured by the revenue from trade taxes as share of total export and import values, as reported in the International Monetary Fund's Government Finance Statistics Yearbook and International Financial Statistics report, combined with the unweighted mean of tariff rates (IMF 2018b). Countries with the highest indicator scores for tariff barriers include Argentina, Egypt, Korea, and Russia; and the scores for Egypt, Korea, and Russia are more than twice the sample average. The indicator for nontariff trade barriers also comes from the Economic Freedom of the World Report and is based on data from the WEF's Global Competitiveness Report (WEF 2018).[23] Ecuador has the highest indicator score for nontariff barriers, followed by Egypt, Argentina, and Columbia. Nontariff barriers in Argentina, Ecuador, and Egypt are at least 120 percent higher than the sample average (see appendix C).

Control variables and the coverage of the sample

Data on population size and GDP per capita come from the World Bank's World Development Indicators. The gravity variables come from the GeoDist database of the Centre d'Etudes Prospectives et d'Informations Internationales (CEPII). The estimation sample covers every year between 2006 and 2015.[24] A detailed description of the data sources for all explanatory variables is included in appendix C (table C.2), along with the summary statistics (table C.3).

The sample of countries used in the model (3.1) estimation is smaller than the sample used in the previous sections because of two limitations. First, countries that received no LCT patent transfers are automatically dropped from the sample when estimating the gravity model (3.1), and the model relies on within-country variation to recover its parameters. The model cannot estimate a parameter for countries with no variation, as is the case for low-income countries. The second limitation reflects the availability of the explanatory variables used in model (3.1). The analysis includes 42 developed countries and 33 developing countries that represent 97 percent and 67 percent, respectively, of the GDP of their respective income groups (table 3.4).[25] The developing countries include 22 upper-middle-income countries that represent 92 percent of their group's GDP, and 11 lower-middle-income countries that represent 17 percent of their group's GDP. No data are available for low-income countries. For lower-middle-income countries, the exclusion of India due to absent data on inbound patent transfers greatly reduces the sample's coverage in terms of GDP and population.[26]

TABLE 3.4 **The coverage of the sample**

GROUP	TOTAL ECONOMIES	NUMBER OF ECONOMIES INCLUDED IN THE SAMPLE	SHARE OF TOTAL ECONOMIES COVERED (%)	SHARE OF GDP COVERED (%)	SHARE OF POPULATION COVERED (%)
Low income	34	0	0	0	0
Lower-middle income	47	11	23	17	14
Upper-middle income	56	22	39	92	91
Total developing	137	33	24	67	44
High income	80	42	53	96	97

Note: The table includes recipient economies for which data are available. GDP coverage and population coverage are computed using 2015 data.

The determinants of LCT transfer to developing countries

In this section, we mainly discuss the estimation of specification C, which is the specification that best mitigates endogeneity issues. Specification B is displayed to show the robustness of the results and that time invariant characteristics such as distance have an expected negative effect on LCT transfer. Specification A, which is more exposed to omitted variable bias, is reported in table C.6 in appendix C.

Specific local capacity for technological absorption has no effect on LCT transfer from high-income economies, but it has a modestly positive effect on LCT transfer from developing countries. On average, the stock of patented LCT technologies has no statistically significant effect on LCT transfer from high-income economies (table 3.5, specification C). However, a 10 percent increase in the stock of patented technologies increases LCT patent transfers from developing countries by 3 percent (table 3.6, specification C). It should be noted that these results apply only to specific local capacity, which is measured by the discounted stock of patented LCTs produced domestically, because the data on generic local capacity are very limited.

TABLE 3.5 **Determinants of LCT transfer to developing countries from high-income economies**

	LCT PATENT TRANSFERS FROM HIGH-INCOME ECONOMIES	
	SPECIFICATION B	SPECIFICATION C
Log (stock of inventions)	−0.145 (0.113)	−0.153 (0.113)
Environmental policy stringency	−0.723** (0.295)	−0.759*** (0.289)
Enforced IPR protections	−0.103 (0.108)	−0.115 (0.110)
FDI controls	−0.134* (0.079)	-0.138* (0.081)
Tariff barriers	−0.130** (0.057)	−0.133** (0.057)
Nontariff barriers	0.190*** (0.053)	0.193*** (0.052)
Log (population)	−1.414 (1.415)	−1.283 (1.385)
Log (GDP per capita)	1.244** (0.500)	1.247** (0.503)
Flexibility of business regulations	0.054 (0.116)	0.074 (0.116)
Flexibility of labor regulations	−0.248 (0.165)	−0.252 (0.166)
Flexibility of credit regulations	−0.189** (0.090)	−0.195** (0.090)
Country pairs with trade agreement (0/1)	0.21 (0.143)	0.045 (0.086)
Contiguous borders	−0.170 (0.139)	
Common official language	0.274* (0.149)	

continued

TABLE 3.5, *continued*

	LCT PATENT TRANSFERS FROM HIGH-INCOME ECONOMIES	
	SPECIFICATION B	SPECIFICATION C
Former colonial ties	0.487*** (0.152)	
Log (distance between most-populated cities)	−0.722*** (0.077)	
Exporter-year FE	X	X
Importer FE	X	X
Country-pair FE		X
Observations	11,339	11,339
Country-pairs	1,142	1,142

Note: Marginal effects for developing countries are calculated separately for upper-middle-income, lower-middle-income, and low-income countries. The dependent variable is the total number of low-carbon technology (LCT) patents filed in the country. Variable definitions and summary statistics are presented in table C.2 and table C.3, respectively, in appendix C. FDI = foreign direct investment; FE = fixed effects; IPR = intellectual property rights. Robust standard errors are clustered at the country level.
* $p < 0.10$, ** $p < 0.05$, *** $p < 0.01$.

TABLE 3.6 Determinants of LCT transfer to developing countries from developing countries

	LCT PATENT TRANSFERS FROM DEVELOPING COUNTRIES	
	B	C
Log (stock of inventions)	0.369** (0.177)	0.302* (0.162)
Environmental policy stringency	−1.203*** (0.225)	−1.082*** (0.214)
Enforced IPR protections	−0.029 (0.108)	−0.052 (0.105)
FDI controls	−0.229*** (0.061)	−0.283*** (0.068)
Tariff barriers	−0.200*** (0.070)	−0.243*** (0.071)
Nontariff barriers	0.134** (0.061)	0.148*** (0.057)
Log (population)	2.227 (1.779)	3.082* (1.792)
Log (GDP per capita)	1.068** (0.506)	1.233*** (0.463)
Flexibility of business regulations	−0.137 (0.083)	−0.066 (0.082)
Flexibility of labor regulations	−0.207 (0.153)	−0.276* (0.159)
Flexibility of credit regulations	−0.225** (0.106)	−0.222** (0.105)
Country pair with trade agreement (0/1)	−0.010 (0.170)	0.158 (0.352)
Contiguous borders	0.375** (0.154)	

continued

TABLE 3.6, *continued*

	LCT PATENT TRANSFERS FROM DEVELOPING COUNTRIES	
	B	C
Common official language	0.462*** (0.168)	
Former colonial ties	1.466*** (0.275)	
Log (distance between most populated cities)	−0.431*** (0.101)	
Exporter-year FE	X	X
Importer FE	X	X
Country-pair FE		X
Observations	3,730	3,730
Country-pairs	426	426

Note: Marginal effects for developing countries include upper-middle-income, lower-middle-income, and low-income countries. The dependent variable is the total number of low-carbon technology (LCT) patents filed in the country. Variable definitions and summary statistics are presented in table C.2 and table C.3, respectively, in appendix C. FDI = foreign direct investment; FE = fixed effects; IPR = intellectual property rights. Robust standard errors are clustered at the country level.
* $p < 0.10$, ** $p < 0.05$, *** $p < 0.01$.

Stringent environmental policies inhibit LCT transfer to developing countries when specific local capacity is accounted for. This finding applies to LCT patents originating in both developed and developing economies. An increase of one standard deviation in the stringency of environmental regulation reduces LCT transfers from developed economies by 65 percent and transfers from developing countries by 78 percent. This negative effect may stem from the fact that the model controls for the stock of LCT innovations, which is itself influenced positively by environmental policy stringency. Therefore, the remaining variation in the stringency of environmental regulation could reflect the crowding-out effect of public support on private innovation and associated patent transfers. In other words, environmental policy stringency may be a measure of LCT supply.

Strong IPR protections have no significant effect on LCT transfer from either high-income or developing economies. This result suggests that the market-power effect and the market-expansion effect described earlier tend to offset each other on average.

FDI restrictions hinder LCT transfer from both high-income and developing economies. Controls on the movement of capital and people have a substantial negative impact on the number of LCT patents transferred by both high-income and developing economies. An increase of one standard deviation in FDI restrictions reduces transfers from high-income economies by 23 percent and transfers from developing countries by 41 percent.

High tariffs also deter LCT transfer from both high-income and developing economies, but nontariff barriers have the opposite effect. An increase of one standard deviation in the tariff barriers indicator decreases LCT patent transfers from high-income economies by 15 percent and transfers from developing countries by 26 percent. An increase of one standard deviation in the nontariff barriers indicator increases transfers from developed economies by 30 percent and transfers from developing countries by 22 percent.

The positive impact of nontariff barriers is counterintuitive, but it has at least one possible explanation. High nontariff barriers may encourage firms to inter-act with foreign markets via FDI rather than trade. Because FDI tends to be more knowledge-intensive than trade in capital goods, the negative effect of nontariff barriers on trade is more than compensated by the positive effect of nontariff barriers on FDI—hence, the positive effect of nontariff barriers on patent transfers. Note that this interpretation works for receiving countries having a reasonably large market, a necessary condition for a profitable investment.

Do tariff barriers encourage firms to choose FDI over trade? High tariffs increase the price of imported products, which leads to lower import volume. That is the negative effect we have estimated in our model. In contrast, nontar-iff barriers can have a more prohibitive effect on trade. For instance, imports quotas set a limit on the quantity of goods that can be imported. When a quota is met, FDI is the only way to exploit the technology further. Other examples of nontariff barriers that might encourage FDI over trade are domestic subsi-dies that incentivize foreign firms to operate domestically to level the playing field with competitors. This shift from trade to FDI is more likely to occur when trade costs are high. When including an interaction term between non-tariff barriers and the distance between the two trading partners as a proxy for trade costs, we find that the positive effect of nontariff barriers on patent trans-fer increases with the distance. This result provides some evidence for our interpretation.

Larger market sizes positively influence LCT transfer. Economies with grow-ing populations receive more patent transfers from developing countries, and wealthier economies receive more transfers from both high-income and devel-oping economies. A 1 percent increase in GDP per capita is associated with a 1.2 percent increase in patent transfers from both high-income and developing economies.

The outsized impact of China on key variables may affect the estimation results. China's contribution to LCT innovation and patent transfers dwarfs that of other developing countries, and China has particularly restrictive inbound FDI policies. However, an estimate of model (3.1) using specification C and excluding China produces results that are highly similar to those presented above (see table C.8 in appendix C).

Results by LCT field

Separately estimating the results for each LCT field yields several important findings. First, the results at the field level are generally consistent with the over-all results.[27] Second, substantial heterogeneity exists between results by technol-ogy fields and economies of origin (table 3.7). For instance, an increase of one standard deviation in the tariff barriers indicator reduces manufacturing-related LCT transfers by 17 percent from high-income economies and by 32 percent from developing countries. By contrast, ICT-related LCT transfers are unaf-fected by tariffs.

The analysis finds two significant differences between LCT transfer from high-income economies and LCT transfer from developing countries. First, the magnitude of the determinants is more important for patent transfers from developing countries than it is for transfers from high-income economies. Second, the effect of local capacity for technological absorption is negative for transfers originating in high-income economies and positive for transfers originating in developing countries. This finding suggests that LCT produced in developing countries tends to complement LCT imported from other developing countries, but not LCT imported from high-income economies.

Conditional on adequate capacity, more stringent environmental policies *reduce* patent transfers from high-income economies in all technologies by 65 percent and for transfers from developing countries by 78 percent.[28] Surprisingly, greater nontariff barriers *increase* LCT patent transfers in all technology fields from both developed and—more significant—developing countries. For high-income economies, stronger IPR protections reduce transfers of LCT used in buildings by 24 percent; higher tariffs and FDI controls *deter* LCT transfers in all technologies by 15 percent and 23 percent respectively. For developing countries, higher tariffs and FDI controls inhibit LCT patent transfers by 26 percent and 41 percent, respectively. Finally, an increase of 1.0 percent in GDP per capita boosts LCT patent transfers from both high-income and developing countries (refer to table 3.7, "Transfers from high-income economies" and "Transfers from developing countries").

TABLE 3.7 **Determinants of patent transfers, by technology field**

Percent

	TRANSFERS FROM HIGH-INCOME ECONOMIES						
	ALL	**BUILDINGS**	**ICT**	**ENERGY**	**MANUFACTURING**	**TRANSPORT**	**WASTE**
Effect of a one-standard-deviation increase in							
Environmental policy stringency	−65	ns	ns	−74	-60	−76	ns
Enforced IPR protections	ns	−24	ns	ns	ns	ns	ns
FDI controls	−23	ns	ns	ns	−28	−25	−28
Tariffs	−15	−15	ns	−16	−17	ns	−18
Nontariff barriers	30	20	ns	40	31	26	28
Effects of a 1 percent increase in							
Log (stock of inventions)	ns	−0.4	ns	ns	−0.3	ns	−0.4
Log (population)	ns	−5.5	ns	ns	−0.6	−3.3	ns
Log (GDP per capita)	1.2	ns	1.6	ns	1.4	1.6	1.2
	TRANSFERS FROM DEVELOPING COUNTRIES						
	ALL	**BUILDINGS**	**ICT**	**ENERGY**	**MANUFACTURING**	**TRANSPORT**	**WASTE**
Effects of a one-standard-deviation increase in							
Environmental policy stringency	−78	ns	−89	−79	−71	−87	−81
Enforced IPR protections	ns	−41	−47	ns	ns	ns	ns
FDI controls	−41	ns	ns	−32	−42	ns	−63
Tariffs	−26	−52	ns	ns	−32	ns	ns
Nontariff barriers	62	ns	ns	41	ns	85	66
Effects of a 1 percent increase in							
Log (stock of inventions)	0.3	ns	1.2	ns	0.3	ns	ns
Log (population)	3.1	ns	10.9	ns	4.7	−14.5	7.4
Log (GDP per capita)	1.2	2.8	ns	2.0	ns	3.1	ns

Note: For clarity, only statistically significant effects are reported. Detailed estimation results are presented in table C.6 and table C.7 in appendix C.
FDI = foreign direct investment; ICT = information and communication technology; IPR = intellectual property rights; ns = not significant.

Effects of relaxing FDI controls and lowering tariffs

Simulations for Brazil, China, and Russia—the three largest carbon emitters in the developing world[29]—indicate that moderately easing FDI controls and lowering tariff rates could greatly increase the transfer of LCT. The impact of relaxing FDI controls is 50 percent greater, on average, than the impact of lowering tariffs, because these countries restrict their capital markets more tightly than their goods markets. A 10 percent decrease in FDI restrictions boosts LCT transfer from high-income economies by 11 percent in China, 7 percent in Russia, and 6 percent in Brazil. Meanwhile, LCT transfer from developing countries increases by 23 percent for China, 16 percent for Russia, and 12 percent for Brazil. A 10 percent decrease in tariffs increases LCT transfer from high-income economies by 7 percent in Russia, 4 percent in Brazil, and 2 percent in China; LCT transfer from developing countries increases by 13 percent for Russia, 7 percent for Brazil, and 4 percent for China (table 3.8).

These findings indicate that easing FDI controls potentially through international investment agreements could significantly accelerate LCT transfer to developing countries.[30] International investment agreements[31] are an important tool for reducing FDI restrictions, but progress appears to have plateaued in China and Russia. Both countries have ratified investment agreements with four of the world's top LCT innovators: China, Germany, Japan, and Korea. Neither, however, has ratified such an agreement with the United States (table 3.9). The share of economies that have investment agreements with China and Russia has increased significantly over the past 20 years.[32] Although the number of those agreements is informative, their impact on FDI restrictions can vary significantly. For example, the agreement between China and Germany contains "negative-list reservations," which explicitly exclude certain sectors and industries from its terms.

TABLE 3.8 **Simulated effects of relaxing controls on FDI and lowering tariffs**

	CO$_2$ EMISSIONS IN 2014 (METRIC TONS)	FDI CONTROLS DECLINE BY 10 PERCENT		TARIFFS DECLINE BY 10 PERCENT	
		CHANGE IN LCT TRANSFER FROM			
		HIGH-INCOME ECONOMIES (%)	DEVELOPING COUNTRIES (%)	HIGH-INCOME ECONOMIES (%)	DEVELOPING COUNTRIES (%)
China	10,292	+11	+23	+2	+4
Russian Federation	1,705	+7	+16	+7	+13
Brazil	530	+6	+12	+4	+7

Sources: Calculations based on estimates reported in table C.7 in appendix C, and the 2014 values for FDI controls and tariffs.
Note: CO$_2$ = carbon dioxide; FDI = foreign direct investment; LCT = low-carbon technology.

TABLE 3.9 **Chinese and Russian investment agreements with major LCT innovators**

PARTNER	CHINA	RUSSIAN FEDERATION
Japan	Yes (1989)	Yes (2000)
United States	No	No
Germany	Yes (2005)	Yes (1991)
Korea, Rep.	Yes (2007)	Yes (1991)
China	Yes	Yes (2009)

Source: Data from UNCTAD Investment Policy Hub.
Note: Effective dates for the latest versions are in parentheses.

Domestic policy changes can also facilitate LCT transfer by easing restrictions on the movement of capital and people. China's FDI regulations divide all industries into four categories: encouraged, permitted, restricted, and prohibited (Liu 2017).[33] In industries considered strategic to China's development, the government encourages FDI by offering government subsidies, tax incentives, and regulatory waivers. FDI in restricted industries is subject to specific regulations, including majority ownership by Chinese shareholders. FDI in prohibited industries is forbidden. Most LCT-related industries are in either the encouraged or permitted categories (see table C.10 in appendix C). Some industries, however, such as the construction and operation of nuclear power plants and power grids, are in the restricted category.

China's new foreign investment law—which will come into effect in 2020—is designed to facilitate FDI in industries categorized as encouraged or permitted. Before the new law, foreign investments in encouraged and permitted industries had to comply with certain requirements and get approval, which could take up to six months. The new law has eliminated the approval process for encouraged and permitted industries and replaced it with a simple registration system (Edelberg 2017; Liu 2017). By easing the administrative burden of FDI, the new law is likely to positively affect inbound LCT transfer.

CONCLUSIONS

Confirming the results of chapter 2, the analysis in this chapter shows that LCT innovations remain concentrated in high-income countries and that almost three-quarters of all LCT transfers occur between high-income countries. Using a dataset of patents from 75 countries observed from 2006 to 2015, this chapter identifies five main drivers of LCT transfer to and from developing countries. Restrictive FDI policies and tariffs inhibit LCT transfer, whereas nontariff barriers, large markets, and local capacity for technological absorption encourage it. Separately analyzing LCT patent transfers originating in high-income and developing economies reveals that these factors have a stronger impact on LCT transfer from developing countries.

The analysis also demonstrates that modestly easing FDI restrictions and lowering tariffs can significantly accelerate LCT transfer. China's new FDI law sets a positive example for other developing countries by easing the administrative burden faced by foreign investors in many LCT-related industries. Meanwhile, the finalization of the EGA, which aims to decrease tariff rates on environmental goods, could significantly increase LCT transfer among WTO member states, as advocated in chapter 2, if negotiations resume and conclude successfully.

It is important, however, to recall the limits of the present study. Although cross-border patent filing is a good indicator of international technologies transfer, it is also an imperfect measure—for several reasons. First, some firms may file strategic patents without actually transferring technology. Second, the number of high-value patents transferred is a count variable, which implicitly assumes that all inventions have the same technological content. Third, the measures of tariff, nontariff, and FDI barriers used in the empirical estimation are the same for all technologies and not specific to LCT[34] and may produce measurement errors in the variables used.[35] Finally, data constraints exclude certain countries—such as India—from the analysis, which greatly reduces the sample's representativeness.

NOTES

1. U.S. and European patent laws differ slightly in form but serve similar purposes.
2. For more information on the EPO Worldwide Patent Statistical Database, see https://www .epo.org/searching-for-patents/business/patstat.html#tab-1.
3. Table C.5 in appendix C details the differences between the three studies in terms of methodology, scope, and results.
4. Because the propensity to patent differs across sectors (Cohen, Nelson, and Walsh 2000), this analysis does not compare sectors or technological fields in absolute terms.
5. The CPC system is an expanded version of the International Patent Classification (IPC) system developed by the World Intellectual Property Organization (WIPO). Previous analyses, notably Dechezleprêtre, Glachant, and Ménière (2013), used the IPC system to identify LCTs; however, the IPC system was not designed for this purpose, and it does not include a dedicated code for LCTs. LCTs can be identified in certain categories—such as renewable energy, motor vehicles, and construction inputs—but several important types of LCTs used in the manufacturing sector are excluded, and the IPC does not identify LCTs used in the agricultural sector. Whereas the IPC covers only 13 LCT subfields, the CPC includes 33 LCT subfields containing dozens of codes.
6. At present, comprehensive data are available only through 2015.
7. This limitation has no significant impact on the results.
8. Indian patent data can be accessed through WIPO but are classified under the IPC system, which differs from the CPC used in the PATSTAT database. The IPC and the CPC classifications can be matched only for a small subset of LCTs, which limits the potential for comparisons between India and other countries.
9. Dechezleprêtre (2017) documents the drop in public R&D for low-carbon innovation using International Energy Agency data.
10. This statistic is deliberately underestimated because of India's absence from the sample.
11. This low rate is not specific to LCTs. Boeing and Mueller (2016) show that China's recent patent expansion has taken place to the detriment of patent quality.
12. Instead of using patents, Glachant et al. (2013) use inbound FDI to measure LCT transfer. Their findings are similar to those presented here, though the FDI data indicate higher levels of LCT transfer to Brazil, Mexico, and Russia.
13. Although we recognize that the 45-degree line is not the optimal allocation of LCT transfer, the distance from it can help to classify countries in terms of transfer priorities.
14. As noted earlier, patents are considered part of the same family if they share the same priority patent. High-value patents are defined as those filed in at least two patent offices.
15. This section draws heavily on Jaffe, Newell, and Stavins (2003).
16. A particularly important channel within FDI is international joint venture between firms operating in developing countries and firms operating in developed countries.
17. Many studies have found that stricter environmental policies promote innovation in LCT (see Johnstone, Haščič, and Popp 2010; Popp 2002).
18. The discounted stock of patented inventions is computed as $K_{jkt} = (1 - \delta) K_{jkt-1} + I_{jkt}$, where δ is a 15 percent discount rate used in the literature (Keller 2004) and I_{jkt} is the number of inventions.
19. A score of 1 indicates no IPR protections, and a score of 7 indicates that IPR is heavily protected.
20. The EOS is administered by 150 partner institutes in their respective economies.
21. EPI data are from 2008, 2010, 2012, 2014, 2016, and 2018. For more information on the EPI, visit https://epi.envirocenter.yale.edu.
22. A survey conducted for the report asks executives, "How prevalent is foreign ownership of companies in your country?" and "How restrictive are regulations in your country relating to international capital flows?" Responses range from 1 (rare foreign ownership, highly restrictive regulations) to 7 (frequent foreign ownership, nonrestrictive regulations).
23. The survey asks executives to rate on a scale of 1 to 7 whether they agree with the statement, "In your country, tariff and nontariff barriers significantly reduce the ability of imported goods to compete in the domestic market."
24. In this analysis, observations of IPR stringency begin in 2006.
25. Note that all technology exporters are included, because they are not subject to data limitations.

26. Table C.4 in appendix C presents the complete list of economies included in the econometric analysis.

27. Although the results at the field level are generally in line with the overall findings, it appears that there are differences regarding the effects of local absorptive capacities and stringency of IPR protections. It is not sound, however, to derive the determinants of overall LCT transfer by aggregating the estimated effects at the field level. The composition of the sample differs when the dependent variable of model (3.1) is the sum of all LCT patents and when it is the sum of patent filings in a given technology field, because the fixed-effects estimation cannot exploit data for country pairs for which there is no variation over time. For instance, the likelihood that the number of patents transferred between two countries will equal zero is much higher for CCS than it is for energy. Therefore, the number of country pairs used in the field-level regression is always lower than in the aggregate regression.

28. The values noted in this section are the average values of significant marginal effects across technology fields.

29. Among the countries that are included in the estimation sample. That is not the case of India as explained earlier in the chapter.

30. Note that this is an interpretation because we do not estimate the effects of international investment agreements directly.

31. Most international investment agreements are bilateral investment treaties that establish the terms and conditions for private investment by firms of one country into another. These treaties are typically designed to ensure that foreign firms receive fair and equitable treatment in the countries in which they are investing.

32. World Bank calculation using data from UNCTAD Investment Policy Hub In 2018, China had investment agreements with 44 percent of the high-income economies and 40 percent of the developing countries included in this analysis. Russia had agreements with 34 percent of the high-income economies and 23 percent of the developing countries.

33. Encouraged, restricted, and prohibited industries are listed in the Catalogue for the Industrial Guidance of Foreign Investments, which is approved by the Party Central Committee and the State Council. The permitted category includes all industries not named in the Catalogue.

34. Data on tariff and nontariff measures exist but for a very limited number of LCT and countries.

35. These measurement errors can bias our estimation if they are correlated with the transfers and their determinants.

REFERENCES

Aghion, P., N. Bloom, R. Blundell, R. Griffith, and P. Howitt. 2005. "Competition and Innovation: An Inverted-U Relationship." *Quarterly Journal of Economics* 120 (2): 701–28.

Boeing, P., and E. Mueller. 2016. "Measuring Patent Quality in Cross-Country Comparison." *Economics Letters* 149 (December): 145–47.

Brunel, C. 2019. "Green Innovation and Green Imports: Links between Environmental Policies, Innovation, and Production." *Journal of Environmental Management* 248 (October): 109290.

Brunnermeier, S. B., and M. A. Cohen. 2003. "Determinants of Environmental Innovation in US Manufacturing Industries." *Journal of Environmental Economics and Management* 45 (2): 278–93.

Calel, R., and A. Dechezleprêtre. 2016. "Environmental Policy and Directed Technological Change: Evidence from the European Carbon Market." *Review of Economics and Statistics* 98 (1): 173–91.

Cohen, W., R. Nelson, and J. Walsh. 2000. "Protecting Their Intellectual Assets: Appropriability Conditions and Why U.S. Manufacturing Firms Patent (or Not)." NBER Working Paper 7552, National Bureau of Economic Research, Cambridge, MA. http://www.nber.org /papers/w7552.pdf.

Dechezleprêtre, A. 2017. "Sustaining Investment in Climate Innovation." Climate Innovation Insights, Series 1.2: Accelerating the Evolution of Climate Innovation Clusters, Climate-KIC. https://www.climate-kic.org/wp-content/uploads/2017/03/Insight02_Proof4.pdf.

Dechezleprêtre, A., M. Glachant, I. Haščič, N. Johnstone, and Y. Ménière. 2011. "Invention and Transfer of Climate Change–Mitigation Technologies: A Global Analysis." *Review of Environmental Economics and Policy* 5 (1): 109–30.

Dechezleprêtre, A., M. Glachant, and Y. Ménière. 2013. "What Drives the International Transfer of Climate Change Mitigation Technologies? Empirical Evidence from Patent Data." *Environmental and Resource Economics* 54 (2): 161–78.

de la Tour, A., M. Glachant, and Y. Meniere. 2011. "Innovation and International Technology Transfer: The Case of the Chinese Photovoltaic Industry." *Energy Policy* 39 (2): 761–70.

Dussaux, D., A. Dechezleprêtre, and M. Glachant. 2018. "Intellectual Property Rights Protection and the International Transfer of Low-Carbon Technologies." Working Paper 288, January, Grantham Research Center for Climate Change and the Environment.

Eaton, J., and S. Kortum. 1996. "Trade in Ideas Patenting and Productivity in the OECD." *Journal of International Economics* 40 (3–4): 251–78.

———. 1999. "International Technology Diffusion: Theory and Measurement." *International Economic Review* 40 (3): 537–70.

Edelberg, P. 2017. "Is China Really Opening Its Doors to Foreign Investment?" *China Business Review*, November 8. https://www.chinabusinessreview.com/is-china-really-opening-its-doors-to-foreign-investment.

EIA (U.S. Energy Information Administration). 2016. "International Energy Outlook 2016 with Projections to 2040." DOE/EIA-0484 (2016). EIA, Washington, DC.

Glachant, M., D. Dussaux, Y. Ménière, and A. Dechezleprêtre. 2013. "Promoting the International Transfer of Low-Carbon Technologies: Evidence and Policy Challenges." Report for the Commissariat général à la stratégie et à la prospective (French Center for Policy Planning), October.

Guellec, D., and B. van Pottelsberghe de la Potterie. 2001. "The Internationalization of Technology Analysed with Patent Data." *Research Policy* 30 (8): 1253–66.

Gwartney, J., R. Lawson, and J. Hall. 2014. *Economic Freedom of the World: 2014 Annual Report.* Fraser Institute.

———. 2015. *Economic Freedom of the World: 2015 Annual Report.* Fraser Institute.

Harhoff, D., F. M. Scherer, and K. Vopel. 2003. "Citations, Family Size, Opposition and the Value of Patent Rights." *Research Policy* 32 (8): 1343–63.

IMF (International Monetary Fund). 2018a. *Annual Report on Exchange Arrangements and Exchange Restrictions.* Washington, DC: IMF, 1950–.

———. 2018b. *Government Finance Statistics Yearbook.* Washington, DC: IMF.

Jaffe, A. B., R. G. Newell, and R. N. Stavins. 2003. "Technological Change and the Environment." In *Handbook of Environmental Economics* Vol. 1, edited by K.-G. Maler and J. Vincent, 461–516. Oxford, U.K.: North-Holland.

———. 2005. "A Tale of Two Market Failures: Technology and Environmental Policy." *Ecological Economics* 54 (2–3): 164–74.

Jaffe, A. B., and K. Palmer. 1997. "Environmental Regulation and Innovation: A Panel Data Study." *Review of Economics and Statistics* 79 (4): 610–19.

Johnstone, N., I. Haščič, and D. Popp. 2010. "Renewable Energy Policies and Technological Innovation: Evidence Based on Patent Counts." *Environmental and Resource Economics* 45 (1): 133–55.

Johnstone, N., and J. Labonne. 2006. "Environmental Policy, Management and R&D." *OECD Economic Studies* 42: 169–203. Paris: OECD Publishing. www.oecd.org/eco/greeneco/38698195.pdf.

Keller, W. 2004. "International Technology Diffusion." *Journal of Economic Literature* 42 (3): 752–82.

Lanjouw, J. O., and A. Mody. 1996. "Innovation and the International Diffusion of Environmentally Responsive Technology." *Research Policy* 25 (4): 549–71.

Lanoie, P., J. Laurent-Lucchetti, N. Johnstone, and S. Ambec. 2011. "Environmental Policy, Innovation and Performance: New Insights on the Porter Hypothesis." *Journal of Economics and Management Strategy* 20 (3): 803–42.

Lawson, R., and J. Lemke 2012. "Travel Visas." *Public Choice* 154 (1–2): 17–36.

Liu, M. 2017. "The New Chinese Foreign Investment Law and Its Implication on Foreign Investors." *Northwestern Journal of International Law and Business* 38 (2): 285–306.

Maskus, K. E. 2000. "Intellectual Property Rights and Economic Development." *Case Western Reserve Journal of International Law* 32 (3): 471–506.

——. 2004. *Encouraging International Technology Transfer.* Issue Paper 7. Geneva: International Centre for Trade and Sustainable Development and United Nations Conference on Trade and Sustainable Development.

Maskus, K. E., and L. Yang. 2013. "The Impacts of Post-TRIPS Patent Reforms on the Structure of Exports." RIETI Discussion Paper Series 13-E-030, Research Institute of Economy, Trade and Industry.

Medvedev, D. 2019. "China: Innovation and the New Technology Revolution." Background paper for *Innovative China: New Drivers of Growth*, World Bank, Washington, DC.

Nesta, L., F. Vona, and F. Nicolli. 2014. "Environmental Policies, Competition and Innovation in Renewable Energy." *Journal of Environmental Economics and Management* 67 (3): 396–411.

Newell, R. G., A. B. Jaffe, and R. N. Stavins. 1999. "The Induced Innovation Hypothesis and Energy-Saving Technological Change." *Quarterly Journal of Economics* 114 (3): 941–75.

Park, W. G., and D. C. Lippoldt. 2008. "Technology Transfer and the Economic Implications of the Strengthening of Intellectual Property Rights in Developing Countries." OECD Trade Policy Working Paper 62, OECD Publishing, Paris.

Popp, D. 2002. "Induced Innovation and Energy Prices." *American Economic Review* 92 (1): 160–80.

Popp, D., T. Hafner, and N. Johnstone. 2011. "Environmental Policy vs. Public Pressure: Innovation and Diffusion of Alternative Bleaching Technologies in the Pulp Industry." *Research Policy* 40 (9): 1253–68.

Scherer, F., D. Harhoff, and J. Kukies 2000. "Uncertainty and the Size Distribution of Rewards from Technological Innovation." *Journal of Evolutionary Economics* 10 (1): 175–200.

Silva, J. S., and S. Tenreyro. 2006. "The Log of Gravity." *The Review of Economics and Statistics* 88 (4): 641–58.

WEF (World Economic Forum). 2018. *Global Competitiveness Report.* Geneva: World Economic Forum.

4 The Rise of Emerging Economies as Leaders in Low-Carbon Innovation

INTRODUCTION

The previous chapters have discussed how a number of emerging economies have succeeded in developing the capacity to absorb, imitate, and indigenously create technology. These countries are now important players in global markets, disrupting the traditional paradigm of North–South technology transfer and introducing new models of South–South technology exchange.

This chapter discusses elements of this transformation with a focus on China, which has achieved remarkable progress in leveraging both technology transfer and domestic innovation to support its transition to low-carbon development. The first section describes the rise of the wind, solar, and ethanol industries in a few emerging economies that have transformed themselves from technology importers to technology innovators and exporters. The second section focuses on a single low-carbon industry, electric vehicles (EVs), in which China has emerged as a global leader. Next, the chapter examines the case of a Chinese EV firm, Build Your Dreams (BYD), and compares it to that of a similarly innovative U.S. firm, Tesla. The last section draws some conclusions.

THE EVOLVING ROLE OF LCT TRANSFER AND INNOVATION IN EMERGING ECONOMIES

The experience of the Republic of Korea, a former emerging economy that is now an industrialized nation, offers important lessons for countries striving to develop their capabilities to absorb and adapt foreign technology. In the 1960s, the Korean government encouraged technology transfer through production arrangements with foreign firms, reverse engineering of imported equipment, and technical training provided as part of turnkey plant investment. Weak intellectual property rights (IPR) protections encouraged imitation and adaptation, whereas foreign direct investment (FDI) played only a modest role in building Korea's technological capacity. In the 1970s, the government shifted to an outward-looking development strategy that forced Korean industries to compete in international markets. Competitive pressures created a strong incentive to adopt new technologies, and Korean industries began investing heavily in technological development and adaptation. In the 1980s, Korean firms became increasingly focused on innovation and made large-scale investments in their domestic research and development (R&D) capabilities. National economic policies played a major role in the country's technological advancement; as the scale and complexity of the domestic technology sector increased, the government moved from setting rules and standards to providing concrete targets and supportive financing.[1]

The rise of the wind industry

Like Korea, a number of emerging countries started off as importers and adaptors of low-carbon technology (LCT) and became innovators, producers, and exporters. Wind, ethanol, and solar industries provide good examples of this transformation.

The manufacturing of wind turbines and related equipment began in Europe in the late 1980s and 1990s, supported by public policies aimed at developing renewable energy sources (Urban 2018). Starting in the early 2000s, Brazil, China, India, and South Africa began increasing their wind energy manufacturing capabilities. This process was driven by the high transport costs for large turbine components combined with surging domestic and regional demand for wind power (CEMAC 2017) and the need to diversify energy sources.

China began developing its wind power industry by importing technology from European firms through licensing agreements and joint ventures (Ru et al. 2012). German–Chinese technological cooperation included joint R&D projects, which resulted in the design of wind turbines on the multimegawatt scale. But soon Chinese firms realized that the imported technology could not suit their needs, and they used their own knowledge and capabilities to create wind turbines tailored to specific local conditions in China, such as low-wind-speed turbines for use in desert regions marked by extreme heat, dryness, and sand exposure. Initially supported by feed-in tariffs, which were recently replaced by an auction system, the industry grew rapidly; China now has the highest installed wind capacity in the world and ranks among the leading countries in publications on strategic wind energy components. Chinese companies manufacture turbines and other large, complex wind power products at prices well below those of major Western manufacturers (Lam, Branstetter, and Azevedo 2017).

India was also late to enter the wind power sector, but it rapidly established itself as one of the world's top producers of wind power generation and distribution systems. Like Chinese firms, Indian firms worked closely with foreign counterparts to assimilate existing technologies and managed to generate new innovations, creating wind turbines designed to suit the Indian context. This "interactive learning" process, combining technology transfer with domestic innovation, generated benefits for both Indian firms and their foreign counterparts (Lundvall 1985).

Local content requirements slowed down the growth of South Africa's wind industry. In 2011, South Africa launched the Renewable Energy Independent Power Producer Procurement Program (REIPPPP), which was intended to support the development of renewable energy, help address the energy supply crisis, and mitigate emissions. The procurement process required project developers to engage at the local level, compensate affected communities, and buy a certain percentage of their equipment locally. Local content requirements were expected to support local industrial development and create jobs, but they have been controversial policy instruments—in South Africa and elsewhere—because their impact on jobs depends on how they are implemented. The value of the REIPPPP was to attract private investors in relatively new sectors thanks to a well-designed and transparent procurement process. The program was less successful, however, in fostering the growth of a local wind industry. High-technology components such as blades continued to be imported. Local manufacturers could not supply turbines and had difficulties proving the required two years of experience. Moreover, investors hesitated because of the perceived lack of government commitment to renewables and the small size of the South African market (Rennkamp and Westin 2013).

In Brazil, the rise of wind energy generation after the 2001 crisis was the result of a strategy to diversify the energy mix, supported by policies and subsidies programs (in 2002 and 2004) and credit programs from the National Development Bank. Brazil is now the largest wind energy market in Latin America, and companies such as Petrobras are moving into the offshore market. The key innovation supporting the development of the sector was the introduction of exclusive renewable energy auctions, which reduced prices, made the market competitive, and attracted foreign companies.

Ethanol and solar industries

In addition to its leadership in wind power, Brazil has emerged as a leading producer of sugarcane-based ethanol for the transportation industry. Sugarcane has been transformed into alcohol for centuries, and ethanol production draws on this age-old technology. In Brazil, the widespread use of ethanol fuel began as a reaction to the variability of oil prices and it culminated in the creation of flex-fuel engines that can run equally well on gasoline or ethanol. Brazil's success with sugarcane ethanol (box 4.1) underscores the key role that consistent, long-term policy support plays in the development of LCT. The ethanol industry was supported through changing political administrations, oil-price shocks, and economic crises, with an array of fiscal and industrial incentives that were maintained until the industry matured. Over time, Brazil developed substantial technological and scientific expertise in ethanol-based technologies, which it began exporting, particularly to Africa, through a combination of technology transfer and private sector investment that became known as "ethanol diplomacy" (Dalgaard 2012).

Expanding its leadership beyond wind power, China is now a leader in solar photovoltaic (PV) systems, a technology developed in the United States but now manufactured predominantly in China. Solar PV has been considered a strategic industry in China since the 2006–10 five-year plan and has benefitted from generous public subsidies. After a crisis in 2011–12, however, the industry was restructured and subsidies became more selective. China is currently the largest producer in the world of solar PV cells (see figure 4.1).

China's experience with solar water heaters is another example of its transformation from a technology importer to an innovator. In the 1980s, China imported flat plate collectors from Canada, but this technology did not function well in the Chinese context. Chinese engineers responded by developing evacuated tube technology, an inexpensive alternative that better serves the needs of the Chinese market. Today, 95 percent of all solar water heaters in China use the

BOX 4.1

Brazil's success with sugarcane ethanol

Brazil has been producing sugarcane-based ethanol since the 1970s, when President Ernesto Geisel initiated the National Alcohol Program (ProAlcohol) in response to the 1973–74 oil crisis. The program was designed to reduce Brazil's dependence on oil imports while addressing the collapse of sugar export prices. ProAlcohol worked closely with the state-owned oil company, Petrobras, to address financing challenges and develop innovations that would allow the shared use of existing infrastructure (for example, technologies that would enable the same pipelines to carry both oil and ethanol while avoiding corrosion or undesired mixing). Ethanol was initially blended with gasoline at rates of 5–10 percent, which was safe for unmodified gasoline engines and lightly modified gas stations. The government incentivized ethanol production by providing low-interest loans to expand sugar mills and distilleries, establishing guaranteed prices set at the average cost of production, and creating demand through blending mandates. Petrobras, which had experience as a gasoline retailer, was granted a monopoly on ethanol distribution.

The 1979 oil crisis spurred a second phase in the ethanol program. Foreign and domestic automakers were pressured to manufacture ethanol-only vehicles, and by 1985 practically all new vehicles ran on pure ethanol. Ethanol pump prices were fixed at 59 percent of the price of gasoline, and ethanol-only vehicles were subject to lower sales taxes and licensing fees than conventional vehicles. Petrobras also built a distribution and pump infrastructure for pure, as opposed to blended, ethanol.

Because oil price projections remained high, however, little effort was made to increase the efficiency of domestic ethanol production. Tumbling oil prices in 1986–87, just as Brazil was experiencing one of its worst economic crises, forced the government to reduce guaranteed prices for ethanol to below the cost of production. Meanwhile, ethanol output fell as sugar prices recovered and exports rebounded. The ethanol industry was compelled to increase production efficiency, but the market remained constrained by technical limitations, because the maximum ethanol blend that could be used in gasoline-powered cars was just 25 percent.

In 2003–04, Brazil's automotive sector launched flex-fuel technology, which radically altered the ethanol market by enabling car owners to use whatever fuel or mix of fuels they wanted. This innovation was introduced by the Brazilian subsidiaries of major international car companies such as Fiat, General Motors, and Volkswagen, which drew on both foreign technology and local research and development. Government incentives ensured that flex-fuel vehicles were priced competitively with traditional gasoline-powered automobiles. To promote the sale of flex-fuel vehicles, the authorities used many of the same policies that had previously bolstered sales of ethanol-only vehicles, including favorable tax treatment at the point of purchase and reduced annual licensing fees.

Source: Adapted from Jiang et al. 2013 and Meyer et al. 2012.

evacuated tube design, and Chinese firms hold 95 percent of the patents for core technologies used in solar water heaters worldwide.

The development of solar PV cells and solar water heaters—two equally successful industries—is instructive. Although China is the world's largest investor, producer, and exporter of solar PV, the diffusion and installation of solar PV remains a challenge because of a number of social and technical barriers, including grid connectivity. Conversely, in the case of solar water heaters—where fewer of these barriers exist—China has the world's largest installed capacity (REN21 2011). These low-cost standalone systems have been very popular and constitute largely overlooked agents in the transition from fossil fuels to low-carbon energy (Tyfield, Ely, and Geall 2015).

FIGURE 4.1

Estimated world solar photovoltaic cell production, 2005–18

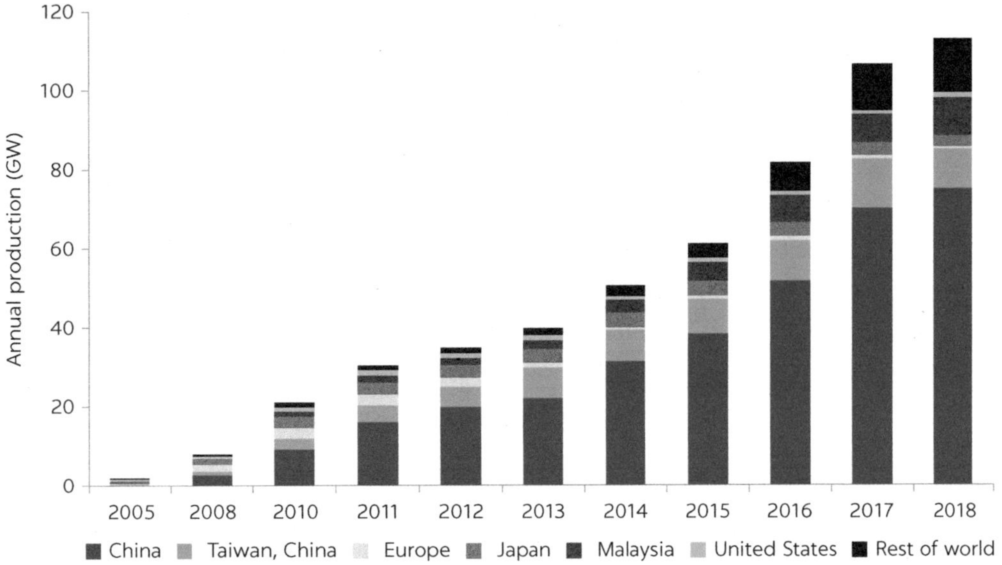

Source: JRC 2019.
Note: Data for 2018 are estimated. GW = gigawatt.

Finally, as discussed in chapter 2, emerging countries are not only becoming innovators but are also transferring technology to developing countries at the same or lower level of development. Is South–South LCT transfer any different from the traditional North–South LCT transfer? Ideally, South–South technology transfer could offer unique advantages, because developing countries share similar characteristics and may benefit from opportunities for collaborative capacity building. Some examples of South–South collaboration are reported in appendix D. Although too few to draw general lessons, they highlight that regardless of its origin, technology transfer takes place within a country-specific political, economic, and social environment that influences the type and amount of technology transferred, who participates in the decision-making process, and who benefits from the new technology. The studies also reveal that, to be sustainable, technology transfer requires not only an adequate policy framework but also an inclusive public consultation process. The rest of this chapter discusses the development of the EV market as a case study to illustrate China's success in technology adoption and innovation; it then compares the strategy and performance of one of China's largest battery and EV producers, BYD with that of an equally successful U.S. EV producer, Tesla.

THE EMERGENCE OF A GLOBAL ELECTRIC VEHICLE MARKET

The dynamic and growing EV industry is a major development in LCT. Initially driven by the energy crises of the 1970s and 1980s, and by the U.S. state of California's push for more fuel-efficient, lower-emissions vehicles, EV production took off in the late 1990s. The major EV designs include battery-powered electric vehicles (BEVs), plug-in hybrid electric vehicles (PHEVs), and fuel-cell electric vehicles (FCEVs). EV sales and production are largely concentrated in China, Europe, Japan, and the United States (see figure 4.2 and figure 4.3). Together, these four markets account for more than 97 percent of global EV sales and 93 percent of production (Lutsey et al. 2018). Surging global demand, progress in building the charging infrastructure, and an ever-expanding array of vehicle models are the key drivers of the EV industry.

Norway, which has the highest number of EVs per capita in the world,[2] aims to have zero-emissions vehicles account for all new cars sold by 2025, and France and the United Kingdom have announced that new gasoline and diesel cars will be banned by 2040. Other countries in Europe, however, are lagging. Among emerging countries, China is expected to lead the EV revolution. According to BloombergNEF (2018) projections, by 2025, 19 percent of all car sales in China will be electric, compared to 14 percent in Europe and only 11 percent in the United States. By 2040, the share of EV sales is expected to reach 60 percent in China. Worldwide EV sales will surge to 30 million in 2030 (figure 4.4).

India, the second-largest emerging economy in the world, is far behind in developing its EV industry. In terms of size, India's automobile industry currently ranks fifth in the world, but its EV industry is in its nascent stages. The overall cost of producing EVs is high because India imports most of the inputs (such as battery packs), and the country has a near absence of charging infrastructure despite initiatives to set up community charging stations.

FIGURE 4.2

New electric car sales, by country, 2013 and 2017

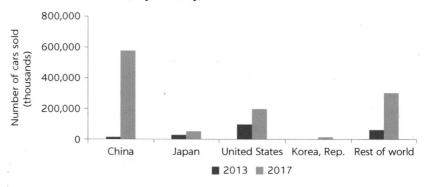

Source: Coffin and Horowitz 2018.

FIGURE 4.3

Exports of lithium-ion batteries, by country, 2013 and 2017

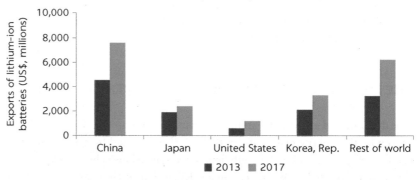

Source: Coffin and Horowitz 2018.

FIGURE 4.4

The electric vehicle market revolution, 2015–40

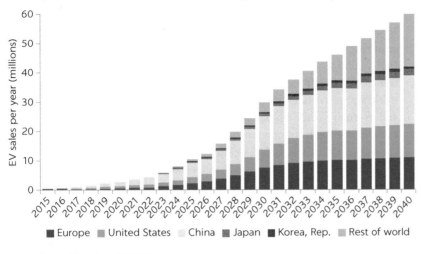

Source: BloombergNEF 2018.
Note: EV = electric vehicle.

Moreover, India produces electricity mainly by burning coal, which defeats the purpose of introducing EVs to reduce greenhouse gas emissions. In early 2019, however, India launched the "National Mission on Transformative Mobility and Battery Storage" to support clean, connected, shared, and sustainable mobility initiatives, and a "Phased Manufacturing Program" to support setting up of large-scale, export-competitive integrated batteries and cell-manufacturing giga plants, as well as localizing production across the entire EV value chain. The two programs are intended to run until 2024.

The rise of China's EV industry

The rapid expansion of China's EV industry was initially underpinned by growing concerns about pollution and energy security, but it also reflects key features of China's industrialization strategy. Over the past 20 years, China has become the world's largest passenger vehicle market, with annual automobile sales rising from fewer than 1.0 million units in 2001 to 22.7 million in 2018 (Yeung 2019). Although the growth of vehicle ownership is an important part of China's economic development, it has also driven a sharp increase in carbon emissions and local air pollution. Thus, in 2009, the Chinese government decided to vigorously develop its EV industry as a means of simultaneously reducing air pollution, moderating oil consumption, and positioning China as a technological leader in the global automotive industry.

The following analysis uses Porter's Diamond Model to shed light on the factors that have driven China's emergence as a major force in the global EV industry.[3] The analysis points to four determinants of China's comparative advantage:

- **China has an abundant endowment of the productive factors necessary to succeed in the EV industry,** and its extensive trade network enables producers to obtain resources that cannot be sourced domestically. China has large lithium reserves, but it also imports high-quality lithium from Africa and

South America. Besides lithium, EV batteries also require a cathode, which is usually made of metals such as nickel and cobalt, as well as a graphite anode. In 2016, China accounted for 66 percent of global graphite production and 35 percent of consumption. To control costs, Chinese companies have been acquiring cobalt and lithium assets around the world. The mining firm China Molybdenum recently spent US$2.6 billion to purchase the rights to the Democratic Republic of Congo's Tenke mine, which is believed to hold the world's largest concentration of cobalt. In addition to its vast natural resources and extensive trade links, China has a large and diverse workforce, and it ranks in the top third of countries in terms of human capital. Moreover, the government's earlier push to develop a domestic automotive sector has provided the new EV industry with engineers and workers who already possess car-manufacturing experience. Chinese firms have access to a range of finance options, including venture capital, and the government has invested heavily in the country's industrial infrastructure.

- **Chinese EV producers benefit from the presence of a well-established cluster of related industries.** China's automotive sector includes over 10,000 auto-parts factories, and local suppliers can produce all of the key components for EVs, such as batteries, motors, and electric control systems. In the early stages of the EV industry's development, China either imported highly complex parts, such as engines, or produced them through joint ventures between foreign and Chinese firms. China has since developed the domestic capability to manufacture all the essential elements of EVs.

- **China's EV sector benefits from a thriving domestic market for automobiles, which is far less saturated than most auto markets in advanced economies.** In 2017 a total of 29 million cars were sold in China; however, China still has just 80 vehicles per thousand people compared to 770 per thousand people in the United States. The considerable margin for growth in China's auto market leaves ample space for alternatives such as EVs. In addition, because the dominance of conventional vehicles is far less entrenched in China than it is in many advanced economies, Chinese consumers are more willing to accept EVs and face lower switching costs.

- **China's automotive sector is concentrated, but regulatory changes are expected to increase competition.** In China, hundreds of car companies produce thousands of models, but the top-10 manufacturers dominate 88 percent of the market, with the top-two firms taking about 20 percent each. The elimination of foreign-ownership restrictions on special purpose vehicles and EVs in 2019, which will be followed by the liberalization of regulations on commercial vehicles in 2020 and passenger cars in 2022, should increase market contestability and intensify competitive pressures.

The role of China's industrial policies in the rapid development of its EV industry

In the early 2000s, China's efforts to develop the EV industry focused on establishing the R&D capacity necessary to overcome critical barriers related to price, infrastructure, and battery technology. Early efforts to support R&D for core EV technologies were included in the 1986 High-Tech Development Plan (known as the "863 program"),[4] which continued through several Five-Year Plans.

The 863 program required cofinancing from the private sector, so most applicants for program funding were automakers partnered with research institutions (Kokko and Liu 2012). After nearly 10 years of R&D promotion efforts, the government began to focus its support on EV production. The Ministry of Science and Technology announced the Strategic Plan for New Energy Vehicles in 2001. Three years later it established the vertical programs on fully electric battery-powered vehicles, gas-electric hybrids, and fuel-cell vehicles, as well as the horizontal programs focusing on battery technology, electric motors, and electronic control systems. These programs provided the framework for building the domestic technological capacity that would underpin the rise of China's EV value chain during the next 10 years.

Engineering the systemic changes necessary to develop a mass-market EV industry proved extremely challenging. In 2008, China launched a pilot program to accelerate the introduction of EVs, initially in 10 cities, each of which was expected to introduce 1,000 EVs within three years. EVs were exempted from the 10 percent purchase tax on new vehicles, with a maximum total financial incentive per vehicle equal to 60 percent of the vehicle's price. Despite intense government support, including tax and price subsidies and infrastructure investment, the experiment failed to achieve its objectives.[5] Zhang et al. (2014) ascribe this failure to weaknesses in EV subsidy policies, local protectionism, inadequate charging infrastructures, and opportunistic behavior by cities and individuals. The pilot's key lesson was that the transition from conventional vehicles to EVs would require not just vision, strategic direction, and government support, but also much higher subsidies and incentives as well as tighter coordination among auto manufacturers, battery developers, infrastructure providers, and consumers.[6]

EV production accelerated in late 2013, when the government significantly increased subsidies to EV manufacturers and developed a network of charging facilities and services based on unified standards. By 2015, China had become the world's largest EV market. In the same year, the Chinese government launched "Made in China 2025," a 10-year industrial plan to make China a global high-tech leader by developing 10 high-tech industries, including new EVs. The 12th Five-Year Plan (2016–20) reaffirmed the government's commitment to the EV industry by including it among six emerging industries prioritized for governmental support.

China's policies in support of the EV industry—from central and local authorities—can be qualified as comprehensive (stretching from R&D to charging stations and consumers), strategic, and aggressive. The EV industry has been supported by subsidies in all countries (box 4.2 describes the key policies adopted in the U.S. EV industry); however, China's subsidies to the industry were huge. According to the Ministry of Industry and Information Technology, by 2018 total central government subsidies for EV purchases reached US$13 billion, despite delays of some subsidy payments. Local government subsidies may have been much higher, but no comprehensive estimates are currently available.

The Chinese government's generous support for the EV industry also led to unintended consequences. In 2016, a nationwide investigation covering 90 companies and 401,000 EVs sold between 2013 and 2015 revealed that manufacturers could cheat the system by faking sales or downgrading key parts, such as batteries and motor controllers. The government publicly identified the companies involved in the scandal and scrutinized its EV subsidy policies. Reforms in

BOX 4.2

U.S. electric vehicle policies

In the United states, as in China, financial incentives, including tax credits and tax exemptions, have played a major role in the expansion of electric vehicle (EV) technology. The U.S. federal government offers a tax credit for plug-in EVs purchased after 2009; that credit ranges from US$2,500 to US$7,500 per vehicle on the basis of battery capacity and gross vehicle weight rating. The full credit is available until a manufacturer sells 200,000 EVs, at which point it begins to phase out.

Over half of all U.S. state governments use rebates, tax exemptions, and tax credits to promote EV purchases. For example, California offers rebates for light-duty zero-emissions vehicles and plug-in hybrids, and low-income families are eligible for an extra US$2,000 in incentives. Washington and New Jersey exempt EVs from motor vehicle sales and use taxes. More than 10 American states—including California, Colorado, Florida, and New York—allow EVs to use high-occupancy vehicle lanes. More than 10 states offer rebates and tax credits for installing charging stations, and as of 2017 the United States had 47,130 charging outlets.

In addition, the federal government's Advanced Research Project Agency–Energy has funded EV projects focusing on batteries, automotive controls, and efficient EV chargers. Fleet procurement is another major EV-promotion policy employed by the United States, especially in large municipalities. Battery-powered EVs made up about 1 percent of all U.S. vehicles sold in 2017, and this share is projected to increase to 12 percent by 2050 in part because of supportive state policies and falling battery costs.

Source: Adapted from Lu 2018.

2017 reduced EV subsidy levels, tightened technical requirements, and introduced stronger oversight and enforcement mechanisms.

In March 2019, China announced a new scheme that almost halves the existing subsidies and raises the threshold for a vehicle to be eligible for these subsidies. The new scheme also cancels local-level passenger EV subsidies to encourage fair competition across regional markets and requires local governments to add more charging stations and hydrogen refueling stations, as well as providing better services. Lithium-ion battery manufacturers are now required to have at least 8 gigawatt-hours of production capacity to qualify for subsidies (Sanderson, Hancock, and Lewis 2019), and manufacturers of advanced batteries, including lithium-ion and nickel metal hydride, are exempt from the 4 percent consumption tax. The government has also restricted EV incentives to vehicles with batteries manufactured in China, prompting foreign battery companies to establish China-based production facilities or joint ventures with Chinese firms.

To expedite the transition from conventional vehicles, the central government has established that 20 percent of new vehicles would be plug-in EVs by 2025. Meanwhile, following the central government's lead, many local authorities are requiring that a certain percentage of new government vehicles be EVs. Shenzhen, a major industrial center, completely transitioned its fleet of more than 16,000 buses to EVs, and by May 2018 it had 13,000 EV taxis in service. Many cities have also promoted the installation of charging stations to encourage private EV ownership. For example, Beijing has set a target of building more than 435,000 chargers by 2020, and Shanghai subsidizes

30 percent of all investment in specialized and public chargers. Since 2019, manufacturers selling at least 30,000 conventional vehicles must have a minimum of 4–5 percent of their sales in EVs. Manufacturers that do not meet this requirement will be fined or must buy credits from other manufacturers. Local governments could receive up to US$14 million to build charging stations if they meet certain conditions, and several provinces and cities have announced additional subsidies (up to 30 percent of the total investment) to support the installation of charging stations.

Indigenous innovation originated from domestic firms, not from joint ventures

China's industrialization policies have resulted in an unusual development pattern of the country's automotive market. In China, multinational automakers dominate the conventional vehicle industry, whereas domestic firms dominate EV production (figure 4.5). This pattern contrasts with the development of auto industries in other emerging economies, where production often focuses on serving international automotive supply chains with cutting-edge technologies and where domestic production of these technologies, such as EVs, is generally limited (Helveston et al. 2017). In China, joint ventures with international firms represent only 12 percent of the EV market, and indigenous firms represent the rest. This feature is partly the result of the Trade-Technology-for-Market (TTM) policy, which has been the cornerstone of China's industrialization strategy since the early 1980s. Devised by Deng Xiaoping, the TTM policy requires foreign firms in strategic sectors to form joint ventures with Chinese state-owned partners. Foreign firms are obliged to share technology with their Chinese counterparts in exchange for access to the Chinese market. During the

FIGURE 4.5

Market shares of joint ventures and domestic firms in the conventional and electric vehicle industries

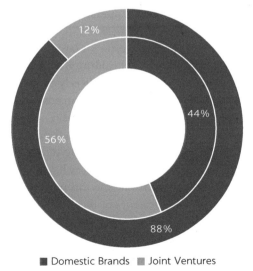

■ Domestic Brands   ■ Joint Ventures

Source: China Association of Automobile Manufacturers and DaaS-Auto.
Note: Inner circle shows market shares in the conventional vehicle industry. Outer circle shows market shares in the electric vehicle industry.

early stages of the TTM policy's implementation, high tariff barriers[7] sharply limited the scope for auto imports, making joint ventures one of very few ways for foreign automakers to access the Chinese market (Howell 2018).

The TTM policy has long been the subject of criticism from China's trading partners. In March 2018, the Office of the U.S. Trade Representative published a report documenting China's "unfair technology transfer regime for U.S. companies" (USTR 2018). The report highlights the auto industry as an area in which compulsory technology transfer is rampant, and it singles out the EV subsector as a place in which "you're simply not going to be able to sell that product in China unless the local partner has mastered the ability to leverage the technology to produce it going forward."

Meanwhile, Chinese critics have argued that the TTM policy has encouraged Chinese firms to rely on imported outdated technologies instead of investing in domestic research. For example, under a 1984 joint venture between Volkswagen and Shanghai Automotive, the latter developed the capacity to build cars based on German technology, and it continued to produce them under a market monopoly until the 2000s. Because of its limited capacity to create new technologies, Shanghai Automotive produced the same increasingly outdated models for almost 20 years. In response to this challenge, the Chinese government has refocused attention from technology transfer to domestic R&D since 2006, and the timing of this shift has coincided with the development of the country's EV industry.

The joint venture model enabled major foreign automakers to dominate China's mid-range to high-end auto market, whereas smaller Chinese firms focused on small, low-cost vehicles and the emerging minicar segment. This pattern of industry segmentation reflects three key features of the Chinese automotive sector. First, joint ventures dominate China's conventional vehicle market because foreign firms can earn high profit margins by licensing and selling older technologies while withholding cutting-edge innovations. Second, few joint ventures can produce EVs while complying with local regulations for EV manufacturing facilities and the requirement that EV batteries be produced in China. Consequently, EVs produced through joint ventures tend to be expensive and are often sold at a loss as taxi fleets rather than to private consumers. Third, the limited use of joint ventures in the EV subsector opened market opportunities for independent Chinese firms, which were able to capture a large domestic market share thanks to a decade-long process of building R&D capacity. Meanwhile, China's conventional automakers continue to rely on their foreign partners for innovation and to focus their R&D efforts on adapting foreign technologies to the Chinese market (Helveston et al. 2017).

The Chinese government's highly active role in the development of the EV sector has given rise to concerns about the long-term sustainability of the industry. The government's incentive policies may have created a protected EV market for independent domestic firms, and this protection could ultimately have negative implications for efficiency and technological advancement, especially as joint venture requirements are relaxed (Helveston et al. 2017).[8] The government's plan to remove the 50 percent cap on foreign ownership of joint ventures by 2022 will effectively end the TTM policy in the automotive sector. Once the cap is lifted, most joint ventures in the Chinese auto industry will likely transition to full foreign ownership. For instance, Tesla's first plant in

China is already wholly owned by Tesla. Meanwhile, Chinese firms that previously partnered with foreign companies will be forced to compete in the market under their own brands.

BYD AND TESLA: THE CONTRASTING TRAJECTORIES OF INNOVATIVE ELECTRIC VEHICLE FIRMS IN CHINA AND THE UNITED STATES

BYD: From imitation to innovation

This section analyzes the experience of a Chinese automaker, BYD, as a successful example of a firm that has made a transition from technology importation to local innovation and how this transition affects the Chinese market. The next section compares BYD's experience with that of Tesla, the legendary U.S. company that has dominated the U.S. EV market in the past 10 years.

BYD is a major Chinese automaker based in Shenzhen, Guangdong Province. Founded in 1995, BYD started out as a battery maker and entered the automobile business in 2003. The company has diversified into areas such as cell phone assembly and solar cell manufacturing. The establishment of BYD's conventional vehicle business followed the standard model of inbound technology transfer and local adaptation. In 1995, chemist Wang Chuanfu learned that Japanese battery producers and electronics firms were transitioning from nickel-cadmium (NiCd) batteries to nickel metal hydride (NiMH) and lithium-ion batteries, which require a more complex, higher-value-added production process. Realizing that the manufacturing base for NiCd batteries could be moved to China, Mr. Wang founded the Shenzhen BYD Battery Company Limited with an initial investment of US$300,000.

The company's first revolutionary act was to replace the capital-intensive Japanese style of production with a labor-intensive style more suited to the Chinese manufacturing sector. With a team of 20 employees, Mr. Wang dismantled the batteries produced by competitors (Burkitt 2017) and learned to reverse engineer the technology. Soon, BYD became the preferred battery supplier for large cell phone companies such as Motorola. By 2002, BYD employed 17,000 workers and had become one of the world's top manufacturers of both NiCd and lithium-ion batteries.

As the battery market for electronics matured and BYD faced increasing competition from new Chinese rivals, the company expanded into the domestic EV industry, perceiving the nascent sector as a way to leverage its manufacturing capabilities while creating new demand for batteries. BYD's initial approach to the auto industry mirrored its approach to battery production: manufacturing processes substituted labor for capital, and foreign products were reverse engineered to expand in-house production capabilities. Although quality control was an issue during the early stages of BYD's entry into the automotive sector, the company developed special tools and worker-training programs to improve its performance. BYD managers regarded these early challenges as part of an ongoing learning process through which BYD adapted international production methods to reflect local conditions (Wang and Kimble 2013).

BYD's automotive wing initially focused on three main business lines: conventional vehicles, fully electric vehicles, and hybrid vehicles. BYD targeted the low-cost, family-oriented passenger vehicle segment, and its first car model, the F3, came off the production line in 2005. In 2008, BYD unveiled the first plug-in hybrid to be produced at a commercial scale anywhere in the world. Despite having a fully electric range of over 60 miles, BYD's hybrid was not as glamorous as the Tesla Roadster, which debuted the same year. BYD struggled with low sales between 2010 and 2012, but it continued working on an innovative technology. In 2011 it introduced the G6 model, which used an engine and transmission system developed in-house. BYD engineers subsequently created a "dual-mode"[9] plug-in hybrid that was cheaper and more efficient than the Toyota Prius at the time. This model required no reverse engineering, because BYD already had the capacity to produce batteries, electric motors, and electronic control systems—the three core EV technologies.

BYD then began producing EV models based on its own internally developed lithium-ion-phosphate battery. This battery boasted a safer design than previous technologies and did not require cobalt or nickel, which were in short supply in the Chinese market. The Chinese government's generous subsidies for domestically produced EVs apply only to models that use Chinese-built batteries, making local components especially important. More recent energy-density requirements have prompted Chinese battery makers to push their technological limits even further.

BYD's focus on R&D sets it apart from other Chinese companies, and its integration of multiple complementary product lines is unique among EV producers. In January 2015, BYD announced that the world's first three-engine, four-wheel drive, dual-mode sport utility vehicle, the Tang, was available for preorder. The Tang's three engines make it able to reach speeds of over 100 kilometers per hour within five seconds. By 2018 BYD had more than 12,000 domestic patents and more than 8,000 international patents (in areas such as environmentally friendly, fire-safe iron phosphate chemistries and advanced EV drive and energy recovery systems). In 2013, BYD received the "Outstanding Patent Innovation and Industrial Design" award from the World Intellectual Patent Organization. BYD's patent for EV batteries also received the China Patent Association's Award of Excellence.

BYD is currently the only company in the world that can design and produce all the essential EV technologies in-house—batteries, electric motors, and electronic control systems and charging facilities—and it has the capacity to coordinate investments and innovate across the entire EV value chain.[10]

In 2015, BYD opened its first Latin American factory in Campinas, Brazil, mostly to avoid import tariffs both in Brazil and across much of the Latin America region, which allowed the company to introduce some of the first all-electric buses to the Brazilian and regional markets. The Campinas factory manufactures and assembles long-range electric buses as well as iron phosphate battery packs. It began production in 2018, coinciding with the launch of a new electric bus model.[11] BYD plans to gradually increase the share of local technology used in production from less than 50 percent to 70 percent by 2022. In addition, BYD opened a new electric bus production facility in the U.S. state of California in October 2017, and it has decided to relocate its European electric bus production from China to plants in Hungary and France.

Tesla: From vision to reality

Tesla is one of the most inspiring examples of American entrepreneurship in the past 20 years. Founded by two Silicon Valley engineers, Martin Eberhard and Marc Tarpenning, the firm is named after the 19th-century scientist Nikola Tesla, who invented the induction motor and alternating current power transmission that make the EV industry possible. Shortly after Tesla Motors was incorporated in July 2003, Elon Musk became Chairman of Tesla's Board of Directors and was tasked with overseeing all aspects of the design and manufacturing of EVs and battery products. Musk, a visionary innovator and entrepreneur, identified strongly with Tesla's mission to "accelerate the world's transition to a sustainable energy future" by producing affordable, mass-market EVs and battery products.[12] The company soon became a major player in the EV industry.

In 2008, Tesla unveiled the Roadster, a two-seater electric sports car that was immediately successful despite its extremely high price tag. The Roadster was six times more efficient than conventional cars and produced just 1/10th of the pollution. It was also the first car to use lithium-ion batteries. In 2012, Tesla released the Model S, a seven-seater EV with an operational range of 208–265 miles that could compete in the premium sedan category. The Model S was named Motor Trend's Car of the Year, underscoring its ability to compete with conventional vehicles.

Tesla introduced several innovations that contributed to build its image as a "disruptive" firm.

- **Seeking alliances and partnerships to overcome the lack of automotive expertise.** To develop the Roadster's concept, Tesla held an international design competition—won by Lotus, a well-known sports car company. Tesla used existing conventional automotive technology developed by Lotus to complement its EV-specific innovations (the power train and batteries). Moreover, it was also able to use the Lotus plant in the United Kingdom to fit the production of Tesla Roadsters. In 2010, Tesla collaborated with Toyota to develop a second-generation sport utility vehicle under the Toyota Motors brand. Tesla provided the power train, software, and battery technologies; Toyota built the remainder of the vehicle. The partnership allowed Tesla to have access to a new production plant and to learn from Toyota's engineering and production systems, helping Tesla reduce production costs and build its automotive expertise.
- **Innovating on battery technology.** Soon after the release of the Roadster, Tesla partnered with Panasonic to improve its battery technology. Tesla's goal was to increase the maximum range of its vehicles while reducing their overall cost. Panasonic invested US$30 million in Tesla, and that investment helped the company meet its margins and cost targets. In 2011, the two companies again joined forces to develop a new generation of nickel-based battery cells that were later incorporated in the Tesla Model S. Later, the company developed a battery cell capable of holding 31 percent more energy than the original Roadster cell, but in the same size and at a lower cost.
- **Multiplying charging stations.** In 2012, Tesla established its first six "supercharger" stations in California. By 2015, Tesla had installed 2,000 superchargers in almost 400 stations in Asia, Australia, Europe, and North America.

- **Direct sales and no advertisements.** Tesla does not advertise or sell its cars through traditional dealers. Instead, it sells directly to consumers through its website and offers test drives at dedicated Tesla Stores.
- **Making patents available to all.** Tesla launched a most remarkable initiative in 2014, the opening of all its patents, including those for batteries and power trains. This decision reflected Tesla's vision as much as its commercial ambitions. Tesla initially regarded patents as a necessary defense against the risk that other car companies would copy its technology and reproduce it on a mass scale. By 2014 it had become apparent that this was not happening: global EV output remained marginal, representing only about 1 percent of total vehicle sales. To realize its vision of an environmentally sustainable global auto industry, Tesla decided to disclose all its patents. This decision was based on the idea that firms should share their technologies and explore new approaches to intellectual property management, spinoffs, licensing, and other methods that may enable companies to better absorb external ideas (Chesbrough 2003). Tesla was convinced that the shift from conventional vehicles to EVs, would not occur simply through isolated experiments. A real transition would require a comprehensive ecosystem supported by close collaboration between battery producers, automotive manufacturers, providers of charging infrastructure, and software developers.

Starting in 2008, Tesla, although innovative and successful, faced serious financial challenges. Elon Musk used a combination of his own wealth, venture capital, bank and government loans, investments by other automakers, and the U.S. stock and debt markets to transform Tesla's vision into a reality. The company struggled to reduce the price of its EVs and capture a larger share of the consumer market. Despite serious production challenges and continuing financial problems, however, Tesla has repeatedly outperformed traditional car companies in the stock market.

CONCLUSIONS

This chapter has discussed some examples of LCT transfer and innovation in a small number of emerging economies, which account for a large fraction of existing LCT deployment. The chapter finds that emerging countries are rapidly deploying LCTs, innovating on the transferred technologies, and introducing new institutional changes that challenge the use of conventional technologies. China stands out as having made the fastest progress in LCT deployment, innovation, and production. Given its large size, China has a key role in contributing to the global transition to low-carbon, more sustainable patterns of development.

China's experience with acquiring technology through joint ventures was critical to its early industrialization, but in recent years that practice has yielded increasingly mixed results. In an industry marked by rapid technological upgrading, joint ventures can discourage foreign parent companies from transferring the latest technologies, and can also create a disincentive for domestic firms to invest in R&D. The relative lack of interest among foreign automobile companies in developing the EV market gave Chinese firms, such as BYD, space to grow.

China succeeded in the EV market because of its ability to learn from mistakes, make adjustments, and move forward. The first pilots were marked by several difficulties that made it impossible to attain the government's objectives. Thus, the policy targets were changed, the industry revised its strategies, and it eventually succeeded in producing cheaper and better-designed EV models—to meet domestic preferences. Although subsidies to promote EV sales were initially expensive and untargeted, they were essential for the industry to take off. The industry is now sufficiently strong to survive the upcoming replacement of most subsidies with targeted regulatory initiatives.

Finally, the contrasting but equally successful experience of two EV companies, BYD in China and Tesla in the United States, provides some insights into different evolutions of the world EV industry. Both companies are led by visionary innovators but differ in their strategies and in their vision on how the global market should develop. Although BYD is the more successful firm—in terms of EV sales—Tesla's most important contribution to the future may be its "open innovation" approach to IPR. Allowing competitors to benefit from a firm's innovations may offer a way for the EV industry to rapidly take hold and develop.

NOTES

1. Appendix D describes how Korea became a global leader in the rapidly growing market for energy storage systems.
2. The Norwegian success story is first and foremost due to a substantial package of incentives developed to promote zero-emission vehicles into the market. Subsidies have included the following: no purchase/import taxes (1990–), exemption from 25 percent value added tax on purchase (2001–20), no annual road tax (1996–), no charges on toll roads or ferries (1997–2017), and a maximum charge of 50 percent of the total amount on ferry fares and on toll roads for EVs (2018–). The government has recently decided that after 2021 the incentives will be revised and adjusted parallel with market development.
3. The model provides a framework for understanding competitive advantage at the national and firm levels (Porter 1990). The four points of the "diamond" represent the determinants of comparative economic advantage: (i) factor endowment, which includes the natural resources, skilled labor, technology, and infrastructure necessary to compete in a given industry; (ii) demand conditions, which influence the quantity of a good or service that will be purchased at different price points; (iii) the presence of related industries, which generate complementarities and facilitate the development of economies of agglomeration; and (iv) firm strategy and market competition, which reflect how firms are created, organized, and managed, as well as the structure and contestability of a given market. In addition to these four factors, government policies and idiosyncratic shocks can significantly affect competitive advantage among firms and industries.
4. The 863 program was launched in 1986 to accelerate the development of high-tech industry and R&D capacity through three successive Five-Year Plans, with the goal of promoting domestic innovation and enhancing China's international competitiveness.
5. The pilot was expanded to 24 cities; however, by 2012 the total number of EVs introduced each year in those 24 cities had reached just 10,000.
6. EV subsidies are directly allocated to manufacturers, and consumers pay the retail price minus the subsidies. In 2010, a subsidy ranging from US$635 to US$7,941 was available for each PHEV purchased, and a subsidy of US$9,530 was available for each BEV. The subsidies covered about 40–60 percent of the costs of EVs. When the subsidy program expired in 2012, the central government took six months to renew it. In 2013, the subsidies for each PHEV were adjusted to US$5,600 and subsidies for each BEV ranged from US$5,600 to US$9,530 depending on a vehicle's driving range. The subsidies decreased by 5 percent in 2014 and by 10 percent in 2015 according to the 2013 standard. The subsidy program was renewed again in 2016—up to US$8,736 for each BEV and up to US$4,765 for each PHEV.

It decreased by 20 percent in 2017 and 2018 according the 2016 standard, and by 40 percent in 2019 (Lu 2018).

7. Tariffs on imported vehicles ranged from 180 to 220 percent through 1994 and from 70 to 150 percent through 2001 before dropping to 30 percent through 2005 and 25 percent thereafter.

8. Howell (2018) and Gallagher (2006) also find that the joint venture model has had an adverse effect on domestic innovation capacity in the automotive sector.

9. "Dual mode" indicates that a vehicle can switch from fully electric to gasoline power.

10. BYD also produces a comprehensive range of solar energy technologies. BYD plans to open its first overseas solar energy R&D center in Brazil, as a partnership with the State University of Campinas. BYD aims to become the first company in Brazil to offer a comprehensive zero-emissions energy system that integrates solar generation, storage, and transportation technology.

11. The new model was designed in partnership with Brazilian bus and coach manufacturer Marcopolo and uses a BYD rolling chassis with a Marcopolo Torino body. The partnership with Marcopolo allows BYD to contribute its strongest technologies—the power train and batteries produced by the Campinas factory—without needing to build the local production capacity necessary to create an entire vehicle.

12. This section is based on Karamitsios (2013), Lehtinen (2015), and Purificato (2014).

REFERENCES

BloombergNEF. 2018. "Electric Vehicle Outlook 2018." BloombergNEF, New York.

Burkitt, L. 2017. "The World's Largest Electric Vehicle Maker Hits a Speed Bump." *MIT Technology Review*, May 8. https://www.technologyreview.com/s/604335/the-worlds-largest-electric-vehicle-maker-hits-a-speed-bump/.

CEMAC (Clean Energy Manufacturing Analysis Center). 2017. "Benchmarks of Global Clean Energy Manufacturing." Golden, CO: CEMAC, U.S. Department of Energy, National Renewable Energy Laboratory.

Chesbrough, H. W. 2003. *Open Innovation: The New Imperative for Creating and Profiting from Technology*. Boston: Harvard Business School Publishing Corporation.

Coffin, D., and J. Horowitz. 2018. "The Supply Chain for Electric Vehicle Batteries." *Journal of International Commerce and Economics*, December. https://www.usitc.gov/publications/332/journals/the_supply_chain_for_electric_vehicle_batteries.pdf.

Dalgaard, Klaus Guimarães. 2012. "The Energy Statecraft of Brazil: Promoting Biofuels as an Instrument of Brazilian Foreign Policy, 2003–2010." PhD thesis, Department of International Relations, London School of Economics.

Gallagher, K. S. 2006. "Limits to Leapfrogging in Energy Technologies? Evidence from the Chinese Automobile Industry." *Energy Policy* 34 (4): 383–94.

Helveston, J., Y. Wang, V. Karplus, and E. R. Fuchs. 2017. "Innovating Up, Down, and Sideways: The (Unlikely) Institutional Origins of Experimentation in China's Plug-in Electric Vehicle Industry." https://papers.ssrn.com/sol3/papers.cfm?abstract_id=2817052.

Howell, S. T. 2018. "Joint Ventures and Technology Adoption: A Chinese Industrial Policy that Backfired." *Research Policy* 47 (8): 1448–62.

Jiang, M. K., L. Mytelka, L. Neij, G. Nemet, and C. Wilson. 2013. "Historical Case Studies of Energy Technology Innovation." Cambridge University Press: Cambridge, UK.

JRC (Joint Research Centre). 2019. *China: Challenges and Prospects from an Industrial and Innovation Powerhouse*. Brussels: European Commission.

Karamitsios, A. 2013. "Open Innovation in EVs: A Case Study of Tesla Motors." Master of Science thesis INDEK 2013:67. KTH Industrial Engineering and Management, Stockholm.

Kokko, A., and Y. Liu. 2012. "Governance of New Energy Vehicle Technology in China: The Case of Hybrid Electric Vehicles." In *Paving the Road to Sustainable Transport: Governance and Innovation in Low-Carbon Vehicles*, edited by M. Nilsson, K. Hillman, A. Rickne, and T. Magnusson, 200–20. London: Routledge.

Lam L. T., L. Branstetter, and I. M. L. Azevedo. 2017. "China's Wind Industry: Leading in Deployment, Lagging in Innovation." *Energy Policy* 106: 588–99.

Lehtinen, P. 2015. "The Advancement of Electric Vehicles—Case: Tesla Motors. Disruptive Technology Requiring Systemic Innovating." Management and Organization Master's thesis, University of Tampere, Department of Management Studies.

Lu, J. 2018. "Comparing U.S. and Chinese Electric Vehicle Policies." Environmental and Energy Study Institute, Washington, DC, February 28.

Lundvall, B.-Å. 1985. *Product Innovation and User-Producer Interaction*. Industrial Development Research Series 31. Aalborg: Aalborg University Press.

Lutsey, N., M. Grant, S. Wappelhorst, and H. Zhou. 2018. "Power Play: How Governments Are Spurring the Electric Vehicle Industry." ICCT White Paper, International Council on Clean Transportation, Washington, DC.

Meyer, D., L. Mytelka, R. Press, E. L. Dall'Oglio, P. T. de Sousa Jr., and A. Grubler. 2012. "Brazilian Ethanol: Unpacking a Success Story of Energy Technology Innovation." In *Energy Technology Innovation: Learning from Historical Successes and Failures*, edited by A. Grubler and C. Wilson, 275–91. Cambridge, U.K.: Cambridge University Press.

Porter, M. 1990. *The Competitive Advantage of Nations*. New York: The Free Press.

Purificato, M. 2014. "The Open Innovation Paradigm in Electric Vehicle Industry: A Case Study of Tesla Motors." Bachelor's thesis, LUISS Guido Carli.

REN21 (Renewable Energy Policy Network for the 21st Century). 2011. "Renewables 2011 Global Status Report." REN21, Paris.

Rennkamp, B., and F. Westin. 2013. "Feito no Brasil? Made in South Africa? Boosting Technological Development Through Local Content Policies in the Wind Energy Industry." Eleventh Globelics International Conference, Ankara, Turkey, September 11–13.

Ru, P., Q. Zhi, F. Zhang, X. Zhong, J. Li, and J. Su. 2012. "Behind the Development of Technology: The Transition of Innovation Modes in China's Wind Turbine Manufacturing Industry." *Energy Policy* 43 (April): 58–69.

Sanderson, H., T. Hancock, and L. Lewis. 2019. "Electric Cars: China's Battle for the Battery Market." *Financial Times*, March 5. https://www.ft.com/content/8c94a2f6-fdcd-11e6-8d8e-a5e3738f9ae4.

Tyfield, D., A. Ely, and S. Geall. 2015. "Low Carbon Innovation in China: From Overlooked Opportunities and Challenges to Transitions in Power Relations and Practices." *Sustainable Development* 23 (4): 206–16.

Urban, F. 2018. "China's Rise: Challenging the North–South Technology Transfer Paradigm for Climate Change Mitigation and Low Carbon Energy." *Energy Policy* 113 (February): 320–30.

USTR (Office of the United States Trade Representative Executive Office of the President). 2018. "Findings of the Investigation into China's acts, policies and practices related to technology transfer, intellectual property and innovation under Section 301 of the Trade Act of 1974," March: https://ustr.gov/sites/default/files/Section%20301%20FINAL.PDF.

Wang, H., and C. Kimble. 2013. "Innovation and Leapfrogging in the Chinese Automobile Industry: Examples from Geely, BYD, and Shifeng." *Global Business and Organizational Excellence* 32 (6): 6–17.

Yeung, K. 2019. "China's January Car Sales in Biggest Drop in Seven Years as Worries over Economy, Spending Deepen." *South China Morning Post*, February 18. https://www.scmp.com/economy/china-economy/article/2186630/chinas-january-passenger-car-sales-biggest-drop-seven-worries.

Zhang, X., R. Rao, J. Xie, and Y. Lang. 2014. "The Current Dilemma and Future Path of China's Electric Vehicles." *Sustainability* 6 (3): 1567–93.

5 Policies to Support Low-Carbon Technology Transfer

INTRODUCTION

The aim of this chapter—the last of the report—is to provide actionable advice to policy makers seeking to transfer low-carbon technologies (LCTs), either inward through import and diffusion or outward through innovation, production, and export. As previous chapters have shown, addressing climate change creates an urgent need for LCT transfer, but economic transformations take time, especially in energy (chapter 1). Meanwhile, the LCT transfer process (proxied for by trade, patents, and foreign direct investment [FDI]) is at present dominated by developed and a few developing countries, but it has seen some progress (chapters 2 and 3). Although experiences among countries remain unique and context-specific, there is much to learn from the few countries that have successfully leveraged industrial and innovation policies[1] to take advantage of the emerging global value chain for LCT (chapter 4). Taking these findings forward, this chapter seeks to provide answers to the question of how developing countries can deploy LCTs at scale while capturing parts of the growing global value chain in LCTs.

The first section of the chapter discusses LCT in the context of the need for large-scale deployment to mitigate climate change while meeting growing energy demand. Next, the chapter presents deployment itself as a potential opportunity for economies seeking export-led growth to become LCT producers and exporters. The third section discusses the critical roles of human capital and state capacity to deploy and develop LCTs, which are unevenly distributed among developing countries. The fourth section introduces policies, practices, and procedures for LCT deployment and production, outlining the need for optimal policy mixes to be tailored according to objectives (LCT deployment versus LCT production) and context (for example, state capacity, income levels, market size, and policy feasibility). Next, recommendations are provided to policy makers and their supporters. The sixth and final section summarizes and concludes the chapter.

NECESSITY OF LCT TRANSFER

Achieving the Paris Agreement's objectives of limiting climate change to 1.5°C or below 2°C entails Herculean efforts in the coming decades. The so-called carbon law provides a road map toward global decarbonization, requiring that global greenhouse gas (GHG) emissions be halved every decade from 2020 onward (Rockström et al. 2017). This level of reduction requires a fundamental transformation of many human systems, particularly those related to energy. It would entail massive changes in fuels (renewables versus nonrenewables) and technologies (low versus high carbon), alongside "different infrastructure, urban planning, consumer products, consumption patterns, built environments, business models, professional training programs, investments and policies" (IEA and IRENA 2017).

Given the scale of the LCT deployment implied by such a radical transformation, however, skepticism is warranted. Energy transitions, for example, tend to be complex and unpredictable processes (chapter 1). These transitions appear to have "no magic formula" and tend to be "path-dependent, rather than revolutionary, cumulative rather than fully substitutive" (Sovacool 2016). For example, very low-tech forms of energy (animal, wood, and steam power) remain prevalent throughout the world, not having been fully replaced by fossil, nuclear, or renewable energy (RE) sources.

Current trends give a mixed picture as to whether the energy transition can be achieved at the scale needed. For example, on the energy supply side, this transition requires additional installed RE capacity of about 300 gigawatts (GW) each year to 2030, but in 2018 only 180 GW were added. On the energy demand side, investments in energy efficiency have slowed (IEA 2019). Across both demand and supply sides, private incentives and public policies are sending mixed signals: "current market and policy signals are not incentivizing the major reallocation of capital to low-carbon power and efficiency that would align with a sustainable energy future" (IEA 2019).

In addition, the specific technologies likely to be needed for achieving the 1.5°C or below 2°C target—for example, carbon removal and sequestration of GHGs from the atmosphere—remain unproven, and presently receive insufficient investment. These technologies have relatively little scholarship and knowledge production, let alone commercial applications, to support them (UNEP 2017). As a result, many of the emissions pathways prevalent in policy analysis (for example, three of the four "illustrative model pathways" in IPCC 2018) rely on a series of as-yet unproven technologies.

Despite the scale of the challenge in narrowing the gap between existing and needed LCT deployment and policies for a global low-carbon transition, there are grounds for optimism. First, achieving most of the emissions reductions needed is feasible through the rapid diffusion of *existing* technologies (figure 5.1). UNEP (2017) states that maintaining more than a 66 percent chance of containing global warming to 1.5°C requires that annual global GHG emissions not exceed 24 gigatons by 2030.[2] Without new mitigation policies, emissions are expected to rise to about 65 gigatons of CO_2 equivalent ($GtCO_2e$) in 2030, implying a gap of roughly 41 $GtCO_2e$. These figures are stark: the gap to 1.5°C is larger than current annual global emissions of CO_2, which were 36 gigatons in 2016 (UNEP 2017).[3] Most of these emissions reductions, however, can be achieved by globally deploying commercially proven LCTs. In four major sectors alone—energy, industry, transport, and buildings—deployment of existing LCTs can narrow the gap by almost two-thirds (24 $GtCO_2e$ in 2030).

FIGURE 5.1

GHG emissions abatement potential across LCT sectors by 2030

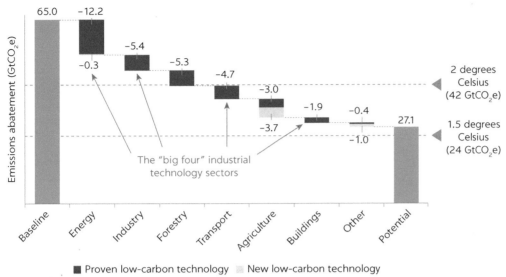

Source: Based on data from UNEP 2017.
Note: Global warming can be contained to 1.5 degrees Celsius by 2030 (lower horizontal line) or to 2 degrees Celsius (higher horizontal line). GHG = greenhouse gas; $GtCO_2e$ = gigatons of carbon dioxide equivalent; LCT = low-carbon technology.

A rapid global deployment of existing technologies to mitigate climate change does entail structural changes that will require a dramatic increase in the supply of capital, intermediate, and consumption goods. These goods include RE capital equipment, electric vehicles, and energy-efficient building components and appliances (figure 5.2), in addition to the various support services needed to build and maintain them. For policy makers who believe in strategically targeting sectors for economic development objectives (for example, via industrial or innovation policies)[4] and who believe mass deployment of LCTs to be likely, this represents a massive opportunity.

A second reason for optimism is that, despite the unprecedented nature of the transition challenge, some LCTs are already progressing rapidly in terms of cost, deployment time, and scale, in addition to the steady increase in transfers of LCTs across borders (chapter 2). The costs to install RE, for example, have declined precipitously in recent years (IEA 2019). Between 2010 and 2018, costs per GW of installed capacity declined for utility solar photovoltaic (by 78 percent), energy storage (54 percent), onshore wind (22 percent), and offshore wind (8 percent). Gross investment in renewables has stalled, but mostly because of this cost decline. Adjusted for prices, annual investment in renewables rose by 55 percent between 2013 and 2018 (figure 5.3 and figure 5.4).

Meanwhile, the average time taken to install 1 GW of RE declined by more than a quarter: from 2.6 years in 2013 to 1.9 years in 2018. Battery manufacturing capacity is surging, and is expected to reach 400 GW capacity by the mid-2020s, up from a 2018 level of 70 GW (IEA 2019). Heat pump sales are growing steadily, by 10 percent annually and as a share of global building heating equipment (currently 2.5 percent).

A third positive sign is the increasing amount of investment globally in LCT research and development (R&D), including in sectors where emissions are

FIGURE 5.2

A rapid increase in the global stock of low-carbon capital goods is needed by 2030 and 2050

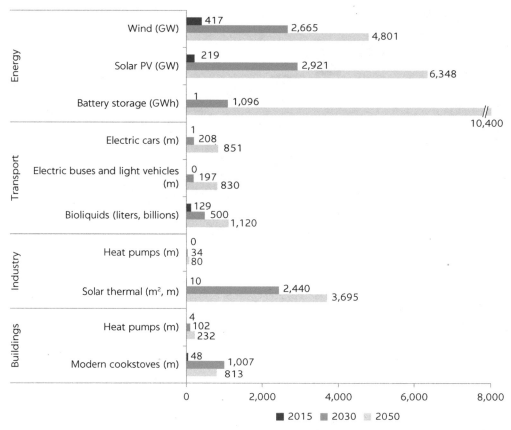

Source: Based on data from IRENA and OECD/IEA 2017.
Note: Units are in parentheses. GW = gigawatt; GWh = gigawatt-hour; m = millions; PV = photovoltaic.

FIGURE 5.3

Renewables investment has remained stable at about US$300 billion a year

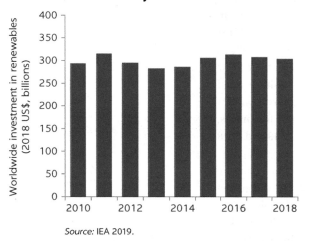

Source: IEA 2019.

FIGURE 5.4

At constant 2018 technology costs, renewables investment is up by 55 percent since 2010

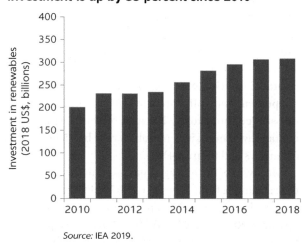

Source: IEA 2019.

difficult to abate (transport) or have the potential to be transformational (storage). For venture capital, 2018 was a record year for investments in clean energy companies, with US$6.9 billion worth of deals, up from a US$2.7 billion average for 2007–11. The bulk of this increase was in transportation—one of the most difficult technologies for which to abate emissions. In addition, investment in energy storage has surged, rising 55 percent to reach US$4 billion in 2018. In these two sectors, companies with complementary inputs are increasingly joining forces.

Overall, the scale of the challenge of mass global deployment of LCTs should not be understated. It remains far from clear whether the "techno-optimistic" or "techno-pessimistic" view of technology's role in mitigating climate change will turn out to be accurate. Despite these challenges and uncertainties, however, the proven nature of many existing LCTs, along with positive trends in certain technologies, means there is significant space for policy to support LCTs, thereby making a global low-carbon transition more likely.

Opportunity of LCT transfer

The global transfer—and deployment—of LCTs is not only a necessity but also an opportunity, on three fronts. First, the policies needed to deploy LCTs could also raise output, employment, innovation, and firm competitiveness. Traditionally, economic analyses have portrayed climate change as a global commons problem, with diffuse benefits of reduced climate damages and concentrated costs from mitigation policies; however, developments in the literature—some recent, others long running—have questioned this logic.[5] Overall, when designed and implemented well, the same policies that induce firms to deploy LCTs could also be good for the economy. This thinking inverts the notion of a necessary trade-off between climate and economic objectives: by embarking on reforms designed to foster LCT transfer, countries can also raise output, employment, innovation, and even firm competitiveness.

Second, many policies that aim to accelerate the deployment of LCTs have other welfare benefits, also known as "development co-benefits." GHG abatement policies tend to also reduce local air and water pollution, providing substantial benefits to human health (Vandyck et al. 2018; West et al. 2013).[6] In addition, when motor fuel prices align more with their social optimum (for example through a carbon tax), costly road accidents and congestion tend to decline (Burke and Nishitateno 2015; Burke and Teame 2018; Chi et al. 2013; Parry, Walls, and Harrington 2007; Santos 2017; Santos et al. 2010). Reductions in fossil fuel consumption can provide a boon for fossil fuel–dependent countries, helping support energy security objectives and shielding economies from fluctuations in global oil prices (IEA 2014; Krupnick, Burtraw, and Markandya 2000; OECD 2000).

Third and finally, global deployment of LCTs offers an opportunity for the increasingly large number of countries seeking export-led growth. LCTs could themselves be a strategic sector, for two reasons: they tend to be relatively sophisticated (as noted in chapter 1, they have specific characteristics, including a higher level of complexity and sophistication, compared with high-carbon technologies); and LCTs offer potential for huge growth in deployment globally, and therefore in trade.

Many economists argue that the theoretical justification remains for active intervention in response to technology market failures (Rodrik 2008; Stiglitz 2010, 2018), that no country has developed without such measures (Yülek 2018), and that many if not most of the transformational technologies have involved the state's proactive use of its own resources to support specific sectors (Mazzucato 2015). Old industrial policies emphasized import-substitution measures that—it is argued—hindered competition, dampened market signals, involved little active encouragement for technological innovation, and incentivized corruption and cronyism. By contrast, new industrial policies emphasize export-orientation, incorporating clear, quantifiable goals for investment in sophisticated (or complex) industries (Hausmann et al. 2014; Yülek 2018), strong incentives for steady improvement through competition, and investment in complementary infrastructure to help firms achieve the needed scale economies (Cherif and Hasanov 2019).

For LCT, a burgeoning literature addresses "green industrial policies" (Altenberg and Assmann 2017). Using a specific set of policies, especially those involving carbon pricing, governments can help shift economic structure toward low-carbon models. These policies include sunset green industrial policies, which support the deployment and production of LCTs, alongside complementary sunset policies that support those negatively affected by a low-carbon transition (Hallegatte, Fay, and Vogt-Schilb 2013). This could require a mission-driven and entrepreneurial state, making strategic investments in key green technologies (Mazzucato 2016; Mazzucato and Semieniuk 2016).

Despite increasing discussions in the literature, evidence remains patchy on which types of industrial policies (including green policies) are most effective. While technology market failures remain, so too do governmental failures. "Directed technical change" (Acemoglu 2002), including toward environmentally friendly technologies (Acemoglu et al. 2009), is possible but potentially difficult. Developing countries cannot simply "import" the needed strategic plans from donor agencies, and doing so could even backfire.[7] Governments should therefore choose for themselves whether to adopt green industrial policies to deploy or produce LCTs, remaining cognizant of the risks of action (through the mismanagement of rents and perverse incentives generated) as well as the opportunity costs of inaction (through missing an opportunity for export-led growth; refer to the section titled "Government objectives" later in this chapter).

NATIONAL CAPABILITY FOR LCT TRANSFER

Having shown the necessity and opportunity for LCT transfer, the chapter turns to developing a typology of LCT transfer and defines and tests which capabilities are needed by countries for importing, diffusing, producing, and finally exporting foreign technologies, including LCTs. Specifically, this section proposes a typology for defining the varying stages of technology transfer (for all technologies), identifies the potential inputs needed for countries to achieve deeper and more complex levels of LCT transfer, and tests empirically whether these proposed inputs are predictive of LCT imports, deployment, and exports across and within countries.

What are the stages of technology transfer?

As previous chapters have discussed, it is not enough to simply import a given technology; technology has not been "transferred" until it is widely used and understood by domestic firms and households (domestic diffusion). In addition, technologies themselves are seldom homogeneous or static: they vary over time with subsequent innovation, including in the importing country. From the perspective of importing countries, the type or quality of transfer matters. Technology transfer can be deemed as occurring along a scale, with stages ranging from initial adoption through indigenous invention and production of the improved or altered technology.

These stages of technology transfer, going from import to domestic production with potential export, are hereafter referred to as the *technology-transfer staircase* (figure 5.5). The staircase ranges from early stages of technology import (adoption and domestic diffusion) to domestic production (imitation, collaborative innovation with foreign firms, or fully indigenous invention) with the possibility for subsequent export. Under this framework, a country that has climbed to a higher step can be said to have transferred the foreign technology more.

Each step has differences in origin and strategy for obtaining the technology, as well as control and ownership of any subsequent innovation on top of that technology (table 5.1). Adoption and domestic diffusion mean reliance on foreign sources of the technology with no control over any subsequent innovation process or ownership of that process's output. By contrast, collaborative innovation between domestic and foreign firms (for example, through joint ventures or other collaborative arrangements) may confer some control and ownership over subsequent innovation outputs.

Why climb?

Countries can "climb the staircase" through deeper levels of diffusion of foreign technology, increasing levels of domestic production, or increasing sophistication of domestic innovation. For developing countries, this climb can be desirable for the following reasons:

• **Entering the technology-transfer staircase through the *adoption and diffusion of foreign technology* can confer large economic benefits.** For all countries, generating technologies internally can be significantly more costly than simply importing those technologies. As a result, the importation of foreign technologies can confer significant domestic cost savings and

FIGURE 5.5

The technology-transfer staircase: From import to production of new technology

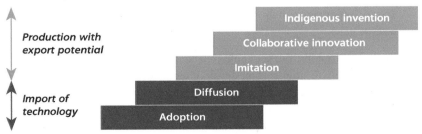

Note: The figure shows different stages of technology transfer, from importing a foreign technology to domestic production with the potential for further innovation. The technology-transfer staircase is an homage to, but separate from, the capabilities escalator of firm and state capabilities needed to achieve higher levels of innovation sophistication (Cirera and Maloney 2017).

TABLE 5.1 Characteristics of technology-transfer stages

	STEPS ON THE TECHNOLOGY-TRANSFER STAIRCASE				
	IMPORT OF TECHNOLOGY		PRODUCTION AND EXPORT		
	ADOPTION	DIFFUSION	IMITATION	COLLABORATIVE INNOVATION	INDIGENOUS INVENTION
Origin of technology	Foreign	Foreign	Foreign	Domestic firms and international firms	Domestic firms and their foreign subsidiaries
Strategy for obtaining technology	Import	Import	Licensing	Joint ventures, R&D cooperation, international donors	Building R&D (international quality), mergers and acquisition
Control of innovation process	No control	No control	No control	Some, but R&D direction is with foreign firms	Domestic firms own R&D processes and commercialization
Ownership of innovation output	No ownership	No ownership	No ownership	R&D direction with foreign partners	Ownership by domestic firms

Source: Elaboration based on Lee et al. 2003.
Note: R&D = research and development.

productivity benefits. This possibility represents a positive externality "of truly historic proportions," allowing countries to pursue a process of "Schumpeterian catch-up" (Cirera and Maloney 2017).

- **Climbing to higher steps through *domestic technology production* entails deeper levels of industrialization, which is strongly linked to economic development.** Industrialization—defined here as rapid growth in the manufacturing sector—can help accelerate productivity growth, and therefore economic growth. For instance, for countries that have outperformed others in the past three decades, more than two-thirds of their gross domestic product (GDP) growth is "attributable to a rise in productivity correlated with industrialization: an annual average productivity gain of 4.1 percent versus 0.8 percent for the other developing economies" (McKinsey Global Institute 2018). As some have observed, all developed countries have gone through a stage of rapid productivity growth driven principally by the manufacturing sector (Mazzucato 2015; Yülek 2018).

- **Climbing to the final steps through *increasingly sophisticated levels of indigenous innovation* confers multiple benefits to domestic firms and workers.** The production structures of industries vary widely, as does the value added by firms nested along value chains. Generally, firms closer to the innovative parts of the value chain (that is, on higher steps of the technology-transfer staircase) receive higher returns, which allows them to invest in more innovation (Yülek 2018). Increasing levels of sophistication in innovation require deeper levels of skills and knowledge among firms and workers, which entail deeper stocks of organizational and human capital. These deeper stocks help support higher levels of income and nonincome welfare gains.

In short, climbing the technology-transfer staircase can help countries achieve sustainable, low-carbon development. Climbing the staircase means getting closer to the technological frontier, catching up through the diffusion of foreign technologies, and reaping the benefits of productivity growth from increasing levels of domestic production and sophistication of innovation outputs.[8] For LCT in particular, the global deployment of LCTs may provide an unparalleled opportunity for countries to climb the staircase rapidly through domestic deployment and production for export (see the earlier section titled "Opportunity of LCT transfer").

Will countries climb?

Climbing the staircase is neither inevitable nor necessarily a linear process. Multiple market failures mean that firms and households in many developing countries do not adopt widely available technologies, despite the potentially large gains from doing so (the "innovation paradox"; refer to Cirera and Maloney 2017). For LCT, other market failures may lead to low diffusion, whether from foreign or domestic sources, and any diffusion tends to be spatially heterogeneous. For example, firms and households may have imperfect information about potential energy saving investments, and may underinvest in energy efficiency measures, despite the potential for large savings—a phenomenon known as the "energy efficiency paradox" (Allcott and Greenstone 2012; Häckel, Pfosser, and Tränkler 2017; Jaffe and Adam 1994). In addition, when energy efficiency technologies are diffused, their spatial distribution within countries is nonuniform, reflecting heterogeneous socioeconomic, contextual, and local policy conditions (Morton, Wilson, and Anable 2018).

Similarly, there is no guarantee that domestic firms and workers will innovate on top of the technology they have imported. As previous chapters have mentioned, the literature debates the quality and quantity of technological spillovers from trade and FDI. A firm importing technology—or even producing and exporting that technology—through FDI may not have any ownership or control over it or any subsequent innovation process, and low knowledge spillovers (for instance due to all workers being from the technology source country) could result in only few firms and workers benefitting from the imported technology.

How can countries climb?

Importing, producing, and innovating technology rely on a complementary set of inputs, such as human, physical, and organizational capital. The absence of these inputs can more than offset the gains from Schumpeterian catch-up, which may explain why so many developing countries underinvest in importing and diffusing foreign technologies, despite the potential gains (Cirera and Maloney 2017). Moreover, developing countries find it harder to climb. Without a sufficient level of these inputs, countries may not be able to catch up; but, perversely, countries with lower levels of these inputs may also be less able to implement measures to increase their inputs (the "innovation policy paradox"; Cirera and Maloney 2017).

The following complementary inputs are referred to as *national capability*:

- **Human capital (workers)** includes the quality of workers in terms of educational levels, health, and composition (such as age). Human capital can potentially be imported through migration, but the ability to attract highly skilled workers varies across countries, tending to be lower in developing countries.
- **Organizational capital (firms)** includes absorptive capacities as well as managerial skills among firms. It can be imported through FDI, though learning-by-doing spillovers from FDI vary.
- **Institutional capital (states)** includes the quality of governance institutions, such as the legal and policy-making framework and administrative effectiveness. This type of capital cannot be imported.

TABLE 5.2 Inputs required to climb the technology-transfer staircase

	INPUTS REQUIRED TO CLIMB THE TECHNOLOGY-TRANSFER STAIRCASE				
	IMPORT OF TECHNOLOGY		PRODUCTION AND EXPORT		
	ADOPTION	DIFFUSION	IMITATION	COLLABORATIVE INNOVATION	INDIGENOUS INVENTION
Human and organizational capital required (workers and firms)	Basic skills to operate and maintain imported technology	Previous + capability to spread learning at scale.	Ability to learn by following guidance and/or reverse-engineer.	Previous + deeper managerial and human capital; Learning by doing, following product design	Previous + capacity to assess technological business opportunities (e.g. network effects) and take risks with a long-term vision.
Institutional and physical capital required (states and economies)	Basic institutions allowing for import of foreign technology	Previous + infrastructure and business environ-ment conducive to scaled-up diffusion	Infrastructure and stable business environment needed for production and distribution networks	Previous + intellectual property rights and/or large market size conducive to foreign participation in joint ventures with local firms	Previous + more proactive supportive state and deeper physical capital levels.
Financial capital required	Basic trade financing	Previous + access to investment financing	Foreign direct investment	Deeper domestic capital markets, along with access to international capital markets and/or public finance	Venture capital and direct public support

- **Physical capital (economies)** includes the quality of buildings and infra-structure (such as transport and energy reliability) as well as complementary infrastructure needed for LCT (for example, electric vehicle charging hubs). It can be imported via, for example, domestic and foreign construction firms, which is costly and takes time.
- **Financial capital (markets)** includes access to financial resources from domestic firms, and, in the case of innovation, the ability to access patient long-term capital. Access also varies by technology (risk levels and capital intensity). Financial capital can be imported through access to international private and public climate finance, though multiple nontechnological aspects may raise the costs of this external finance (for example, political risk and exchange rate risk).

Subsequent steps of the technology-transfer staircase require deeper and more complex levels of these complementary inputs (table 5.2). Firms and workers need a range of skills, from the most basic to the capacity to innovate and develop new products. States need to be more effective to help firms and workers become more technologically sophisticated, with deeper levels of complementary physical capital such as infrastructure required. Given the larger risks present at the earlier stages of innovation (the top of the staircase), more patient financial capital is required from investors and governments (Mazzucato 2015).

Presumably, the requirement for deeper levels of complementary inputs should be the case for LCTs, as it is for other technologies. Although LCTs have a set of defining features compared with other technologies (such as higher cap-ital costs; refer to chapter 1), these features tend to imply that even deeper levels of inputs would be required to diffuse and produce LCTs. Few studies, however, have explicitly tested the link between such inputs and LCT diffusion and production.

NATIONAL CAPABILITY MATTERS FOR LCT TRANSFER

To examine whether national capabilities are linked to deeper levels of LCT trade and deployment, the analysis tests in two stages. First, it operationalizes measures of the national capability and links them observationally to metrics of LCT transfer (import and export of LCT[9] per capita), as well as to general innovation outcomes. This stage allows for better identification of factors that matter *across* countries. Second, the analysis uses multivariate regression, with controls for country and year fixed effects, to identify what factors matter for rising to higher levels of the technology-transfer staircase (proxied through deeper levels of LCT trade and deployment) *within* countries over time.

National capabilities are operationalized using different proxies. Human capital is proxied for by either the World Bank's Human Capital Index, which compares countries on metrics of education and health, or the United Nations' Human Development Index, education subindex, which ranks countries by educational outcomes.[10] Organizational capital is proxied by the United Nations' Competitive Industrial Performance Index, which compares the competitive performance of domestic firms, particularly manufacturing firms, across countries.[11] Institutional capital is proxied for by the World Bank's Worldwide Governance Indicators Government Effectiveness index scores, which capture perceptions of the quality of public services, the civil service, the quality of policy formulation and implementation, and the credibility of the government's commitment to such policies.[12] Physical capital uses productive capital per capita (which includes physical capital such as infrastructure and buildings) from the World Bank's Changing Wealth of Nations dataset (Lange, Wodon, and Carey 2018). Last, the depth of financial capital is proxied by domestic credit to the private sector as a percentage of GDP.[13]

The extent to which countries diffuse and produce LCT is proxied using different measures (table 5.3). LCT trade intensity (imports and exports of LCT per capita) provides some evidence as to how much LCT is being transferred to that country (via imports) as well as produced by that country (exports). Similarly, domestic RE deployment (installed renewable capacity per capita) should also give some supportive evidence as to domestic LCT deployment.

TABLE 5.3 **Proxies for LCT transfer depth across and within countries**

TECHNOLOGY-TRANSFER STAIRCASE STAGE	DEPENDENT VARIABLES	MEASURE	DATA	SOURCE
Import and diffusion of LCT	LCT imports	Value of imports of 107 6-digit identified LCTs (refer to chapter 2) per capita	2008–17, 250 countries	UN Comtrade; Gautier and Zigzag 2019
	Diffusion of renewable energy	Renewable energy capacity installed per capita	2009–18, 220 countries	IRENA Data and Statistics
Production and export of LCT	LCT exports	Value of LCT exports per capita	2008–17, 250 countries	UN Comtrade; Gautier and Zignago 2019
	Innovation outputs	Global Innovation Index 2018, Innovation Output subindex scores	2014–18, 186 countries	Cornell University, INSEAD, and WIPO 2018

Sources: Cornell University, INSEAD, and WIPO 2018; Gaulier and Zignago 2019; IRENA Data and Statistics, https://www.irena.org/Statistics; UN Comtrade, https://comtrade.un.org/.

Note: IRENA = International Renewable Energy Agency; LCT = low-carbon technology; UN = United Nations.

Finally, the potential for a country to innovate on top of existing LCT should depend on its ability to innovate generally, and hence innovation outputs (the Global Innovation Index–Innovation Output subindex scores) are also examined across countries.

Across countries: Exports, imports, and general innovation

Across economies, national capability appears to matter for all stages of LCT transfer. Importing and operating technologies require some basic level of capability among firms and workers, and the environment they operate in. Accordingly, economies with higher institutional, organizational, and physical capital tend to import more LCTs (figure 5.6) though financial capital is not a strong predictor. Additionally, the same four factors are also strongly associated with exports of LCTs: economies with more human, institutional, organizational, and physical capital tend to export more LCTs (figure 5.7). Economies with more innovation also tend to have higher levels of these capital measures (figure 5.8), in addition to financial capital (figure 5.9).

Five observations can be made. First, the different types of capital—human, organizational, institutional, and physical—appear to matter for both LCT trade and for innovation. These factors are heavily correlated with LCT exports, imports, and innovation performance. Combined into normalized scores, they can, for example, explain 87 percent of the variance in innovation outputs across countries (figure 5.10). This finding supports the idea that such complementary inputs matter for innovation.

Second, human capital emerges as the strongest predictor of LCT trade and innovation performance, although institutional capital and physical capital are also highly correlated with LCT trade and innovation. Organizational capital and financial capital appear to be the weakest predictors, which could perhaps indicate that firm-level knowledge and access to finance are less stringent constraints to climbing the technology-transfer staircase than skills of workers.

Third, developed economies have much more national capability (inputs), and tend to trade more LCTs and be more innovative (outputs). This finding is in line with other studies that have shown, for example, that economies with better institutions export more complex products (Berkowitz, Moenius, and Pistor 2003; Teza, Caraglio, and Stella 2018). As a result, although the global deployment of LCT could be an economic opportunity, it could also be the case that developed economies are best placed to take advantage of it.

Fourth, within developing economies, there is significant heterogeneity, with China emerging as a major outlier, both in terms of LCT exports and in innovation performance. This finding reemerges when considering another dimension of LCT trade: green complexity potential (GCP) of exports (Mealy and Teytelboym 2018). Broadly, GCP measures how close an economy's exports are to other green (that is, low-carbon) goods. An economy with high GCP and high performance in innovation should theoretically be well placed to take advantage of the global deployment of LCT. China emerges as a major outlier (figure 5.11) among developing economies, in having both green complex exports and high innovation performance. India, Malaysia, Thailand, Turkey, and Ukraine are also comparatively well placed, but they lag far behind China in terms of innovation performance or green complexity of exports.

FIGURE 5.6

LCT import intensity across economies

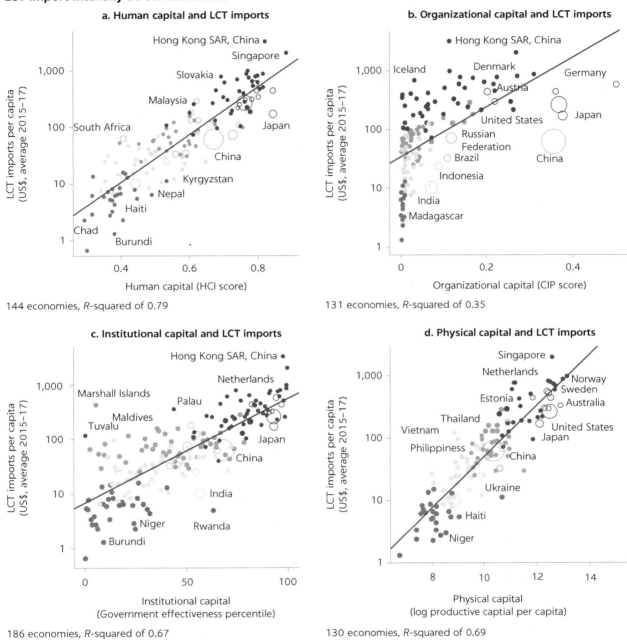

a. Human capital and LCT imports

144 economies, *R*-squared of 0.79

b. Organizational capital and LCT imports

131 economies, *R*-squared of 0.35

c. Institutional capital and LCT imports

186 economies, *R*-squared of 0.67

d. Physical capital and LCT imports

130 economies, *R*-squared of 0.69

● High income ● Upper-middle income ○ Lower-middle income ● Low income

Sources: Gaulier and Zignago 2019; UN Comtrade, https://comtrade.un.org/; UNIDO Statistics database (CIP), https://stat.unido.org/database/CIP 2018; World Bank 2018; World Bank Government Effectiveness data catalog, https://datacatalog.worldbank.org/government-effectiveness-estimate-0; World Bank Human Capital Index (HCI), https://datacatalog.worldbank.org/dataset/human-capital-index.
Note: Bubbles represent carbon dioxide (CO_2) emissions in 2014. LCT = low-carbon technology.

Fifth, despite being an outlier on LCT exports, China underperforms relative to what could be expected given its level of organizational capital (panel b in figure 5.7). The same is true in terms of China's general innovation performance relative to its organizational capital (panel b in figure 5.8), though it outperforms relative to its human, institutional, and physical capital base. China is well placed to take further advantage of global deployment

FIGURE 5.7

LCT export intensity across economies

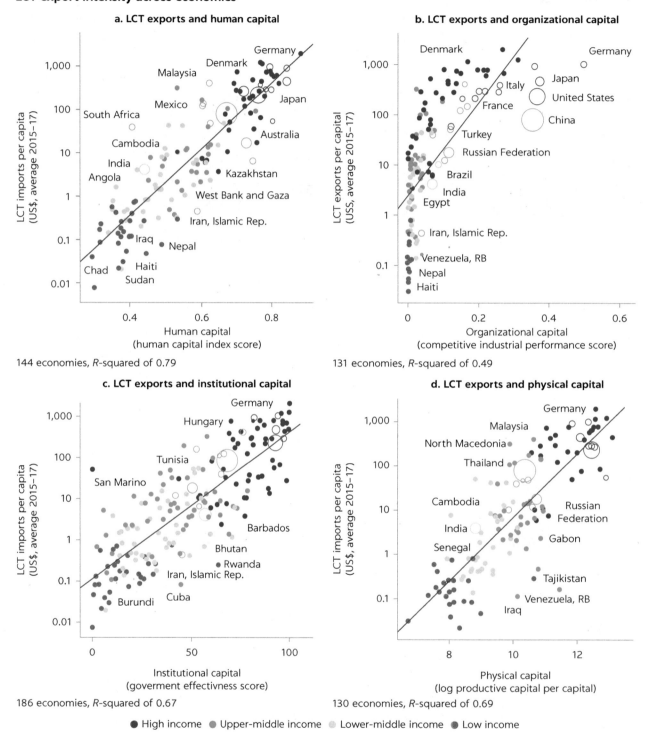

a. LCT exports and human capital

144 economies, *R*-squared of 0.79

b. LCT exports and organizational capital

131 economies, *R*-squared of 0.49

c. LCT exports and institutional capital

186 economies, *R*-squared of 0.67

d. LCT exports and physical capital

130 economies, *R*-squared of 0.69

● High income ● Upper-middle income ○ Lower-middle income ● Low income

Sources: Gaulier and Zignago 2019; UN Comtrade, https://comtrade.un.org/; UNIDO Statistics database (CIP), https://stat.unido.org /database/CIP 2018; World Bank 2018; World Bank Government Effectiveness data catalog, https://datacatalog.worldbank.org/government -effectiveness-estimate-0; World Bank Human Capital Index (HCI), https://datacatalog.worldbank.org/dataset/human-capital-index.
Note: Bubbles represent carbon dioxide (CO_2) emissions in 2014. LCT = low-carbon technology.

FIGURE 5.8

Innovation performance across economies

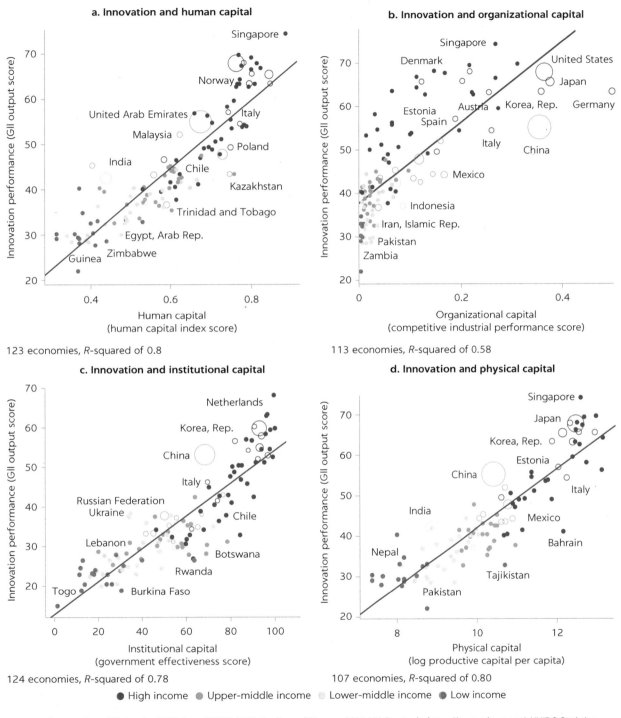

Sources: Cornell University, INSEAD, and WIPO 2018; Gaulier and Zignago 2019; UN Comtrade, https://comtrade.un.org/; UNIDO Statistics database (CIP), https://stat.unido.org/database/CIP 2018; World Bank 2018; World Bank Government Effectiveness data catalog, https://datacatalog.worldbank.org/government-effectiveness-estimate-0; World Bank Human Capital Index (HCI), https://datacatalog.worldbank.org/dataset/human-capital-index.

Note: Bubbles represent relative carbon dioxide (CO_2) emissions in 2014. GII = Global Innovation Index.

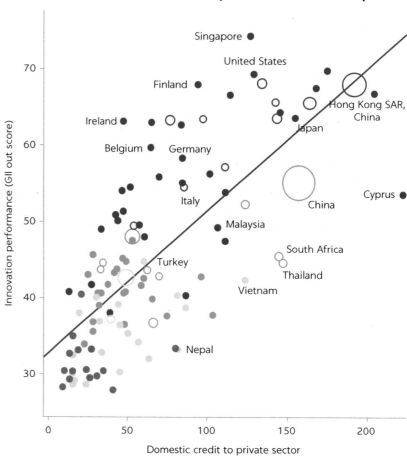

FIGURE 5.9

More-innovative economies have deeper stocks of financial capital

117 economies, *R*-squared of 0.53

● High income ● Upper-middle income ● Lower-middle income ● Low income

Sources: Cornell University, INSEAD, and WIPO 2018; Gaulier and Zignago 2019; UN Comtrade, https://comtrade.un.org/; UNIDO Statistics database (CIP), https://stat.unido.org/database/CIP 2018; World Bank 2018; World Bank Government Effectiveness data catalog, https://datacatalog.worldbank.org/government-effectiveness-estimate-0; World Bank Human Capital Index (HCI), https://datacatalog.worldbank.org/dataset/human-capital-index.

Note: Bubbles represent relative CO_2 emissions in 2014. GII = Global Innovation Index.

of LCTs, but other economies may have room to catch up through interventions to augment their capital base. Indeed, although China's LCT exports continue to grow, other countries such as Mexico, Turkey, and Vietnam are also increasing their LCT export intensity (figure 5.12).

Observations across economies in one time period, however, are not sufficient for determining which type of capital matters most for increasing LCT trade intensity (as a proxy for LCT transfer) within economies. The next section therefore assesses which of the national capabilities matter most for changing LCT trade intensity within economies.

Within countries across time: LCT trade

Whereas the previous section identified factors that appear to matter across countries in one time period, this section analyzes the same factors within

FIGURE 5.10

Combined, four factors are strongly associated with innovation performance

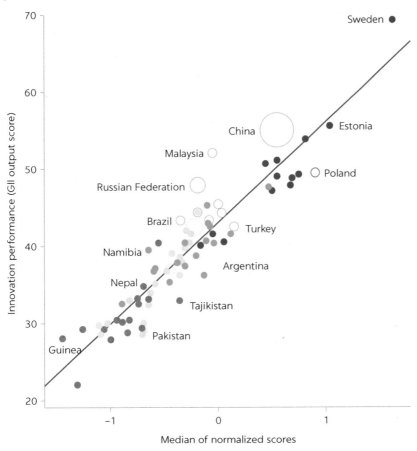

83 economies, *R*-squared of 0.87

● High income ● Upper-middle income ● Lower-middle income ● Low income

Sources: Cornell University, INSEAD, and WIPO 2018; Gaulier and Zignago 2019; UN Comtrade, https://comtrade.un.org/; UNIDO Statistics database (CIP), https://stat.unido .org/database/CIP 2018; World Bank 2018; World Bank Government Effectiveness data catalog, https://datacatalog.worldbank.org/government-effectiveness-estimate-0; World Bank Human Capital Index (HCI), https://datacatalog.worldbank.org/dataset/human-capital -index.
Note: Bubbles represent relative CO_2 emissions in 2014. Factors are human, organizational, institutional, and physical capital metrics. Scores are normalized (z-scores) and a median taken. GII = Global Innovation Index.

countries across several time periods. Using a panel dataset comprising 90,000 observations across countries, within-country analysis of the links between national capability and LCT transfer metrics is conducted through multivariate regression controlling for time and country fixed effects. This regression estimates the effect on measures of LCT trade depth from identified proxies for national capability (see table 5.4).

Taking this approach offers interpretive benefits. Fixed effects regressions (using the "within" estimator) control for unobserved, time-invariant heterogeneity across countries and years. As a result, interpretation can be made as to which national capability inputs matter most for LCT transfer within countries over time, with more assurance that unobserved (albeit, time-invariant) confounders have been controlled for (Imai and Kim 2019; Mummolo and

FIGURE 5.11

More-innovative countries tend to have more green complex exports

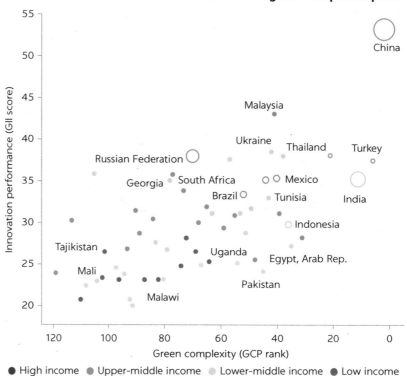

Sources: Cornell University, INSEAD, and WIPO 2018; Mealy and Teytelboym 2018.
Note: Bubbles represent relative CO_2 emissions in 2014. GCP = green complexity potential; GII = Global Innovation Index.

Peterson 2018). The downside of this approach is some loss in statistical power due to the limitation of variation within countries. Nonetheless, it still yields statistically significant results on the links between national capability and identified metrics for LCT transfer (table 5.5).

Six observations can be made about these results. First, for LCT transfer, economic growth matters, especially for exports. A 10 percent increase in GDP within a country is associated with about a 3 percent increase in LCT imports and a 9 percent increase in LCT exports (hereafter, unless otherwise stated, holding other factors constant). This finding reinforces the finding in chapter 3 that market size and economic growth matter for exports of LCT patents. One explanation could be that, for countries with a growing domestic market, LCT deployment and production objectives become complementary: having a larger domestic market makes it more likely that domestic firms can achieve scale economies needed to become competitive in producing LCT.

Second, human capital appears to be the most important factor for accelerating LCT transfer within countries. A 10 percent increase in human development (Human Development Index, education subindex) scores is associated with about a 6 percent increase in LCT imports and a 16 percent increase in LCT exports. This finding is robust to using alternative measures to proxy for human capital, such as the Human Capital Index scores. Human capital therefore appears to be among the most important factors in allowing countries to increasingly import, diffuse, and export LCT.

FIGURE 5.12

LCT exports increasing for some developing countries and shrinking for others

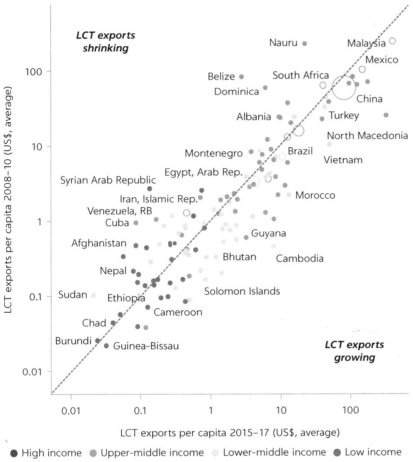

Source: Gaulier and Zignago 2019; UN Comtrade, https://comtrade.un.org/.
Note: Bubbles represent relative CO_2 emissions in 2014. LCT = low-carbon technology.

TABLE 5.4 **National capability proxy measures for within-country regression**

EXPLANATORY VARIABLES	MEASURE	DATA	SOURCE
Domestic market size	GDP PPP, constant 2011 international $	1990–2018, 217 countries	WDI
Population	Population levels	1990–2018, 217 countries	WDI
Human capital	Human Development Index: Education subindex scores	1990–2017, 189 countries	UNDP
Organizational capital	Competitive Industrial Performance Index scores	1990–2016, 150 countries	UNIDO
Institutional capital	Government Effectiveness Index scores	1990–2017, 214 countries	World Bank Government Effectiveness Index
Physical capital	Gross fixed capital formation per capita, constant 2010 US$	1990–2018, 217 countries	WDI
Financial capital	Domestic credit to private sector, percent of GDP	1990–2018, 217 countries	WDI

Sources: UNDP Human Development Report, http://hdr.undp.org/en/content/education-index; UNIDO Statistics database (CIP), https://stat.unido.org
/database/CIP 2018; World Bank Government Effectiveness data catalog, https://datacatalog.worldbank.org/government-effectiveness-estimate-0;
World Bank World Development Indicators (WDI), https://datacatalog.worldbank.org/dataset/world-development-indicators.
Note: GDP = gross domestic product; PPP = purchasing power parity; UNDP = United Nations Development Programme; UNIDO = United Nations
Industrial Development Organization; WDI = World Development Indicators.

TABLE 5.5 **Cross-country regressions of LCT transfer on national capability metrics, 2008–17**

DEPENDENT VARIABLE (LOG):	1 LCT IMPORTS	2 LCT EXPORTS
Explanatory variables (log)		
GDP[a]	0.277*	0.937***
	(0.16)	(0.35)
Population	0.224	-0.002
	(0.26)	(0.57)
Human capital[b]	0.645**	1.6**
	(0.32)	(.71)
Organizational capital[c]	0.094*	0.59***
	(0.05)	(0.12)
Institutional capital[d]	0.043	0.198*
	(0.05)	(0.12)
Physical capital[e]	0.713***	0.407**
	(0.06)	(0.13)
Financial capital[f]	0.004***	0.002
	(0.00)	(0.00)
Constant	4.967	-5.55
	(4.22)	(9.21)
Observations	980	980
Countries	119	119
Years	2008-17	2008-17
Country x year fixed effects	Yes	Yes
R-squared	0.81	0.86

Source: Based on data from Gaulier and Zignago 2019; IRENA Data and Statistics, https://www.irena.org/Statistics; UN Comtrade, https://comtrade.un.org/; and World Bank World Development Indicators, https://datacatalog.worldbank.org/dataset/world-development-indicators.
Note: All dependent and explanatory variables are expressed in logarithmic transformation form (that is, all regressions are log-log). Fixed effects were controlled for using the within estimator to control for unobserved time-invariant heterogeneity. Standard errors in parentheses.
GDP = gross domestic product; LCT = low-carbon technology.
a. Based on GDP.
b. Based on Human Development Index-Education score.
c. Based on Competitive Industrial Performance Index score.
d. Based on Government Effectiveness Index score.
e. Gross fixed capital formation (constant 2010 US$) per capita.
f. Financial credit to domestic firms as percent of GDP.
g. Value (US$) of LCT per capita, including 104 identified 6-digit LCT traded goods (refer to chapter 2).
h. Measured as installed renewable energy capacity per capita.
i. Value of exports of LCT per capita.
*p < 0.10 **p < 0.05 ***p < 0.01

Third, the depth of physical capital stocks matters for LCT trade. A country growing its per capita stock of gross fixed capital by 10 percent can expect to increase imports of LCT by about 7 percent and exports by about 4 percent. This finding underpins the important role that infrastructure plays in the transfer of LCTs. Having a deeper base of productive capital may be an important precursor to importing LCTs that rely on preexisting infrastructure, such as electric vehicles that depend on the existence of available and reliable electricity. This same capital may also be needed by firms seeking to develop and export LCTs.[14] That the growth in LCT trade with respect to growth in capital is below unity may also indicate, however, that existing physical capital–deepening efforts are not especially low-carbon at present. For a low-carbon transition to take place, countries need to increase the low-carbon intensity of existing efforts to deepen physical capital—that is, through policies aimed at accelerating the deployment of LCTs.

Fourth, organizational capital matters for LCT exports, but not necessarily for LCT imports. A country experiencing a 10 percent bump in competitive industrial performance can expect to export about 6 percent more LCT but to import only about 1 percent more LCT. This finding suggests that countries wanting to export more LCT should focus on improving their broad industrial competitiveness. The factors that matter for LCT exports appear to be the same factors that matter for industrial competitiveness generally.

Fifth, institutional capital (government effectiveness) does not appear to matter that much. Institutional capital is mildly positively associated with LCT exports but not with LCT imports. A country whose government becomes 10 percent more effective (in terms of Government Effectiveness Index scores) can expect to export about 2 percent more LCT. This effect is not nearly as strong as that of human capital. It does point, however, to the role that governments have in at least not preventing technology transfer through their own ineffectiveness—for instance, by allowing unchecked corruption to prevent firms from investing in new technologies or workers to invest in their own education. This role is in addition to their central role in proactively raising other forms of national capability, especially human capital.

Sixth, financial development does not have an important effect on LCT transfer. Domestic capital provided to firms is found to be statistically significant only for LCT imports, but the effect is very small: a 10-percentage-point increase of GDP in domestic credit to the private sector is associated with a 0.04 percent increase in LCT imports. Other studies also find that financial market deepening does not have a strong effect on RE deployment (Pfeiffer and Mulder 2013). To the extent that finance constrains LCT transfer, efforts to support specific climate finance[15] may be warranted; however, this suggests that the extent to which finance per se holds back LCT transfer may be overstated. For LCT transfer, raising core capabilities—such as education levels of workers and organizational effectiveness of firms—may be more effective at accelerating LCT diffusion and development than simply increasing access to finance. The most important policy question for accelerating LCT, therefore, may not be "Who will finance it?" but, rather, "Who will have the skills to design, build, and operate it?"

Despite these findings, four caveats are warranted. First, the above analysis may still be subject to statistical bias if, for example, confounders vary with time, whereas reverse causation (for example, that LCT imports cause increases in human capital) appears unlikely but cannot be ruled out (Imai and Kim 2019). Second, given the low variation of dependent variables within countries over time (for example, Government Effectiveness scores do not change much, perhaps reflecting the path-dependent nature of institutional quality), interpretation should be confined to marginal changes, rather than huge, systemic changes in national capability (Mummolo and Peterson 2018). Third, quantitative approaches have inherent limits compared with qualitative methods, such as surveys or case studies. Qualitative methods, although harder to generalize, can incorporate a richer variety of contextual considerations, especially when considering the interactions with policies (Kemp and Pontoglio 2011). Finally, the above analysis of capabilities says nothing about how those capabilities can change over time. Specifically, it does not tell us much about policies.

Given the necessity and opportunity for LCT deployment, what policies can developing countries implement to accelerate LCT diffusion or production? The next section turns to policies, highlighting how developing countries can enact policies to import and diffuse, as well as potentially produce and export, LCTs. First, the section discusses the varying initial conditions of developing countries, with country "types" identified. Second, it outlines varying objectives of countries. Third, it introduces a policy typology that links country types to objectives. The following section therefore turns to a more qualitative assessment of policies, identifying instruments that countries can implement to achieve their specific objectives for LCT diffusion or production.

POLICIES FOR LCT TRANSFER

Policy rationale and features: Market failures

The economic justification for government intervention in technology traditionally focuses on market failures that lead to socially suboptimal levels of investment in technology (table 5.6). Put simply, multiple market failures hold back technologies on every step of the technology-transfer staircase (from import of foreign technologies all the way to indigenous invention and export). These failures prevent firms from investing in developing and transferring technologies that would otherwise be socially desirable.

All market failures are not equal: they vary in their significance across the technology development chain. Market failures can be partial or complete, or even nonexistent, for specific technologies (Krupnick et al. 2010). For example, network externalities may be a more significant barrier for investment in utility-scale solar (which relies on the preexistence of a reliable electric grid) than for off-grid solar systems (which are stand-alone). Financial frictions may be more important for deployment stages, where private finance seems to matter more, than in the early innovation stages where state-owned or state-controlled companies play a more significant role (Mazzucato and Semieniuk 2016).

In addition, our knowledge of these market failures, and the degree of consensus on their importance, is also not equal. Less is known, for instance, about the deployment and diffusion stages of innovation (the first steps on the technology-transfer staircase) than about the R&D stages (Mazzucato and Semieniuk 2016). The importance of intellectual property rights, and the effectiveness of measures designed to protect intellectual property, remains controversial (refer to chapter 1 and to Rai, Schultz, and Funkhouser 2014). Finally, in the realm of imperfect information and inattention, the energy efficiency paradox has been hotly contested, with some studies questioning its existence (Allcott and Greenstone 2012; Allcott and Knittel 2019; Jaffe and Adam 1994), and others showing evidence of such an effect (Coste et al. 2019).

Government failures

Market failures, which lead to underinvestment in LCT within and across countries, justify government intervention. These market failures can be tackled by

TABLE 5.6 **Market failures holding back LCT transfer and potential policy responses**

MARKET FAILURE	DESCRIPTION	EXAMPLE POLICY RESPONSES
Knowledge spillovers	Firms cannot internalize all the benefits of the knowledge they generate (positive externalities of knowledge spillovers). They therefore underinvest in developing new knowledge.	Demand-pull measures (priority feed-in tariffs, trading systems/taxes, levies, green public procurement) and tech-push measures (R&D subsidies and tax incentives)
Network externalities	Many LCTs have inherent network effects, in that the value of the network does not grow in line with the number of actors in the network and may rely on other, complementary networks. For instance, electric vehicle deployment relies on the existence of a reliable electric grid as well as charging stations.	Public and PPP-based investment in complementary infrastructure
Increasing returns to scale	The costs to produce LCTs may decline rapidly and not in line with production (for instance, refer to the section, "Necessity of LCT Transfer," that discusses the recent rapid reduction in solar PV costs). As a result, first-movers face prohibitive costs and may underinvest in the production of LCTs compared with other technologies.	Demand-pull measures (priority feed-in tariffs, trading systems/taxes, levies, green public procurement) and tech-push measures (R&D subsidies and tax incentives)
Incomplete property rights	Where property rights are incomplete, firms may not be able to internalize all benefits from technological investment, and they therefore underinvest.	IPR/patent law, IPR exploitation support, and enforcement efforts
Financial market frictions and mismatches	Investors in the financial sector may have shorter time horizons than is required for investment in LCT, which may have large up-front capital costs but low variable costs over time.	Green investment portfolio mandates, green indexes, de-risking instruments
Imperfect information and inattention	Households and firms may have imperfect information that prevents them investing in LCT. For instance, imperfect knowledge of or inattention to the savings from energy efficiency investments may prevent firms and households from investing in energy efficiency (the "energy efficiency paradox").	Informational campaigns, direct regulatory measures (labeling standards, fuel-efficiency standards, and supply-side bans)

Note: IPR = intellectual property rights; LCT = low-carbon technology; PPP = purchasing power parity; PV = photovoltaic; R&D = research and development.

pushing down costs (for example, through R&D subsidies), pulling up demand (such as through feed-in tariffs), or through informational interventions such as green labelling and public information campaigns. The particular instruments that are suited to overcome market failures are highly context-specific and will change over time (Altenberg and Assmann 2017).

Five caveats are noteworthy, however. First, developing countries are in a disadvantageous position when it comes to both diffusing and producing LCTs. As earlier sections of this chapter have highlighted, despite the potential opportunity—and necessity—for all countries in globally deploying LCTs, developed countries are better placed with deeper stocks of the needed inputs for trading and producing LCTs. Compounding this disparity is the reality that developing country policy makers face more market failures impeding innovation and perversely have less capability to address them (the "innovation policy dilemma"; Cirera and Maloney 2017).

Second, developing countries have very different starting positions. For instance, China is a significant outlier in terms of innovation outputs and the intensity and complexity of its low-carbon exports compared with other developing countries (figure 5.13). It therefore has an advantageous position compared with other countries for the production and export of LCTs (latter stages of the technology-transfer staircase). In general, countries that are more well-placed to take advantage of LCT export opportunities are those that are already innovative.

Countries are also in different starting positions in terms of their ability to import and diffuse LCT (figure 5.13). For RE specifically, countries vary in their attractiveness to private investors and in the quality of existing policies for renewables. China is again at the frontier among developing countries, but it is joined by Brazil, India, Mexico, and Thailand. From a climate mitigation perspective, it is good news that these countries are at the upper end of the RE deployment spectrum: together, these countries account for two-thirds of developing country emissions. Some countries are less attractive to private investors in RE or have policy environments less conducive to RE deployment. Many Commonwealth of Independent States countries, for instance, have moderate or high policy quality but low financial attractiveness for RE investment, so they may fail to attract financing. By contrast, many countries in Africa and South Asia have moderate financial attractiveness but lack the policy quality required for a large-scale ramp-up in renewables deployment.

Third, the traditional focus on market failures as a justification for intervention obscures a central reality: governments have already been intervening and failing. To the extent that states and markets are codependent, as well as path-dependent, existing institutional structures help predetermine future economic outcomes (Mazzucato 2015). The fact that helping accelerate LCT diffusion and development invariably requires policy changes points to the insufficiency of existing interventions: globally, policy is currently biased in the direction of unsustainability.

FIGURE 5.13

Developing countries have different starting positions for renewable energy deployment

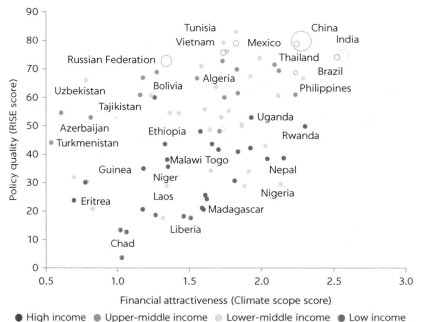

Sources: BloombergNEF 2018; World Bank Regulatory Indicators for Sustainable Energy (RISE), http://rise.worldbank.org/scores.
Note: Policy quality for renewable energy is proxied by the World Bank's Regulatory Indicators for Sustainable Energy (RISE), which rank countries by the quality of their energy sector policies and regulations for renewable energy. Financial attractiveness for private investors is proxied by BloombergNEF's "ClimateScope," which ranks developing countries by attractiveness to inward investment in renewable energies. Higher scores on both axes may indicate a great ability to deploy renewable energy domestically. Bubbles represent relative CO_2 emissions in 2014.

Worse, because of the path-dependent nature of investment, historical policy failures have helped lock in a carbon-intensive structure of economic production well into the future ("carbon lock-in"). Economies and the policy mixes that direct them "co-evolve" (Edmondson, Kern, and Rogge 2018). Economies are complex systems, and the technological frontier changes slowly on the basis of historical incentives. Accordingly, the fossil fuel subsidies mentioned earlier have helped lock in a global path of carbon-intensive economic development (Grubb 2014), and create what some have called a "techno-institutional complex" of fossil fuel–dominated energy mixes (Unruh 2002; Wilson et al. 2012). As a result, corrective interventions need to be much stronger—and potentially costlier—than they otherwise would have been.

Fourth, LCT faces strong obstacles in the form of multiple market failures. For example, carbon-intensive energy production leads to negative externalities (such as air pollution and climate change), which are not internalized in prices. Only 20 percent of global GHG emissions is covered by a carbon price well below the US$40–80 required by 2020 for achieving the Paris Agreement goals, for example (High-Level Commission on Carbon Prices 2017; World Bank 2019). In addition, as with all technologies, firms investing in low-carbon energy production technologies may not be able to internalize all of their benefits and will therefore tend to underinvest.

As a result, a single policy instrument may not be effective in isolation or may need to be so stringent as to be overly costly. For example, a corrective tax—such as a carbon price set at the right level from incumbent carbon-intensive energy producers—may not be high enough to allow low-carbon energy producers to innovate, enter the market, and compete. As a result, even with a carbon tax, the energy sector may not decarbonize. Further, relying only on taxes as an instrument may necessitate overly high carbon taxes to allow new low-carbon market entrants.

The existence of multiple market failures of LCT necessitates multiple interventions through policy mixes. For negative environmental externalities—whereby prices do not reflect social costs from energy production—a corrective tax or tax-like instrument (like an emissions trading scheme) may be the most effective instrument warranted. For knowledge spillovers—whereby firms cannot internalize all the benefits of innovation—subsidies for low-carbon R&D may also be needed. Finally, for scale economies and network effects, the government may need to provide strong support through preferential feed-in tariffs while investing directly in complementary infrastructure, such as electricity grids that can support the heterogeneous characteristics of renewables. As a result, policies need to be combined into mixes, varying in terms of both their economic efficiency and their political and administrative feasibility, across country contexts (IEA 2017b).

Fifth, in enacting policies to address market failures, governments can also fail. Government policy is not set in stone, and can be subject to amendments, changes, or even complete reversals. Firms and households know this in advance, and therefore incorporate the risks of policy changes into expectations of future revenues and costs (Dixit, Pindyck, and Dixit 1994), and they underinvest relative to what they would have without this uncertainty. As a result, some claim that "government-induced policy risk is the biggest deterrent to [low-carbon] investment worldwide" (Stern 2016). By contrast, reducing uncertainty about the future for firms by ensuring that policies are credible, reliable, and consistent can help accelerate LCT diffusion (Pfeiffer and Mulder 2013).

Overall, the strong case for government intervention to support LCT diffusion and production comes with certain stipulations. Countries come from diverse starting positions, so policies should be tailored to country circumstances and policies that, at present, are biased toward fossil fuel–intensive consumption and production. To be effective and efficient, policies must also be packaged in mixes of supporting measures addressing multiple, separate market failures. These policy mixes should be as consistent and reliable as possible to maximize their effect on fostering positive incentives toward LCTs. When enacting such policy measures, governments need to carefully manage any economic rents generated, to ensure that policy support is temporary—and known to be temporary—rather than permanent.

Government objectives

Governments have diverse objectives, including for LCT transfer. Some governments may simply want to deploy RE specifically to meet rising energy demand. Many countries in the world with the lowest energy access, at present, also have among the highest potential for solar energy, especially in Africa (Kabir et al. 2018). Deployment of solar-based renewables would be a win-win in these contexts, raising access to energy while mitigating climate change. Similarly, countries may seek to deploy energy efficiency technologies to induce investments in those very technologies, thereby helping domestic firms become more cost competitive (Coste et al. 2019).

Government objectives for LCT transfer can include deployment, production, or both. Countries seeking to deploy LCT may be called "strong deployers." By contrast, governments in other countries may see LCT as predominately an opportunity for export-led growth. Such countries may wish to develop domestic industries in LCT, thereby potentially reaping productivity gains from industrialization. These countries might be labeled "strong industrializers."

Last, governments may want to deploy and produce LCT jointly. Objectives of domestic LCT production and deployment can be synergistic, especially for large countries. For large markets, deployment can mean the generation of a large domestic market, which benefits LCT producers through the achievement of scale economies. Countries seeking to achieve both deployment and production of LCT might be called "green industrializers." Despite multifaceted government objectives, these three simplified categories can help countries identify policy mixes for LCT transfer.

Policy typology

A plethora of policies can be identified to help facilitate the deployment or production of LCTs. At the lower end of the technology-transfer staircase (import and diffusion of foreign LCT), policies can be identified to overcome the market failures that prevent LCT deployment. To address negative externalities, policies such as carbon pricing and environmental taxes can help rebalance incentives away from fossil fuel–intensive technologies and toward LCT. For imperfect information and inattention, governments could engage in informational campaigns, subsidies for energy efficiency investment, and direct regulatory measures (like performance standards).

At the upper end of the staircase (indigenous invention), policies can be identified to address negative externalities that prevent investment in innovation and development of industries. For instance, innovation policies such as R&D subsidies, publicly supported venture capital and government-backed loan guarantees can help firms overcome increasing market failures due to knowledge spillovers, increasing returns to scale, and network externalities (a summary of 1,600 empirical studies on innovation policies can be found in appendix E, "Empirical Evaluations of Innovation Policy Instruments.") For governments seeking to proactively support specific sectors, policies can be identified for a controversial area of policy making: industrial policy.

Policies for LCT transfer can be distinguished on two dimensions: the instrument mechanism (systemic, demand-pull, and tech-push) and the type of national capability they primarily raise (human, organizational, institutional, physical, or financial capital).

First, on the mechanism of instruments, policies can accelerate technology transfer by fostering a more supportive environment at the system level (systemic policies), creating demand for technologies (demand-pull), or more proactively supporting the supply side of technologies ("tech-push"; Rogge and Reichardt 2016). For example, demand-pull feed-in tariffs increase the expected future revenues of renewables investment, creating more demand for solar panels and wind turbines. By contrast, tech-push regulations, like mandates for clean technologies in power generation (for example, sulfur dioxide scrubbers in coal- and gas-fired power plants), force the adoption of specific technologies.

Second, policies affect different levels of national capability needed for technology transfer. For example, expenditure policies that provide subsidies for energy efficiency investments can raise capability among firms by expanding firm-level knowledge and absorption of such technologies. By contrast, direct provision of complementary infrastructure, such as smart grids or electric vehicle charging stations, raises the level of physical and institutional capital—that is, the business environment faced by firms.

Note that this typology is neither mutually exclusive nor collectively exhaustive. Policies can have multiple mechanisms and affect multiple types of national capability. For example, tax policies can raise the human and organizational capital needed for LCT transfer (by making energy efficiency savings more salient and increasing adoption and therefore knowledge of LCT), while also raising institutional capital (as national and local governments gain knowledge of such technologies through absorption). Distinguishing policies according to their primary mechanism and the national capability targeted can help policy makers better target recommendations towards specific objectives, technologies, and countries.

Accordingly, the next section further develops this policy delineation, providing recommendations to policy makers on optimal policy mixes given their diverse objectives and circumstances.

RECOMMENDATIONS

Whether governments are seeking primarily to deploy LCT (initial steps of the technology-transfer staircase) or produce LCT (higher steps) will elucidate the general policy mix they should adopt. For instance, governments seeking LCT deployment should focus on policies that facilitate the first two steps of the technology-transfer staircase (adoption and diffusion), focusing principally on demand-pull policies. Governments seeking LCT production should focus on implementing policies that facilitate rising to the upper steps of the technology-transfer staircase (imitation to indigenous invention), which entail mostly tech-push policies. Countries seeking both deployment and production should focus on further strengthening systemic policies beyond those entailed by seeking deployment and production alone. This section provides recommendations for policy makers based on their respective objectives for LCT. General recommendations are provided on policy mixes, followed by specific suggestions for policy makers seeking LCT deployment or production, or both.

1. Be consistent, coherent, credible, comprehensive, and strategic

As noted earlier, the multiple market failures in technology markets give rise to a need for combining policies together into mixes. Key design features of the mix and of each instrument matter, potentially more than the selection of policies in the mix (Kemp and Pontoglio 2011). There is a burgeoning "sustainability transitions" literature on such policy mixes, which blends findings from environmental economics, policy studies, and national innovation system or technological innovation systems studies, identifying a number of core components for ensuring the effectiveness of policy mixes (Cunningham et al. 2013; Kern, Kivimaa, and Martiskainen 2017; Rogge and Reichardt 2016; Schmidt and Sewerin 2018).

Policy makers must first carefully consider the stringency of each instrument and balance across instruments. Relying only on a single instrument may not facilitate the government's desired end objective, or that instrument may need to be so stringent as to carry politically unacceptable costs. In addition, an unbalanced policy mix—that is, one that overly relies on one or two instruments—is less likely to address all the issues relevant for policy objectives, and hence is less likely to be effective (Schmidt and Sewerin 2018).[16] In order to be effective, policy mixes should be balanced across instrument types in relation to the objective (Hallegatte, Fay, and Vogt-Schilb 2013). For instance, policy stringency could vary relative to the perceived scale of the market failure the mix seeks to address.[17]

Second, policy mixes should be internally consistent and the processes underlying them coherent. Policy mix consistency is the property of alignment between the objectives of the instruments, individually and collectively. Mixes should provide a diagnosis of the problem, identify the beneficiaries of the intervention, and compose instruments that reinforce rather than contradict each other (Cirera and Maloney 2017; Kern and Howlett 2009). Policies can often send contradictory signals to markets. For instance, many countries have subsidies for fossil fuels as well as for LCTs, which can undermine the overall effectiveness of policies at achieving their objectives. Policy process coherence here refers to alignment between the processes of design, implementation, and enforcement of policies with their underlying objectives (Rogge and Reichardt 2016). To achieve an effective mix, policy makers need the capability to create consistent policies, and governance structures need to implement and enforce them in a manner aligned with the mix's underlying objectives (Kemp and Pontoglio 2011).

Third, policy mixes should be both credible and comprehensive. They need to be credible by being both durable and, ex ante, perceived to be durable, which entails both well-signaled intention and substantive action by policy makers (Rogge and Reichardt 2016). To be comprehensive, mixes should comprise enough instruments to address all the relevant market failures, in addition to any institutional or system failures.

Fourth, to help ensure policy credibility, policy mixes should take account of political economy dynamics. For instance, the policy mix could be designed to create incentives among beneficiaries to maintain political support for the policy over time (Edmondson, Kern, and Rogge 2018) while avoiding concentrated costs on organized and politically powerful actors.

Fifth, instruments in the policy mix should collectively target areas where they can make the most impact. Because of technology market failures—for instance, the existence of scale economies and network effects—nonlinearities exist in LCTs, which can significantly affect their deployment or production. For RE, however, the existence of "tipping point" costs can mean that renewable capacity can be deployed rapidly, or not at all. For example, in South Africa, renewables costs have declined so significantly (along with energy efficiency improvements) that new RE installations will "provide more than sufficient capacity to cover projected demand and decommissioning of [coal] plants" (Department of Energy 2018).

Sixth, policy mixes should be designed and implemented as part of a long-term strategic vision. Strategic plans, and their long-term signaling, are important for reducing uncertainty while providing a sense of direction to households and firms, especially when it comes to investments in new technologies that entail large risks and up-front capital costs like some LCTs (Grubb 2014; Mazzucato 2016). Increasingly, governments and others are using long-term plans to encourage LCT deployment and production (Altenberg and Assmann 2017).

2. Get systemic policies right

Policies in the mix can be defined by their primary mechanism (systemic, demand-pull, or tech-push) and the national capability they most affect (table 5.7). Countries should first focus on getting the overarching systemic policy environment right. For all countries, irrespective of their specific objectives, it is important to get the underlying systemic framework aligned with the overall policy objectives. Otherwise, targeted measures are likely to be ineffectual. For example, if fossil fuels are heavily subsidized, then labeling programs are unlikely to be effective at driving deployment and targeted grants ineffective for helping firms make low-carbon innovations. As a result, all countries should work to ensure that systemic incentives facing the private sector are aligned with the overall policy objectives before embarking on demand-pull or tech-push policies.

As a priority, all governments should get energy prices right through fiscal policy. Pricing is the most important single instrument for affecting systemic, economy-wide change through the incentivization of LCT deployment or production (Parry et al. 2014). By reducing or eliminating fossil fuel subsidies and implementing carbon pricing, governments can systematically shift the incentives faced by firms and households—not only encouraging statically efficient reduction of emissions through abatement in least-cost locations but also helping foster dynamic efficiency by encouraging investment in innovation. Faced with increasing input costs for fossil fuel–based energy, most firms and households will choose either to abate emissions (for example, through import and adoption of existing LCTs) or to otherwise pay the tax. Some will choose,

TABLE 5.7 **Policy types for LCT transfer, by primary mechanism and capability affected**

PRIMARY NATIONAL CAPABILITY AFFECTED BY POLICY	PRIMARY MECHANISM OF POLICY		
	SYSTEMIC	DEMAND-PULL	TECHNOLOGY-PUSH
Human and organizational capital (workers and firms)	**Fiscal tax policies:** Tax and subsidy reforms (fossil fuel subsidy reform, carbon pricing, and other environmental tax reforms) **Human capital deepening:** Expanding educational and health spending	**Fiscal expenditure policies:** Direct subsidies, feed-in tariffs, deposit-refund systems, green public procurement **Regulations:** Technology and performance standards, supply-side restrictions (for example, coal in energy) **Informational:** Public information campaigns, rating and labeling programs	**Innovation policies:** Joint venture and local content requirements, skilled migration, employment protection, subsidized professional training and qualifications, entrepreneurship and technological training, scientific workshops, IPR policy or program support measures, early-stage accelerators and incubators, vertical chain tax incentives, innovation inducement prizes, high-tech clusters, R&D grants/loans, equity finance
Institutional and physical capital (states and economies)	**Low-carbon capital deepening:** Physical infrastructure provision (EV charging networks, electric grid infrastructure, public transportation)	**Energy market reforms:** Energy market design, renewable quotas/mandates, grid access guarantees, public energy auction rules, grid management	**Green industrial policies:** Green precommercial public procurement, patent law, support for exploiting low-carbon IPR, technology centers and transfer offices, cooperative R&D programs
Financial capital	**Derisking private investment:** Policy derisking and financial derisking instruments	**Greening the financial system:** Brown penalizing factors, mandatory disclosure of climate-related financial risks and emissions	**State-driven green finance:** Direct funding of early-stage LCT (green investment banks/ low-carbon portfolio mandates in development banks)

Sources: Elaboration based on Cirera and Maloney 2017; Edler and Shapira 2013; Rogge and Reichardt 2016.
Note: Table does not include trade policies (for example, tariffs, border-adjustment measures, export credit guarantees), which are discussed in chapter 3. Note that policy types are not mutually exclusive: specific instruments can affect multiple national capability metrics through multiple mechanisms. EV = electric vehicle; IPR = intellectual property rights; LCT = low-carbon technology; R&D = research and development.

however, to innovate in LCTs, for example creating more-efficient energy capital goods or cheaper low-carbon energy supply goods.

By contrast, nonpricing instruments—such as performance standards or technology mandates—may not provide the dynamic incentives needed for innovation. As a result, such nonpricing measures may lock in existing technologies, forestalling a more efficient and socially desirable low-carbon transition. By contrast, tax policies can help firms and households deploy LCT while also fostering innovation. These policies push the technological frontier itself (Grubb 2014; IEA 2017b), while also pushing firms toward the existing technological frontier. As a result, all policy makers should prioritize getting energy prices right through socially efficient taxation.

That said, pricing policies cannot address all market failures, and political economy obstacles to pricing remain large in many countries. Significant opposition to pricing reforms may exist because of, for instance, the salience of fossil fuel energy, the politically powerful position of fossil fuel–based and energy-intensive sectors, or often misplaced concerns over the distributional effects of such reforms (Baranzini et al. 2017; Dolphin, Pollitt, and Newbery 2016; Hallegatte, Fay, and Vogt-Schilb 2013; Mathys and de Melo 2011). As a result, nonpricing instruments remain important complements to pricing policies.

Nonpricing systemic reforms can also help accelerate LCT deployment and production. Investing in human capital, particularly in educational outcomes, is especially important for increasing the capability of firms and households to deploy and produce LCTs. Such investment could be funded, for example, through environmental taxes (for example, on CO_2, fine particulate matter, and sulfur dioxide). Externalities can offer a less economically distortionary source of revenues compared to capital or labor taxes, which can be especially costly in developing countries by increasing informality (Bento, Jacobsen, and Liu 2018; Erasmo and Moscoso 2012; Heine and Black 2019; Loayza 2018).

In addition, countries should pursue low-carbon capital deepening. Given the pervasive presence of multiple market failures in LCT and the need for complementary infrastructure—because of scale economies and network effects—countries should invest directly in low-carbon infrastructure. This infrastructure includes low-carbon public transportation and renewable-friendly energy infrastructure, which can provide a basis for LCT deployment and production while also raising governmental knowledge and awareness (institutional capital).

Last, developing countries should seek to foster private investment in LCT deployment through derisking mechanisms. As noted above, firms in developing countries tend to underinvest in technology, including in LCT. Access to finance plays an important part: although the returns to investment in technologies should be higher in developing countries than in developed countries, in fact several perceived and actual risks reduce expected returns for investors (Waissbein et al. 2013). As a result, financing costs may be prohibitively high, rendering investment in LCT. Countries therefore need derisking instruments to crowd in the private sector (Waissbein et al. 2013). Derisking instruments seek to remove the underlying causes of policy risks, such as uncertainty in RE policy design or institutional volatility. Examples include loan guarantees, public equity co-investments, and political risk insurance.

No one-size-fits all approach exists for derisking, given the diversity of market conditions and capability across countries. For example, UNDP (2017, 2018) analysis suggests that in Tunisia the largest sources of additional risk to equity investors into renewables are grid/transmission risk (an additional 1 percentage point to the cost of equity) and currency/macroeconomic risks (1 percentage point), whereas in neighboring Lebanon the highest-cost risks are political (1.7 percentage points) and power market risk (1.5 percentage points). Because of this heterogeneity, countries should seek to identify the underlying risks faced by potential LCT investors (for example, in renewables) and implement matching policy and financial derisking instruments.[18]

3. For LCT deployment, mix demand-pull and technology-push policies

Beyond the needed base of systemic policies, especially pricing, policy makers seeking LCT deployment should vary demand-pull and tech-push policies by the specific technology. Countries have built up a rich experience of policies for low-carbon deployment, and broadly find that different technologies respond to policies in varying ways. Generally, LCT deployment requires strong demand-pull policies, but effective policies vary by technology type and may need to be supplemented by tech-push policies in the short or long term. For example, LCTs in energy and transport appear to respond more strongly to certain types of demand-pull policies in the short term, though policy makers should also implement tech-push policies for the long term. By contrast, industrial and building LCTs may respond more strongly in short-term deployment to tech-push policies, though strong demand-pull policies are needed in the long term.

In the energy sector, removing coal provides a particularly promising opportunity to reap welfare gains in the short and medium term. A major polluter in terms of both local air and water pollution Coal negatively affects the health of local populations, with costs often concentrated on the poorest (Hsiang, Oliva, and Walker 2018), and contributes significantly to global GHGs (Cohen et al. 2017; Landrigan et al. 2017). In addition, many countries import coal, making local power supply costs dependent on globally volatile coal prices. Accelerating energy access while phasing out coal in developing countries would lead to significant improvements in health and welfare, helping governments achieve their Sustainable Development Goals (SDGs) for universal energy access (SDG7), reducing the severe impacts of air pollution (part of SDG3), and mitigating climate change (SDG13).[19] Without reforms, these high-carbon assets and the welfare costs they inflict will likely remain locked in.

A policy mix for reversing the lock-in of coal in the power sector could look as follows. First, government should set a public commitment to a coal phaseout date. Doing so would send a strong signal to markets, preventing investment in additional coal energy assets, which would be at risk of stranding. Second, countries should ensure that prices reflect the social costs of coal-sourced electricity through fossil fuel subsidy reform and taxes like those on CO_2, fine particulate matter, and nitrous oxide. These reforms would send further signals to investors of the direction of the domestic energy system. Third, countries should embark on power sector reforms conducive to market entry for RE suppliers. Reforms could include tweaking energy auctions to allow for bidding across hours of the day when renewables are especially cost-competitive (for example, during daylight hours for solar), priority and "clean-first" dispatch of renewables in the power sector, and investment in complementary infrastructure like energy storage facilities (box 5.1). Fourth, countries should seek to directly regulate existing plants through, for example, fleet-wide GHG emissions performance standards, and regulated lifetime and carbon capture and storage retrofit mandates (IEA

BOX 5.1

Reforming power markets for renewables

Power market design is one of the major impediments to deployment of renewables. Many developing countries have monopolistic electricity markets at one or more points on the electricity production chain (generation, transmission, and distribution), in addition to long-term (often 20 to 35 years) power purchasing agreements, some of which contain "take or pay" clauses. These frictions prevent entry of renewable energy supply technologies, which have relatively high variability in their levelized costs, as well as up-front capital costs. As a result, the current power sector design in many countries does not suit the large-scale deployment of renewable power.

Reform of the energy market to allow low-carbon technology penetration includes general reform of pricing structures in addition to deeper flexibilization measures. General reforms include energy auction tweaks that introduce spot price signals for investors, to allow pricing based on marginal costs rather than long-term power purchasing agreements. Such reforms can improve the efficiency and reliability of the system overall (for examples from Peru and the Philippines, see Rudnick and Velasquez 2019a, 2019b) and also make the power market more conducive to renewables investment (IEA 2019).

2017a, 2017b). Fifth, governments should provide direct support measures to those negatively affected by the phaseout of coal, including those affected by mine closures (World Bank 2018).

For technologies with low-carbon energy demand, countries should focus on the demand-pull measures mentioned earlier while fostering a domestic market in energy supply companies. Energy efficiency technologies can help address concerns about energy access, security, and environmental protection jointly (Aznar et al. 2019). Such technologies, however, face strong obstacles to penetration: firms may be unaware of the cost savings potential from adopting such LCTs. In addition, firms may be capital-constrained. More efficient energy pricing—for example, through environmental taxation—can help make such cost savings more salient, but informational and capital constraints may remain nonetheless. Energy service companies (ESCOs), buttressed by public informational campaigns (for example, standards and labeling), can help address these frictions through the procurement and installation of energy efficiency technologies as well as the finance to cover them (Fang, Miller, and Yeh 2012; Lee et al. 2003). Governments could also create super ESCOs, which serve as public entities established to help firms realize efficiency gains while also fostering the development of private sector ESCOs (Sarkar and Moin 2018). Joint efforts and partnerships by government, utilities, the private sector, nonprofits, and academia to supply energy efficiency technologies to low-income households can help raise institutional and human capacity (Aznar et al. 2019), both of which are especially important for LCT deployment (refer to the earlier section titled "National Capability for LCT Transfer"), and can help support energy access and distributional objectives.

In the long term, governments should focus on scaling up complementary infrastructure for low-carbon energy supply and demand technologies. Measures include deeper investment in energy storage technologies, better metering networks, and more efficient, integrated, and responsive grid infrastructure (smart grids). Storage and end-use technologies will become increasingly important as renewables penetrate the power sector. Countries should look to invest in long-duration energy storage, including novel forms like flow batteries (Winsberg et al. 2017).[20]

4. For LCT production, focus on tech-push policies and the long term

Countries seeking to produce LCTs should focus on tech-push, or innovation, policies. A plethora of policies exists to support innovation, and a long literature examines their effectiveness empirically, albeit mostly in developed countries. Unfortunately, despite this history, knowledge on what works remains low for innovation in general and LCT production and export in particular. Invariably, countries embarking on tech-push policies will be taking risks. In spite of the risks, countries can benefit from three broad lessons.

First, countries seeking to climb the technology-transfer staircase and produce and export LCT need deeper levels of capability and more strategic and long-term planning. Innovation and production are notoriously difficult to predict and direct, but countries with higher capability tend to be more innovative. In addition, countries that deepen their physical infrastructure and, especially, raise their human development levels tend to export more LCT.

At the top of the technology-transfer staircase, commercialization and export of indigenous inventions require even deeper demand-pull and tech-pull policies. A pervasive gap exists between new inventions and their commercialization, which prevents new technologies from being widely diffused domestically or exported. Countries with firms reaching this last step on the technology-transfer staircase may need a final push in policy terms to help firms leap this gap. Specifically, this push may entail even deeper demand-pull and tech-push policies. As with industrial policies generally, however, policy makers will need to compare the potential benefits of supporting such early-stage inventors with the risks they create by generating rents.

Second, countries should eschew the ambition to pursue technologically neutral policies (box 5.2). Some policy makers have sought to make innovation policies neutral under the rationale that governments fail and should avoid picking winners. In reality, past and current policies have consistently favored fossil-fuel policies. In addition, technologies face different levels of market failures, with entrant technologies facing more of such obstacles than incumbent technologies. As a result, a technologically neutral approach could simply lock in existing technologies, including fossil fuel–based and energy-intensive technologies. Instead of seeking to *pick* winners, countries hoping to be strong industrializers should instead seek to *create* winners.

BOX 5.2

Why technological neutrality is not neutral

One design feature often sought by policy makers seeking technological diffusion or innovation is technological neutrality, but existing approaches to technological neutrality are rarely neutral. Newer technologies face more and deeper market failures than incumbent technologies. As a result, policies that profess technological neutrality favor incumbent technologies, locking in more mature technologies and forestalling technological change by locking out new technologies (Azar and Sandén 2011; de Mello Santana 2016; Schmidt et al. 2016).

For example, biomass-based power generation ("biopower") is both more mature than solar photovoltaic and wind and easier to integrate into existing electricity systems. Biomass can be co-fired with coal in existing coal-based power plants and is less intermittent and dispatchable than solar or wind power. As a result, when policy mixes are relatively more neutral, markets tend to choose biopower over wind and solar technologies (Schmidt and Sewerin 2018). A technologically "neutral" approach therefore ends up favoring both more mature technologies (biopower) and supporting incumbent technologies (coal). In addition, by favoring lower-cost abatement options,

technological neutrality may fail to effect the deeper decarbonization required for achieving the Paris Agreement goals (Vogt-Schilb, Meunier, and Hallegatte 2018).

Tackling this problem requires new paradigms that quantify the scale of failures in technology markets. New technologies face multiple compounding market failures, which can forestall the pace of technological change. Addressing these market failures, however, entails some degree of targeting, which is difficult given imperfect information available to policy makers and the uncertainty of the pace and direction of technological change. In addition, overcoming barriers to new technologies requires public investments in the needed complementary infrastructure to overcome network effects and externalities. Such infrastructure investments are costly and irreversible, entailing a loss of "option value" (Avner, Rentschler, and Hallegatte 2014). Economists, and the policy makers they support, should therefore seek new, innovative ways to quantify market failures to aid efforts to accelerate innovation, especially in low-carbon technology, where the necessity and opportunity for deployment are both high.

Creating winners entails adopting a more proactive approach to technology, cognizant of the risks involved with directing technological change. One potential approach is through targeting of specific LCT subsectors with complex products, dense backward and forward linkages, and high-growth potential. Other criteria include learning depth (depth of technology spillovers) and uncertainty over future market size. These and other criteria could be systematically incorporated into targeting of sectors. For example, battery storage technologies are strategic, because they have high global market potential, learning and technological depth, dense links in the value chain, and relatively more growth certainty compared with other LCTs (for example, hydrogen fuel cells). Although imperfect and imprecise, approaches such as these can help policy makers seeking to endogenously innovate, produce, and export LCT to more systematically target sectors for tech-push policies.

Third, governments should focus on facilitating technology intermediaries such as accelerators and technology centers. Governments should not attempt to be artificially technologically neutral given the large differences in market failures faced by different technologies, but they should also not seek to pick winning firms themselves. As noted earlier, picking winners generates large rents and creates perverse political economy incentives through vested interests. Despite justification for government intervention, "creative destruction" is a necessary process in innovation. As a result, governments should seek to create winners through technology intermediaries, such as technology centers or institutes and accelerator programs. These intermediaries can help firms and workers generate the capabilities needed for innovation, such as managerial and absorptive capacities, while fostering positive knowledge spillovers (Cirera and Maloney 2017). In this way, the proactive support of technology intermediaries, and the innovation ecosystems they are embedded in, can help create low-carbon winners while avoiding the risks of generating rents within specific firms.

5. For both deployment and production, deepen demand-pull and systemic policies

The objectives of deploying and developing LCT are not mutually exclusive; for many contexts, they are complementary. Firms and households that deploy LCTs are much more likely to understand and therefore innovate on top of those technologies. For LCT transfer to developing countries, the ultimate goal of technology transfer should be not only deployment, but also "to enhance their endogenous capabilities, which will enable future innovation and ensure long-term adoption of low-carbon technologies" (Liu and Liang 2011). Countries that want to deploy LCTs may also want to produce them, and vice versa.

Countries seeking to both deploy and develop LCT ("green industrializers") should further deepen their demand-pull and systemic policies. By incorporating higher carbon pricing levels, supported by complementary policies to minimize any trade-offs while addressing hard-to-abate sectors, countries can help foster joint deployment and production of LCT. Further, by supplementing these policies with deeper demand-pull policies, they can help domestic firms realize the scale economies needed to achieve competitiveness in LCT.

Deeper demand-pull policies will be most effective in large markets. As chapter 2 and this chapter have shown, market size matters for both deployment and production of LCT. This could be because, for large countries, the goals of deployment and production are complementary: countries with large markets can reap the scale economies from large-scale national deployment. Large countries that can make use of the complementary nature of the two objectives should therefore seek to be green industrializers, reaping the various benefits of LCT deployment and the productivity gains from industrialization in a potential major growth sector. Smaller countries, which cannot make use of this complementary nature, may nonetheless seek to integrate their domestic markets through regional integration while also being more targeted on strategic sectors of LCT (for example, those with high levels of trade and integration into global value chains).

6. Alter policy mixes by national capability, with additional support needed for low-income countries

Finally, developing countries should alter the policy mix according to their respective national capabilities. As this chapter has shown, national capability matters for determining outcomes in LCT (in terms of import, deployment, innovation, and export), but it varies significantly across developing countries. Poorer countries, in particular, face more and deeper market failures in technology while perversely having lower national capability to address those failures effectively (the "innovation paradox"; Cirera and Maloney 2017). Countries should therefore alter their policy mixes depending on national capability, in addition to other country- and technology-specific considerations.

Less capable middle-income countries should focus on derisking instruments while deepening national capabilities. These countries are simultaneously less able to attract FDI (for example, because of incomplete property rights or pervasive political risks) and less able to use domestic deployment of LCT to support endogenous innovation. Depending on national objectives for LCT (deployment, production, or both), derisking instruments may be especially necessary to attract FDI, whereas national capability–deepening efforts may need to be more strategic, with policy mixes avoiding certain demand-pull measures (for example, green public procurement) because of the risks of regulatory or political capture.

The situation is especially stark in low-income countries, which may be stuck in technology traps. This chapter has argued that climbing the technology-transfer staircase requires ever-deeper levels of national capability. Deepening these capabilities, in turn, requires state capabilities to enact strategic and effective policy mixes. For low-income countries—where national capability, state capabilities, and the ability to attract foreign technology through FDI, patents, or skilled foreign workers are all very low—these obstacles may be virtually insurmountable. Such countries may therefore remain perpetually in a "technology trap" (Fofack 2008), with capabilities far from the global technological frontier. This problem is significantly exacerbated in the context of LCT, which has a set of defining features (such as higher complexity and capital intensity) that make it more capability-intensive to deploy compared with other technologies. Low-income countries in technology traps are likely to be in even deeper LCT traps.

CONCLUSION

Overall, this chapter has shown both the necessity and the opportunity of LCT transfer, providing recommendations to policy makers in developing countries seeking to deploy or produce LCT. Without transferring LCT to developing countries en masse, the world is unlikely to achieve the Paris Agreement's objectives. This mass deployment is also an opportunity: policies that help deploy LCT—especially carbon pricing—can help countries achieve economic and other development objectives, like improving human health, in addition to reducing GHGs. Additionally, LCT deployment offers an opportunity for countries seeking export-led growth: LCT tends to be more sophisticated with denser linkages along value chains than high-carbon technologies, and global deployment creates the potential for a huge and growing export market.

One particular challenge for global LCT deployment is that national capabilities matter for LCT, and those capabilities vary significantly from one developing country to another. The complementary inputs of human, organizational, institutional, and physical capital appear to matter for LCT transfer across countries. Within countries, human development is the strongest predictor of raising LCT transfer, as proxied by LCT trade intensity. This finding suggests that policies should be aligned with government objectives while raising necessary capabilities in countries. Policies should also be mixed depending on objectives and national capabilities.

That said, the topic of LCT transfer to developing countries is broad, and this chapter has not captured all of its complexities. For example, this chapter has not sought to elucidate in detail the dynamics of political economy, which necessarily constrain policy makers. A large literature exists on this topic, including on the political economy of carbon pricing (see, for example, Dolphin, Pollitt, and Newbery 2016), mitigation instruments (Jakob et al. 2014; Mathys and de Melo 2011), and environmental policies in general (Oates and Portney 2003), but the literature pays comparatively less attention to the political economy of innovation policies.

Finally, future research could more precisely match LCTs to specific developing countries and subnational regions, for instance under the rubric of "smart specialization" (Balland et al. 2018). Despite the plethora of projections for Paris-aligned emissions trajectories, surprisingly few analyses examine what those trajectories mean for trade in LCTs. More precise projections of which technologies are likely to surge in the coming decade, and what countries and regions are most well-placed to take advantage of them, would help provide more granularity on how countries can take advantage of opportunities presented by the low-carbon transition.

NOTES

1. The definitions of "industrial" and "innovation" policies overlap significantly in the literature. Industrial policies have been defined as measures that encourage "restructuring, diversification, and technological dynamism beyond what market forces on their own would generate" (Rodrik 2004). Under the neoclassical paradigm, innovation policies tend to be framed as measures that remedy market failures, whereas the National Innovations Systems (NIS) literature discusses them as measures that enhance the interaction between governments, industry, and nonmarket institutions to generate new knowledge (Cirera and Maloney 2017).

More recently, "true industrial policy" has been explicitly equated with "technology and innovation policy" (Cherif and Hasanov 2019). This chapter will adopt a mixed and broad definition, referring to policies that aim to accelerate technological adoption and the generation of new knowledge as "innovation policies," and measures that seek to promote the creation of new industries as "industrial policies," noting that many policies could be defined as both.

2. There is a high degree of uncertainty on the 1.5°C goal at the 66 percent probability level. Lower levels of probability provide more certainty, but with higher implied thresholds of emissions. For example, to achieve below 1.5°C with a 50 percent probability level, GHG emissions cannot exceed roughly 37 $GtCO_2e$, which is only 12 percent lower than the 2°C target with a 66 percent probability level.

3. The gap between the 2°C and 1.5°C targets and existing Nationally Determined Contributions (NDCs) is lower, because UNEP's (2017) baseline case does not assume that NDCs are fully implemented. The gap between full implementation of NDCs and the 2°C goal is 11.0–13.5 $GtCO_2e$ for conditional and unconditional pledges, respectively. The emissions gap in the case of 1.5°C with 50 percent probability is 16–19 $GtCO_2e$ for conditional and unconditional NDCs, respectively.

4. Refer to note 1 on the definitions of industrial versus innovation policies.

5. Specifically, authors debate the possibility of reducing GHG emissions while raising economic output or employment (the "double dividend hyphothesis"; see Freire-González 2018; Heine and Black 2019). Empirical evidence historically has been mixed. For developing countries, recent studies suggest that "tax shifting" environmental tax reforms (using taxes on carbon to fund reductions in labor taxes) can yield negative abatement costs in many developing countries (Bento, Jacobsen, and Liu 2018; Carson, Jacobsen, and Liu 2014).

6. Note that "co-harms" and trade-offs can also exist within certain mitigation policies. For instance, the installation of scrubbers in power plants to reduce sulfur dioxide emissions can reduce the plants' efficiency, resulting in increased fossil fuel consumption and therefore GHG emissions. Such co-harms and trade-offs tend to be minor, however, compared with co-benefits (Rizzi et al. 2014).

7. In one cross-country study, a developing country's having a donor-funded strategic plan for LCT was negatively associated with renewable deployment (Pfeiffer and Mulder 2013).

8. Note, however, that the steps are not mutually exclusive, and graduation from one stage to another does not entail leaving behind all previous stages. In reality, countries can be at different steps of the staircase at the same time. For example, collaborative innovation happens among firms in countries at the most advanced stages of technological development as well.

9. This chapter uses the list of 107 products identified as LCT in chapter 2.

10. Data from the United Nations Development Programme's Human Development Index, education subindex, http://hdr.undp.org/en/content/education-index (accessed June 2, 2019), and from the World Bank's Human Capital Index data catalog, https://datacatalog.worldbank.org/dataset/human-capital-index (accessed June 2, 2019).

11. Data from the United Nations Industrial Development Organization, https://stat.unido.org/database/CIP 2018 (accessed June 2, 2019).

12. Scores from the World Bank's Government Effectiveness data catalog, https://datacatalog.worldbank.org/government-effectiveness-estimate-0.

13. Data from the World Bank's World Development Indicators, https://datacatalog.worldbank.org/dataset/world-development-indicators (accessed June 2, 2019).

14. One somewhat concerning finding in regression 2, however, is that a growing per capita capital stock appears to also imply *lower* installed RE capacity per capita. This effect could indicate that existing capital-deepening efforts may not be very green, but the effect did not reemerge under non-fixed effects or random effects specifications, or when using an alternative measure to proxy for physical capital—changes in per capita productive capital stocks from the Changing Wealth of Nations dataset (Lange, Wodon, and Carey 2018).

15. Broadly defined as finance that supports mitigation or adaptation objectives (UNFCCC 2016).

16. Note, however, that early evidence suggests that national policies have less variation in terms of balance across instruments and more variation in terms of specificity of the technologies targeted (Schmidt and Sewerin 2018).

17. Although systematic frameworks for estimating the scale of technology market failures do not exist at present, this conceptualization is similar to how binding constraints are to economic

growth, as described in the "growth diagnostics" literature (Hausmann, Rodrik, and Velasco 2008). Theoretically, one could envisage technology market failure diagnostics, which examine the relative strengths of technology market failures, adopting similar methods.

18. For renewables investments, refer to the United Nations Development Programme's "Deriskizing Renewable Energy Investment" (DREI) methodology and tool kit, which seeks to assist policy makers in developing countries in selecting public instruments to promote RE investment, at www.undp.org/DREI.

19. From the International Energy Agency's Sustainable Development Scenario web page, https://www.iea.org/weo/weomodel/sds/.

20. Given the variability of production from renewable sources (especially wind and solar), storage is required to allow deeper renewable penetration into the power sector. Possible storage technologies include pumped hydro, compressed air, thermal, flywheel, supercon-ducting magnetic, electric double layer, and electrochemical energy storage systems. Flow or "redox-flow" batteries (RFB) are rechargeable batteries where rechargeability is pro-vided by two chemicals dissolved in liquid and separated by a membrane; they allow for almost instant recharging (Winsberg et al. 2017).

REFERENCES

Acemoglu, D. 2002. "Directed Technical Change." *Review of Economic Studies* 69 (4): 781–809.

Acemoglu, D., P. Aghion, L. Bursztyn, and D. Hemous. 2009. "The Environment and Directed Technical Change." NBER Working Paper 15451, National Bureau of Economic Research, Cambridge, MA.

Allcott, H., and M. Greenstone. 2012. "Is There an Energy Efficiency Gap?" NBER Working Paper 17766, National Bureau of Economic Research, Cambridge, MA.

Allcott, H., and C. Knittel. 2019. "Are Consumers Poorly Informed about Fuel Economy? Evidence from Two Experiments." *American Economic Journal: Economic Policy* 11 (1): 1–37.

Altenberg, T., and C. Assmann, eds. 2017. *Green Industrial Policy: Concept, Policies, Country Experiences.* Geneva, Bonn: UN Environment, German Development Institute. http://wedocs.unep.org/handle/20.500.11822/22277.

Avner, P., J. Rentschler, and S. Hallegatte. 2014. "Carbon Price Efficiency: Lock-In and Path Dependence in Urban Forms and Transport Infrastructure." Policy Research Working Paper 6941, World Bank, Washington, DC.

Azar, C., and B. A. Sandén. 2011. "The Elusive Quest for Technology-Neutral Policies." *Environmental Innovation and Societal Transitions* 1 (1): 135–39.

Aznar, A., J. Logan, D. Gagne, and E. Chen. 2019. "Advancing Energy Efficiency in Developing Countries: Lessons Learned from Low-Income Residential Experiences in Industrialized Countries." National Renewable Energy Laboratory, Golden. https://www.nrel.gov/docs/fy19osti/71915.pdf.

Balland, P.-A., R. Boschma, J. Crespo, and D. L. Rigby. 2018. "Smart Specialization Policy in the European Union: Relatedness, Knowledge Complexity and Regional Diversification." *Regional Studies* 53 (9): 1252–68. doi.org/10.1080/00343404.2018.1437900.

Baranzini, A., J. C. J. M. van den Bergh, S. Carattini, R. B. Howarth, E. Padilla, and J. Roca. 2017. "Carbon Pricing in Climate Policy: Seven Reasons, Complementary Instruments, and Political Economy Considerations." *WIREs Climate Change* 8: e462. doi: 10.1002/wcc.462.

Bento, A., M. Jacobsen, and A. Liu. 2018. "Environmental Policy in the Presence of an Informal Sector." *Journal of Environmental Economics and Management* 90 (July): 61–77. doi.org/10.1016/j.jeem.2018.03.011.

Berkowitz, D., J. Moenius, and K. Pistor. 2003. "Trade, Law, and Product Complexity." *Review of Economics and Statistics* 88 (2): 363–73.

BloombergNEF. 2018. "ClimateScope 2018." BloombergNEF, New York.

Burke, P. J., and S. Nishitateno. 2015. "Gasoline Prices and Road Fatalities: International Evidence." *Economic Inquiry* 53 (3): 1437–50. doi.org/10.1111/ecin.12171.

Burke, P. J., and A. Teame. 2018. "Fuel Prices and Road Deaths in Australia." *Economic Papers: A Journal of Applied Economics and Policy* 37 (2): 146–161. doi.org/10.1111/1759-3441.12207.

Carson, R. T., M. R. Jacobsen, and A. A. Liu. 2014. "Comparing the Cost of a Carbon Tax in China and the United States." https://www.aeaweb.org/conference/2015/retrieve .php?pdfid=634.

Cherif, R., and F. Hasanov. 2019. "The Return of the Policy That Shall Not Be Named: Principles of Industrial Policy." IMF Working Paper WP/19/74. International Monetary Fund, Washington, DC. https://www.imf.org/en/Publications/WP/Issues/2019/03/26 /The-Return-of-the-Policy-That-Shall-Not-Be-Named-Principles-of-Industrial -Policy-46710.

Chi, G., J. R. Porter, A. G. Cosby, and D. Levinson. 2013. "The Impact of Gasoline Price Changes on Traffic Safety: A Time Geography Explanation." *Journal of Transport Geography* 28 (April): 1–11. doi.org/10.1016/j.jtrangeo.2012.08.015.

Cirera, X., and W. Maloney. 2017. *The Innovation Paradox: Developing-Country Capabilities and the Unrealized Promise of Technological Catch-Up.* Washington, DC: World Bank.

Cohen, A. J., M. Brauer, R. Burnett, H. R. Anderson, J. Frostad, K. Estep, K. Balakrishnan, B. Brunekreef, L. Dandona, R. Dandona, V. Feigin, G. Freedman, B. Hubbell, A. Jobling, H. Kan, L. Knibbs, Y. Liu, R. Martin, L. Morawska, C. A. Pope III, H. Shin, K. Strait, G. Shaddick, M. Thomas, R. van Dingenen, A. van Donkelaar, T. Vos, C. J. L. Murray, and M. H. Forouzanfar. 2017. "Estimates and 25-Year Trends of the Global Burden of Disease Attributable to Ambient Air Pollution: An Analysis of Data from the Global Burden of Diseases Study 2015." *The Lancet* 389 (10082): 1907–18. doi.org/10.1016/S0140-6736(17)30505-6.

Cornell University, INSEAD, and WIPO (World Intellectual Property Organization). 2018. *Global Innovation Index 2018: Energizing the World with Innovation.* Ithaca, Fontainebleau, and Geneva. https://www.wipo.int/edocs/pubdocs/en/wipo_pub_gii_2018.pdf.

Coste, A., M. Cali, N. Cantore, and D. Heine. 2019. "Staying Competitive: Productivity Effects of Environmental Taxes." In *Fiscal Policies for Development and Climate Action*, edited by M. A. Pigato, 65–114. Washington, DC: World Bank.

Cunningham, P., J. Edler, K. Flanagan, and P. Larédo. 2013. "Innovation Policy Mix and Instrument Interaction." In *Compendium of Evidence on the Effectiveness of Innovation Policy.* Manchester Institute of Innovation Research, University of Manchester, U.K. http:// www.innovation-policy.org.uk/share/19_Policy%20mix_linked.pdf.

de Mello Santana, P. H. 2016. "Cost-Effectiveness as Energy Policy Mechanisms: The Paradox of Technology-Neutral and Technology-Specific Policies in the Short and Long Term." *Renewable and Sustainable Energy Reviews* 58 (May): 1216–1222. doi.org/10.1016/J .RSER.2015.12.300.

Department of Energy. 2018. "Request for Comments: Draft Integrated Resource Plan 2018." Department of Energy, Republic of South Africa, Pretoria. http://www.energy.gov.za/IRP /irp-update-draft-report2018/IRP-Update-2018-Draft-for-Comments.pdf.

Dixit, A. K., R. S. Pindyck, and R. K. Dixit. 1994. *Investment Under Uncertainty.* Princeton: Princeton University Press.

Dolphin, G. G., M. G. Pollitt, and D. G. Newbery. 2016. "The Political Economy of Carbon Pricing: A Panel Analysis." Cambridge Working Paper in Economics 1633, University of Cambridge, U.K.

Edler, J., and P. Shapira. 2013. "Impacts of Innovation Policy: Synthesis and Conclusion." In *Compendium of Evidence on the Effectiveness of Innovation Policy.* Manchester Institute of Innovation Research, University of Manchester, U.K. http://www.innovation-policy.org.uk /compendium/.

Edmondson, D. L., F. Kern, and K. S. Rogge. 2018. "The Co-evolution of Policy Mixes and Socio-technical Systems: Towards a Conceptual Framework of Policy Mix Feedback in Sustainability Transitions." *Research Policy,* March 28. doi.org/10.1016/j.respol.2018.03.010.

Erasmo, P. N. D., and H. J. Moscoso. 2012. "Financial Structure, Informality and Development." *Journal of Monetary Economics* 59 (3): 286–302. doi.org/10.1016/j.jmoneco.2012.03.003.

Fang, W. S., S. M. Miller, and C. C. Yeh. 2012. "The Effect of ESCOs on Energy Use." *Energy Policy* 51 (December), 558–68. doi.org/10.1016/j.enpol.2012.08.068.

Fofack, H. 2008. "Technology Trap and Poverty Trap in Sub-Saharan Africa." Policy Research Working Paper 4582, World Bank, Washington, DC.

Freire-González, J. 2018. "Environmental Taxation and the Double Dividend Hypothesis in CGE Modelling Literature: A Critical Review." *Journal of Policy Modeling* 40 (1): 194–223. doi.org/10.1016/j.jpolmod.2017.11.002.

Gaulier, G., and S. Zignago. 2019. "BACI: International Trade Database at the Product-Level. The 1994–2007 Version." CEPII Working Paper 2010-23, Centre d'Etudes Prospectives et d'Informations Internationales. http://www.cepii.fr/CEPII/fr/publications/wp/abstract .asp?NoDoc=2726.

Grubb, M. 2014. *Planetary Economics: Energy, Climate Change and the Three Domains of Sustainable Development.* Oxon, U.K., and New York: Routledge.

Häckel, B., S. Pfosser, and T. Tränkler. 2017. "Explaining the Energy Efficiency Gap - Expected Utility Theory versus Cumulative Prospect Theory. *Energy Policy* 111 (December): 414–26. doi.org/10.1016/j.enpol.2017.09.026.

Hallegatte, S., M. Fay, and A. Vogt-Schilb. 2013. "Green Industrial Policies: When and How." Policy Research Working Paper 6677, World Bank, Washington, DC.

Hausmann, R., C. A. Hidalgo, S. Bustos, M. Coscia, A. Simoes, and M. A. Yíldirim. 2014. *The Atlas of Economic Complexity: Mapping Paths to Prosperity.* Cambridge, MA: MIT Press.

Hausmann, R., D. Rodrik, and A. Velasco. 2008. "Growth Diagnostics." In *The Washington Consensus Reconsidered: Towards a New Global Governance,* edited by N. Serra and J. E. Stiglitz. Oxford Scholarship Online. doi.org/10.1093/acprof:oso/9780199534081 .003.0015.

Heine, D., and S. Black. 2019. "Benefits Beyond Climate: Environmental Tax Reform in Developing Countries." In *Fiscal Policies for Development and Climate Action,* edited by M. A. Pigato, 1–64. Washington, DC: World Bank.

High-Level Commission on Carbon Prices. 2017. *Report of the High-Level Commission on Carbon Prices.* Washington, DC: World Bank.

Hsiang, S., P. Oliva, and R. Walker. 2018. "The Distribution of Environmental Damages." *Review of Environmental Economics and Policy* 13 (1): 83–103. doi.org/10.1093/reep/rey024.

IEA (International Energy Agency). 2014. *Capturing the Multiple Benefits of Energy Efficiency: A Guide to Quantifying the Value Added.* Paris: IEA. doi.org/10.1787/9789264220720-en.

———. 2017a. *Energy, Climate Change and the Environment. The Global Energy Challenge.* Paris: IEA.

———. 2017b. "Real-World Policy Packages for Sustainable Energy Transitions: Shaping Energy Transition Policies to Fit National Objectives and Constraints." Insights Series 2017. IEA, Paris.

———. 2019. *World Energy Investment 2019.* Paris: IEA.

IEA (International Energy Agency) and IRENA (International Renewable Energy Agency). 2017. "Perspectives for the Energy Transition: Investment Needs for a Low-Carbon Energy System." Organisation for Economic Co-operation and Development, IEA, and IRENA. http://www.irena.org/DocumentDownloads/Publications/Perspectives_for_the_Energy _Transition_2017.pdf.

Imai, K., and I. S. Kim. 2019. "When Should We Use Unit Fixed Effects Regression Models for Causal Inference with Longitudinal Data?" *American Journal of Political Science* 63 (2): 467–90. doi.org/10.1111/ajps.12417.

IPCC (Intergovernmental Panel on Climate Change). 2018. "Summary for Policymakers." In *Global Warming of 1.5°C.* Geneva: IPCC.

Jaffe, R. N., and B. Adam. 1994. "The Energy Paradox and the Diffusion of Conservation Technology." *Resource and Energy Economics* 16 (2): 91–122. http://linkinghub.elsevier.com /retrieve/pii/0928765594900019.

Jakob, M., J. C. Steckel, S. Klasen, J. Lay, N. Grunewald, I. Martínez-Zarzoso, S. Renner, and O. Edenhofer. 2014. "Feasible Mitigation Actions in Developing Countries." *Nature Climate Change* 4 (11): 961–68. doi.org/10.1038/nclimate2370.

Kabir, E., P. Kumar, S. Kumar, A. A. Adelodun, and K. H. Kim. 2018. "Solar Energy: Potential and Future Prospects." *Renewable and Sustainable Energy Reviews* 82 (September): 894–900. doi.org/10.1016/j.rser.2017.09.094.

Kemp, R., and S. Pontoglio. 2011. "The Innovation Effects of Environmental Policy Instruments: A Typical Case of the Blind Men and the Elephant?" *Ecological Economics* 72 (December): 28–36. doi.org/10.1016/j.ecolecon.2011.09.014.

Kern, F., and M. Howlett. 2009. "Implementing Transition Management as Policy Reforms: A Case Study of the Dutch Energy Sector." *Policy Sciences* 42 (4): 391–408. doi.org/10.1007/s11077-009-9099-x.

Kern, F., P. Kivimaa, and M. Martiskainen. 2017. "Policy Packaging or Policy Patching? The Development of Complex Energy Efficiency Policy Mixes." *Energy Research and Social Science* 23 (January): 11–25. doi.org/10.1016/j.erss.2016.11.002.

Krupnick, A., D. Burtraw, and A. Markandya. 2000. "The Ancillary Benefits and Costs of Climate Change Mitigation: A Conceptual Framework." In *Ancillary Benefits and Costs of Greenhouse Gas Mitigation*, 53–94. Paris: OECD Publishing.

Krupnick, A. J., I. W. H. Parry, M. Walls, T. Knowles, and K. Hayes. 2010. *Toward a New National Energy Policy: Assessing the Options*. Washington, DC: Resources for the Future.

Landrigan, P. J., R. Fuller, N. J. R. Acosta, O. Adeyi, R. Arnold, N. Basu, A. B. Baldé, R. Bertollini, S. Bose-O'Reilly, J. I. Boufford, P. N. Breysse, T. Chiles, C. Mahidol, A. M. Coll-Seck, M. L. Cropper, J. Fobil, V. Fuster, M. Greenstone, A. Haines, D. Hanrahan, D. Hunter, M. Khare, A. Krupnick, B. Lanphear, B. Lohani, K. Martin, K. V. Mathiasen, M. A. McTeer, C. J. L. Murray, J. D. Ndahimananjara, F. Perera, J. Potocnik, A. S. Preker, J. Ramesh, J. Rockström, C. Salinas, L. D. Samson, K. Sandilya, P. D. Sly, K. R. Smith, A. Steiner, R. B. Stewart, W. A. Suk, O. C. P. van Schayck, G. N. Yadama, K. Yunkella, and M. Zhong. 2017. "The Lancet Commission on Pollution and Health." *The Lancet* 391 (10119): P462–512. doi.org/10.1016/S0140-6736(17)32345-0.

Lange, G., Q. Wodon, and K. Carey. 2018. *The Changing Wealth of Nations 2018: Building a Sustainable Future*. Washington, DC: World Bank. doi.org/10.1596/978-1-4648-1046-6.

Lee, M. K., H. Park, J. Noh, and J. P. Painuly. 2003. "Promoting Energy Efficiency Financing and ESCOs in Developing Countries: Experiences from Korean ESCO Business." *Journal of Cleaner Production* 11 (6): 651–57. doi.org/10.1016/S0959-6526(02)00110-5.

Liu, H., and X. Liang. 2011. "Strategy for Promoting Low-Carbon Technology Transfer to Developing Countries: The Case of CCS." *Energy Policy* 39 (6): 3106–16. doi.org/10.1016/j.enpol.2011.02.051.

Loayza, N. V. 2018. "Informality: Why Is It So Widespread and How Can It Be Reduced?" Research & Policy Briefs 20, World Bank, Washington, DC.

Mathys, N. A., and J. de Melo. 2011. "Political Economy Aspects of Climate Change Mitigation Efforts." *World Economy* 34 (11): 1938–54. doi.org/10.1111/j.1467-9701.2011.01417.x.

Mazzucato, M. 2015. *The Entrepreneurial State: Debunking Public vs. Private Sector Myths*. New York: Public Affairs.

———. 2016. "The Green Entrepreneurial State." *SSRN Research Journal* 92: 134–52.

Mazzucato, M., and G. Semieniuk. 2016. "Financing Renewable Energy: Who is Financing What and Why It Matters." SPRU Working Paper Series 2016-12, Social Policy Research Unit, University of Sussex, U.K.

McKinsey Global Institute. 2018. "Outperformers: High-Growth Emerging Economies and the Companies that Propel Them." McKinsey & Company, September.

Mealy, P., and A. Teytelboym. 2018. "Economic Complexity and the Green Economy." INET Oxford Working Paper 2018-03, Institute for New Economic Thinking at the Oxford Martin School, University of Oxford, Oxford.

Morton, C., C. Wilson, and J. Anable. 2018. "The Diffusion of Domestic Energy Efficiency Policies: A Spatial Perspective." *Energy Policy* 114 (April): 77–88. doi.org/10.1016/j.enpol.2017.11.057.

Mummolo, J., and E. Peterson. 2018. "Improving the Interpretation of Fixed Effects Regression Results." *Political Science Research and Methods* 6 (4): 829–35.

Oates, W. E., and P. R. Portney. 2003. "The Political Economy of Environmental Policy." In *Handbook of Environmental Economics*, Volume 1, edited by K.-G. Maler and J. R. Vincent, 325–54. Amsterdam: Elsevier Science B.V.

OECD (Organisation for Economic Co-operation and Development). 2000. *Ancillary Benefits and Costs of Greenhouse Gas Mitigation*. Paris: OECD Publishing.

Parry, I., D. Heine, E. Lis, and S. Li. 2014. *Getting Energy Prices Right: From Principle to Practice*. Washington, DC: International Monetary Fund.

Parry, I. W. H., M. Walls, and W. Harrington. 2007. "Automobile Externalities and Policies." *Journal of Economic Literature* 45 (2): 373–99.

Pfeiffer, B., and P. Mulder. 2013. "Explaining the Diffusion of Renewable Energy Technology in Developing Countries." *Energy Economics* 40 (November): 285–96. https://doi.org/10.1016/j.eneco.2013.07.005.

Rai, V., K. Schultz, and E. Funkhouser. 2014. "International Low Carbon Technology Transfer: Do Intellectual Property Regimes Matter?" *Global Environmental Change* 24 (1): 60–74. doi.org/10.1016/j.gloenvcha.2013.10.004.

Rizzi, L., C. De La Maza, L. Cifuentes, and J. Gómez. 2014. "Valuing Air Quality Impacts Using Stated Choice Analysis: Trading Off Visibility Against Morbidity Effects." *Journal of Environmental Management* 146 (December): 470–80. doi.org/10.1016/J.JENVMAN.2014.08.009.

Rockström, J., O. Gaffney, J. Rogelj, M. Meinshausen, N. Nakicenovic, and H. J. Schellnhuber. 2017. "A Roadmap for Rapid Decarbonization." *Science* 355 (6331): 1269–71. doi.org/10.1126/science.aah3443.

Rodrik, D. 2004. "Industrial Policy for the Twenty-First Century." John F. Kennedy School of Government, Harvard University, Cambridge, MA.

———. 2008. "Normalizing Industrial Policy." Commission on Growth and Development Working Paper 3, World Bank, Washington, DC.

Rogge, K. S., and K. Reichardt. 2016. "Policy Mixes for Sustainability Transitions: An Extended Concept and Framework for Analysis." *Research Policy* 45 (8): 1620–35. https://doi.org/10.1016/j.respol.2016.04.004.

Rudnick, H., and C. Velasquez. 2019a. "Learning from Developing Country Power Market Experiences: The Case of Peru." Policy Research Working Paper 8772, World Bank, Washington, DC.

———. 2019b. "Learning from Developing Country Power Market Experiences: The Case of the Philippines." Policy Research Working Paper 8721, World Bank, Washington, DC.

Santos, G. 2017. "Road Transport and CO_2 Emissions: What Are the Challenges?" *Transport Policy* 59 (July): 71–74. doi.org/10.1016/j.tranpol.2017.06.007.

Santos, G., H. Behrendt, L. Maconi, T. Shirvani, and A. Teytelboym. 2010. "Part I: Externalities and Economic Policies in Road Transport." *Research in Transportation Economics* 28(1): 2–45. doi.org/10.1016/j.retrec.2009.11.002.

Sarkar, A., and S. Moin. 2018. "Transforming Energy Efficiency Markets in Developing Countries: The Emerging Possibilities of Super ESCOs." Live Wire 2018/92, World Bank, Washington, DC.

Schmidt, T. S., B. Battke, D. Grosspietsch, and V. H. Hoffmann. 2016. "Do Deployment Policies Pick Technologies by (Not) Picking Applications?—A Simulation of Investment Decisions in Technologies with Multiple Applications." *Research Policy* 45 (10): 1965–83. doi.org/10.1016/J.RESPOL.2016.07.001.

Schmidt, T. S., and S. Sewerin. 2018. "Measuring the Temporal Dynamics of Policy Mixes – An Empirical Analysis of Renewable Energy Policy Mixes' Balance and Design Features in Nine Countries." *Research Policy*, March 30. doi.org/10.1016/j.respol.2018.03.012.

Sovacool, B. K. 2016. "How Long Will It Take? Conceptualizing the Temporal Dynamics of Energy Transitions." *Energy Research and Social Science* 13 (March): 202–15. doi.org/10.1016/j.erss.2015.12.020.

Stern, N. H. 2016. "The Stern Review +10: New Opportunities for Growth and Development." Speech given at The Royal Society, October 28. http://www.lse.ac.uk/GranthamInstitute/news/the-stern-review-10-new-opportunities-for-growth-and-development/.

Stiglitz, J. E. 2010. "Development-Oriented Tax Policy." Chapter 1 in *Taxation in Developing Countries: Six Case Studies and Policy Implications*, edited by R. H. Gordon, 11–36. New York: Columbia University Press.

———. 2018. "Industrial Policies and Development Cooperation for a Learning Society." *Asia-Pacific Review* 25 (2): 4–15. doi.org/10.1080/13439006.2018.1548816.

Teza, G., M. Caraglio, and A. L. Stella. 2018. "Growth Dynamics and Complexity of National Economies in the Global Trade Network." *Scientific Reports* 8 (1): 1–8. doi.org/10.1038/s41598-018-33659-6.

UNDP (United Nations Development Programme). 2017. "Lebanon: Derisking Renewable Energy Investment." UNDP, New York.

———. 2018. "Tunisia: Derisking Renewable Energy Investment." UNDP, New York.

UNEP (United Nations Environment Programme). 2017. *The Emissions Gap Report 2017: A UN Environment Synthesis Report.* Nairobi: UNEP.

UNFCCC (United Nations Framework Convention on Climate Change). 2016. *Report on the Workshop on Financing and Use of the Clean Development Mechanism by International Climate Finance Institutions.* Retrieved from https://unfccc.int/sites/default/files /resource/20062016_workshop%20report_final.pdf.

Unruh, G. C. 2002. "Escaping Carbon Lock-In." *Energy Policy* 30 (4): 317–25. doi.org/10.1016 /S0301-4215(01)00098-2.

Vandyck, T., K. Keramidas, A. Kitous, J. V. Spadaro, R. Van Dingenen, M. Holland, and B. Saveyn. 2018. "Air Quality Co-benefits for Human Health and Agriculture Counterbalance Costs to Meet Paris Agreement Pledges." *Nature Communications* 9 (1): 4939. doi.org/10.1038/s41467 -018-06885-9.

Vogt-Schilb, A., G. Meunier, and S. Hallegatte. 2018. "When Starting with the Most Expensive Option Makes Sense: Optimal Timing, Cost and Sectoral Allocation of Abatement Investment." *Journal of Environmental Economics and Management* 88 (March): 210–33. doi.org/10.1016/j .jeem.2017.12.001.

Waissbein, O., Y. Glemarec, H. Bayraktar, and T. Schmidt. 2013. *Derisking Renewable Energy Investment: A Framework to Support Policymakers in Selecting Public Instruments to Promote Renewable Energy Investment in Developing Countries.* New York: United Nations Development Programme.

West, J. J., S. J. Smith, R. A. Silva, V. Naik, Y. Zhang, Z. Adelman, M. M. Fry, S. Anenberg, L. W. Horowitz, and J.-F. Lamarque. 2013. "Co-benefits of Mitigating Global Greenhouse Gas Emissions for Future Air Quality and Human Health." *Nature Climate Change* 3 (September): 885–89. doi.org/10.1038/nclimate2009.

Wilson, C., A. Grubler, K. S. Gallagher, and G. F. Nemet. 2012. "Marginalization of End-Use Technologies in Energy Innovation for Climate Protection." *Nature Climate Change* 2 (11): 780–88. doi.org/10.1038/nclimate1576.

Winsberg, J., T. Hagemann, T. Janoschka, M. D. Hager, and U. S. Schubert. 2017. "Redox-Flow Batteries: From Metals to Organic Redox-Active Materials." *Angewandte Chemie: International Edition* 56 (3): 686–711. doi.org/10.1002/anie.201604925.

World Bank. 2018. *Managing Coal Mine Closure: Achieving a Just Transition for All Achieving a Just Transition for All.* Washington, DC: World Bank. https://openknowledge.worldbank .org/handle/10986/31020.

——— 2019. *State and Trends of Carbon Pricing 2019.* Washington, DC: World Bank. doi .org/10.1596/978-1-4648-1435-8.

Yülek, M. A. 2018. *How Nations Succeed: Manufacturing, Trade, Industrial Policy, and Economic Development.* Singapore: Palgrave Macmillen.

Key Legal Provisions Related to Low-Carbon Technology Transfer

TABLE A.1 **Key legal provisions related to LCT transfer**

SOURCE	STATEMENT OF PARTY COMMITMENTS
United Nations Framework Convention on Climate Change (UNFCCC) Article 4.1(c)	"Promote and cooperate in the development, application and diffusion, including transfer, of technologies, practices and processes that control, reduce or prevent anthropogenic emissions of greenhouse gases not controlled by the Montreal Protocol in all relevant sectors, including the energy, transport, industry, agriculture, forestry and waste management sectors." (United Nations 1992)
UNFCCC Article 4.1(h)	"Promote and cooperate in the full, open and prompt exchange of relevant scientific, technological, technical, socio-economic and legal information related to the climate system and climate change, and to the economic and social consequences of various response strategies." (United Nations 1992)
UNFCCC Article 4.3	"The developed country Parties and other developed Parties included in Annex II shall provide new and additional financial resources to meet the agreed full costs incurred by developing country Parties in complying with their obligations under Article 12, paragraph 1 […] including for the transfer of technology, needed by the developing country Parties to meet the agreed full incremental costs of implementing measures that are covered by paragraph 1 of this Article and that are agreed between a developing country Party and the international entity or entities referred to in Article 11, in accordance with that Article. The implementation of these commitments shall take into account the need for adequacy and predictability in the flow of funds and the importance of appropriate burden sharing among the developed country Parties." (United Nations 1992)
UNFCCC Article 4.5	"The developed country Parties and other developed Parties included in Annex II shall take all practicable steps to promote, facilitate and finance, as appropriate, the transfer of, or access to, environmentally sound technologies and know-how to other Parties, particularly developing country Parties, to enable them to implement the provisions of the Convention. In this process, the developed country Parties shall support the development and enhancement of endogenous capacities and technologies of developing country Parties. Other Parties and organizations in a position to do so may also assist in facilitating the transfer of such technologies." (United Nations 1992)
UNFCCC Article 4.7	Article 4.7: "The extent to which developing country Parties will effectively implement their commitments under the Convention will depend on the effective implementation by developed country Parties of their commitments under the Convention related to financial resources and transfer of technology and will take fully into account that economic and social development and poverty eradication are the first and overriding priorities of the developing country Parties." (United Nations 1992)
Paris Agreement Articles 10.1 and 10.2	"Parties share a long-term vision on the importance of fully realizing technology development and transfer in order to improve resilience to climate change and to reduce greenhouse gas emissions. Parties, noting the importance of technology for the implementation of mitigation and adaptation actions under this Agreement and recognizing existing technology deployment and dissemination efforts, shall strengthen cooperative action on technology development and transfer." (United Nations 1995)

continued

TABLE A.1, *continued*

SOURCE	STATEMENT OF PARTY COMMITMENTS
Paris Agreement Article 10.6	"Support, including financial support, shall be provided to developing country Parties for the implementation of this Article, including for strengthening cooperative action on technology development and transfer at different stages of the technology cycle, with a view to achieving a balance between support for mitigation and adaptation." (United Nations 1995)
Paris Agreement Article 13.10	"Developing country Parties should provide information on financial, technology transfer and capacity-building support needed and received under Articles 9, 10 and 11." (United Nations 1995)

REFERENCES

United Nations. 1992. "United Nations Framework Convention on Climate Change." United Nations, New York. https://unfccc.int/resource/docs/convkp/conveng.pdf.

——. 2015. "Paris Agreement." United Nations, New York. https://unfccc.int/sites/default /files/english_paris_agreement.pdf.

APPENDIX B

Full List of Low-Carbon Technology Products

TABLE B.1 **Full list of LCT products, by HS classification and broad economic category**

HS CODE	PRODUCT DESCRIPTION	BROAD ECONOMIC CATEGORY
252390	Hydraulic cements (e.g., slag cement, super sulphate cement), whether/not colored/in the form of clinkers (excl. cement clinkers, Portland cement & aluminous cement)	Processed
392010	Plates, sheets, film, foil & strip, of polymers of ethylene, non-cellular & not reinforced, laminated, supported/similarly combined with other materials (excl. self-adhesive)	Processed
441872	Assembled flooring panels, multilayer	Processed
560314	Nonwovens, whether/not impregnated/coated/covered/laminated, of man-made filaments, weighing >150 g/m2	Processed
680610	Slag wool, rock wool & similar mineral wools (incl. intermixtures thereof), in bulk/sheets/rolls	Processed
680690	Mixtures & articles of heat-insulating/sound-insulating/sound-absorbing mineral materials (excl. of 68.11/68.12/Ch.69)	Processed
700800	Multiple-walled insulating units of glass	Processed
701931	Mats of glass fibers	Processed
701939	Webs, mattresses, boards & similar nonwoven products of glass fibers	Processed
730820	Towers & lattice masts of iron/steel	Processed
730900	Reservoirs, tanks, vats & similar containers for any material other than compressed/liquefied gas, of iron/steel, of a capacity >300 l, whether/not lined/heat-insulated but not fitted with mechanical/thermal equip.	Capital goods (except for transport equipment)
732111	Cooking appliances & plate warmers, for gas fuel/for both gas & other fuels	Durable
732190	Parts of the non-electric domestic appliances of 7321.11-7321.83, of iron/steel	Processed
732490	Sanitary ware & parts thereof, of iron/steel (excl. of 7324.10-7324.29)	Processed
761100	Aluminum reservoirs, tanks, vats & similar containers, for any material (other than compressed/liquefied gas), of a capacity >300 l, whether/not lined/heat-insulated but not fitted with mechanical/thermal equip.	Capital goods (except for transport equipment)
761290	Aluminum casks, drums, cans, boxes & similar containers, incl. rigid tubular containers but excl. collapsible tubular containers, for any material (other than compressed/liquefied gas), of a capacity not >300 l, whether/not line/heat-insulated, but not fitted	Capital goods (except for transport equipment)
840110	Nuclear reactors	Capital goods (except for transport equipment)
840120	Machinery & apparatus for isotopic separation, & parts thereof	Capital goods (except for transport equipment)
840140	Parts of nuclear reactors	Parts and accessories
840219	Vapor generating boilers, incl. hybrid boilers (excl. of 8402.11 & 8402.12; excl. central heating hot water boilers capable also of producing low pressure steam)	Capital goods (except for transport equipment)
840290	Parts of the boilers of 8402.11-8402.20	Parts and accessories

continued

TABLE B.1, *continued*

HS CODE	PRODUCT DESCRIPTION	BROAD ECONOMIC CATEGORY
840410	Auxiliary plant for use with boilers of 84.02/84.03 (e.g., economisers, super-heaters, soot removers, gas recoverers)	Capital goods (except for transport equipment)
840420	Condensers for steam/other vapor power units	Capital goods (except for transport equipment)
840490	Parts of the auxiliary plant of 8404.10 & 8404.20	Parts and accessories
840510	Producer gas/water gas generators, with/without their purifiers; acetylene gas generators & similar water process gas generators, with/without their purifiers	Capital goods (except for transport equipment)
840681	Steam turbines & other vapor turbines (excl. for marine propulsion), of an output >40MW	Capital goods (except for transport equipment)
840690	Parts of the steam turbines & other vapor turbines of 8406.10-8406.82	Parts and accessories
841011	Hydraulic turbines & water wheels, of a power not >1000kW	Capital goods (except for transport equipment)
841012	Hydraulic turbines & water wheels, of a power >1000kW but not >10000kW	Capital goods (except for transport equipment)
841013	Hydraulic turbines & water wheels, of a power >10000kW	Capital goods (except for transport equipment)
841090	Parts (incl. regulators) of the hydraulic turbines & water wheels of 8410.11-8410.13	Parts and accessories
841181	Gas turbines other than turbo-jets/turbo-propellers, of a power not >5000kW	Parts and accessories
841182	Gas turbines other than turbo-jets/turbo-propellers, of a power >5000kW	Parts and accessories
841199	Parts of the other gas turbines of 8411.81 & 8411.82	Parts and accessories
841290	Parts of the engines & motors of 8412.10-8412.80	Parts and accessories
841581	Air-conditioning machines incorporating a refrigerating unit & a valve for reversal of the cooling/heat cycle (reversible heat pumps)	Capital goods (except for transport equipment)
841780	Industrial/laboratory furnaces & ovens (excl. of 8147.10 & 8417.20), incl. incinerators, non-electric	Capital goods (except for transport equipment)
841790	Parts of the industrial/laboratory furnaces & ovens of 8417.10-8417.80	Parts and accessories
841861	Compression-type refrigerating/freezing equip. whose condensers are heat exchangers	Capital goods (except for transport equipment)
841869	Refrigerating/freezing equip. n.e.s. in 84.18; heat pumps	Capital goods (except for transport equipment)
841919	Instantaneous/storage water heaters, non-electric (excl. of 8419.11)	Capital goods (except for transport equipment)
841939	Dryers for use as machinery/plant/laboratory equip., whether/not electrically heated (excl. of 8419.31, 8419.32, 84.36-84.38 & 84.51)	Capital goods (except for transport equipment)
841940	Distilling/rectifying plant, whether/not electrically heated	Capital goods (except for transport equipment)
841950	Heat exchange units, whether/not electrically heated	Capital goods (except for transport equipment)
841960	Machinery for liquefying air/other gases, whether/not electrically heated	Capital goods (except for transport equipment)
841989	Machinery, plant & equip., n.e.s. in Ch.84, other than for making hot drinks/for cooking/heating food, whether/not electrically heated	Capital goods (except for transport equipment)
841990	Parts of machinery, plant/laboratory equipment, whether/not electrically heated (excl. furnaces, ovens & other equipment of heading 85.14), for the treatment of materials by a process involving a change of temperature such as heating, cooking, roasting	Parts and accessories
842121	Filtering/purifying machinery & apparatus for filtering/purifying water	Capital goods (except for transport equipment)

continued

TABLE B.1, *continued*

HS CODE	PRODUCT DESCRIPTION	BROAD ECONOMIC CATEGORY
842129	Filtering/purifying machinery & apparatus for liquids (excl. of 8421.21-8421.23)	Capital goods (except for transport equipment)
842139	Filtering/purifying machinery & apparatus for gases, other than intake air filters for internal combustion engines	Capital goods (except for transport equipment)
842199	Parts of the filtering/purifying machinery & apparatus of 84.21 (excl. of centrifuges, incl. centrifugal dryers)	Parts and accessories
847420	Crushing/grinding machines for earth/stone/ores/other mineral substance, in solid (incl. powder/paste) form	Capital goods (except for transport equipment)
847982	Mixing/kneading/crushing/grinding/screening/sifting/homogenising/emulsifying/stirring machines, n.e.s. in Ch.84	Capital goods (except for transport equipment)
847989	Other machines & mechanical appliances, other than Machines & mechanical appliances for treating metal, incl. electric wire coil-winders/Mixing/kneading/crushing/grinding/screening/sifting/homogenising/emulsifying/stirring machines	Capital goods (except for transport equipment)
847990	Parts of Machines & mechanical appliances having individual functions, not specified/incld. elsewhere in this Ch.	Parts and accessories
848340	Gears & gearing (excl. toothed wheels, chain sprockets & other transmission elements presented sep.); ball/roller screws; gear boxes & other speed changers, incl. torque converters	Parts and accessories
848360	Clutches & shaft couplings (incl. universal joints)	Parts and accessories
850161	AC generators (alternators), of an output not >75kVA	Capital goods (except for transport equipment)
850162	AC generators (alternators), of an output >75kVA but not >375kVA	Capital goods (except for transport equipment)
850163	AC generators (alternators), of an output >375kVA but not >750kVA	Capital goods (except for transport equipment)
850164	AC generators (alternators), of an output >750kVA	Capital goods (except for transport equipment)
850231	Wind-powered electric generating sets	Capital goods (except for transport equipment)
850239	Electric generating sets n.e.s. in 85.02	Capital goods (except for transport equipment)
850300	Parts suit. for use solely/principally with the machines of 85.01/85.02	Parts and accessories
850490	Parts of the machines of 85.04	Parts and accessories
850680	Primary cells & primary batteries n.e.s. in 85.06	Non-durable
850710	Electric accumulators, incl. separators therefor, whether/not rectangular (incl. square), lead-acid, of a kind used for starting piston engines	Parts and accessories
850720	Electric accumulators, incl. separators therefor, whether/not rectangular (incl. square), lead-acid (excl. of 8507.10)	Parts and accessories
850730	Electric accumulators, incl. separators therefor, whether/not rectangular (incl. square), nickel-cadmium	Parts and accessories
850740	Electric accumulators, incl. separators therefor, whether/not rectangular (incl. square), nickel-iron	Parts and accessories
850780	Electric accumulators, incl. separators therefor, whether/not rectangular (incl. square), n.e.s. in 85.07	Parts and accessories
850790	Parts of the electric accumulators & separators therefor of 85.07	Processed
851410	Resistance heated furnaces & ovens	Capital goods (except for transport equipment)
851420	Furnaces & ovens functioning by induction/dielectric loss	Capital goods (except for transport equipment)

continued

TABLE B.1, *continued*

HS CODE	PRODUCT DESCRIPTION	BROAD ECONOMIC CATEGORY
851430	Other furnaces & ovens other than resistance heated furnaces & ovens/ furnaces & ovens functioning by induction/dielectric loss	Capital goods (except for transport equipment)
851490	Parts of Industrial/laboratory electric furnaces & ovens (incl. those functioning by induction/dielectric loss); other industrial/laboratory equipment for the heat treatment of materials by induction/dielectric loss	Parts and accessories
853120	Indicator panels incorporating liquid crystal devices (chemically defined)/light emitting diodes (LED)	Capital goods (except for transport equipment)
853224	Fixed electrical capacitors, other than those of 8532.10, ceramic dielectric, multilayer	Capital goods (except for transport equipment)
853710	Boards, panels, consoles, desks, cabinets & other bases, equipped with 2/more apparatus of 85.35/85.36, for electric control/distribution of electricity, incld. Those incorporating instruments/apparatus of Ch. 90 & numerical control apparatus	Parts and accessories
853931	Electric discharge lamps (excl. ultra-violet lamps), fluorescent, hot cathode	Processed
854140	Photosensitive semiconductor devices, incl. photovoltaic cells whether/not assembled in modules/made up into panels; light emitting diodes	Parts and accessories
854390	Parts of electrical machines & apparatus, having individual functions, not specified/incld. elsewhere in this Ch.	Parts and accessories
860120	Rail locomotives powered by electric accumulators	Industrial
870390	Vehicles principally designed for the transport of persons (excl. of 87.02 & 8703.10-8703.24), with C-I internal combustion piston engine (diesel/semi-diesel), n.e.s. in 87.03	Passenger motor cars
900190	Lenses (excl. of 9001.30-9001.50), prisms, mirrors & other optical elements, of any material, unmounted, other than such elements of glass not optically worked	Processed
900290	Lenses, prisms, mirrors & other optical elements, of any material, mounted, being parts of/fittings for instr./apparatus (excl. such elements of glass not optically worked), n.e.s. in 90.02	Processed
901380	Liquid crystal devices not constituting articles provided for more specifically in other headings; other optical appliances & instr., n.e.s. in Ch.90	Capital goods (except for transport equipment)
901390	Parts & accessories of the articles of 90.13	Parts and accessories
901580	Surveying/hydrographic/oceanographic/hydrological/meteorological/geophysical instr. & appliances (excl. compasses), n.e.s. in 90.15	Capital goods (except for transport equipment)
902610	Instruments & apparatus for measuring/checking the flow/level of liquids	Capital goods (except for transport equipment)
902620	Instruments & apparatus for measuring/checking pressure	Capital goods (except for transport equipment)
902680	Instruments & apparatus for measuring/checking the flow/level/pressure/other variables of liquids/gases (e.g., flow meters, level gauges, manometers, heat meter), exclude instru/apparatus of heading 90.14 & 90.15, 90.28	Capital goods (except for transport equipment)
902690	Parts & accessories of the instr. & appliances of 90.26	Parts and accessories
902710	Gas/smoke analysis apparatus	Capital goods (except for transport equipment)
902720	Chromatographs & electrophoresis instr.	Capital goods (except for transport equipment)
902730	Spectrometers, spectrophotometers & spectrographs using optical radiations (UV, visible, IR)	Capital goods (except for transport equipment)
902750	Instruments & apparatus for physical/chemical analysis, using optical radiations (UV, visible, IR), n.e.s. in 90.27	Capital goods (except for transport equipment)

continued

TABLE B.1, *continued*

HS CODE	PRODUCT DESCRIPTION	BROAD ECONOMIC CATEGORY
902780	Instruments & apparatus for physical/chemical analysis, n.e.s. in 90.27	Capital goods (except for transport equipment)
902790	Microtomes; parts & accessories of instr. & apparatus of 90.27	Capital goods (except for transport equipment)
903149	Other optical instruments & appliances, other than 9031.41	Capital goods (except for transport equipment)
903180	Measuring/checking instr., apparatus& machines, n.e.s. in Ch. 90	Capital goods (except for transport equipment)
903190	Parts & accessories of the instr., apparatus & machines of 90.31	Parts and accessories
903210	Thermostats	Capital goods (except for transport equipment)
903220	Manostats	Capital goods (except for transport equipment)
903289	Automatic regulating/controlling instr. & apparatus, n.e.s. in 90.32	Capital goods (except for transport equipment)
903290	Parts & accessories of the instr. & apparatus of 90.32	Parts and accessories
903300	Parts & accessories n.e.s. in Ch.90. for machines/appliances/instr./apparatus of Ch.90	Parts and accessories

Source: United Nations International Trade Statistics Knowledgebase, https://unstats.un.org/unsd/tradekb/Knowledgebase/50018/Harmonized-Commodity-Description-and-Coding-Systems-HS.
Note: AC = alternating current; HS = Harmonized Commodity Description and Coding Systems; IR = infrared; kVA = kilovolt-ampere; kW = kilowatt; l = liter; n.e.s. = not elsewhere specified; UV = ultraviolet.

TABLE B.2 **Products, by 6-digit HS, appearing on multiple select lists**

LIST	NUMBER OF SHARED PRODUCT CODES	DESCRIPTION OF PRODUCTS
WBG43 and APEC54	6	**840290** - Boilers; parts of steam or other vapor generating boilers;
		840490 - Boilers; parts of auxiliary plant, for use with boilers of heading no. 8402 and 8403 and parts of condensers for steam or other vapor power units;
		841182 - Turbines; gas-turbines (excluding turbo-jets and turbo-propellers), of a power exceeding 5000kW;
		841989 - Machinery, plant and laboratory equipment; for treating materials by change of temperature, other than for making hot drinks or cooking or heating food;
		841990 - Machinery, plant and laboratory equipment; parts of equipment for treating materials by a process involving a change of temperature;
		850164 - Electric generators; AC generators, (alternators), of an output exceeding 750kVA
WBG43 and GDD30	6	**841011** - Turbines; hydraulic turbines and water wheels, of a power not exceeding 1000kW;
		841090 - Turbines; parts of hydraulic turbines and water wheels, including regulators;
		841861- Heat pumps; other than air conditioning machines of heading no. 8415;
		841950 - Heat exchange units; not used for domestic purposes;
		850720 - Electric accumulators; lead-acid, (other than for starting piston engines), including separators, whether or not rectangular (including square);
		903210 - Regulating or controlling instruments and apparatus; automatic type, thermostats;
APEC54 and GDD30	0	n.a.

continued

TABLE B.2, *continued*

LIST	NUMBER OF SHARED PRODUCT CODES	DESCRIPTION OF PRODUCTS
APEC54, GDD30, and WBG43	4	**840410** - Boilers; auxiliary plant, for use with boilers of heading no. 8402 or 8403 (e.g. economisers, super-heaters, soot removers, gas recovers);
		841919 - Heaters; instantaneous or storage water heaters, non-electric, other than instantaneous gas water heaters;
		850231 - Electric generating sets; wind-powered, (excluding those with spark-ignition or compression-ignition internal combustion piston engines);
		851140 - Ignition or starting equipment; starter motors and dual-purpose starter-generators, of a kind used for spark or compression-ignition internal combustion engines;

Sources: Calculations based on Asia-Pacific Economic Cooperation List of Environmental Goods; Glachant et al. 2013; UN Comtrade; World Bank 2008.
Note: APEC54 = Asia-Pacific Economic Cooperation List of [54] Environmental Goods; GDD30 = Glachant, Dussaux, and Dechezleprêtre List of [30] Climate Change-Related Technologies; HS = Harmonized Commodity Description and Coding Systems; WBG43 = World Bank Group [43] Climate-Friendly and Clean-Energy Technologies List; n.a. = not applicable.

TABLE B.3 **Number of economies in each income group classification, select years**

	1992	1997	2002	2007	2012	2017
High income	39	50	56	65	76	81
Upper-middle income	37	35	33	40	55	56
Lower-middle income	70	58	53	54	48	47
Low income	55	61	64	49	36	34
Unclassified[a]	17	14	12	10	3	0

a. For a full list of unclassified countries by year, see https://datahelpdesk.worldbank.org/knowledgebase/articles/906519-world-bank-country-and-lending-groups.

TABLE B.4 **China's role in LCT exports, by income group classification**

	1992	1997	2002	2007	2012	2016
China's income classification	LIC	LMIC	LMIC	LMIC	UMIC	UMIC
Total exports, China (US$, billions)	0.8	2.6	7.5	55.9	115.5	117.6
Total exports, income group (US$, billions)	1.1	4.1	12.8	61.5	169.2	175.9
China's share of total exports, by value (%)	**68.5**	**65.1**	**58.4**	**90.8**	**68.2**	**66.8**

Source: World Bank World Integrated Trade Solution (database), https://wits.worldbank.org.
Note: LIC = low income; LMIC = lower-middle income; UMIC = upper-middle income.

TABLE B.5 **Top-five economies, by share of LCT imports, by income group, 1992, 2002, and 2016**

1992		2002		2016	
IMPORTER	SHARE (%)	IMPORTER	SHARE (%)	IMPORTER	SHARE (%)
Top-five importers among high-income economies, by share					
United States	23.8	United States	22.5	United States	21.3
Germany	22.4	Germany	11.9	Germany	11.1
Netherlands	8.5	United Kingdom	7.2	Hong Kong SAR, China	5.3
Canada	8.4	Canada	6.2	Japan	5.2
Japan	8.1	Japan	6.1	Korea, Rep.	5.1
Top-five importers among upper-middle-income economies, by share					
Korea, Rep.	35.9	Mexico	39.9	China	51.2
Mexico	18.9	Malaysia	17.4	Mexico	11.5
Malaysia	13.6	Czech Republic	8.3	Russian Federation	6.4
Saudi Arabia	8.0	Poland	8.1	Turkey	5.9
Portugal	5.8	Hungary	7.9	Thailand	4.7
Top-five importers among lower-middle-income economies, by share					
Thailand	40.5	China	59.6	India	29.4
Turkey	19.2	Brazil	9.0	Vietnam	20.8
Algeria	10.4	Thailand	7.4	Indonesia	13.1
Chile	9.1	Turkey	6.2	Pakistan	7.7
Colombia	5.1	Russian Federation	5.2	Nigeria	4.6
Top-five importers among low-income economies, by share					
China	57.8	Bangladesh	41.0	Ethiopia	31.8
Indonesia	30.1	Papua New Guinea	16.2	Tanzania	11.5
India	8.7	Nicaragua	11.2	Nepal	9.0
Bangladesh	1.9	Kenya	8.9	Mozambique	7.9
Sri Lanka	0.8	Zambia	8.3	Uganda	5.7

Source: World Bank World Integrated Trade Solution (database), https://wits.worldbank.org.

TABLE B.6 Top-five economies, by share of LCT exports and income group, 1992, 2002, and 2016

1992		2002		2016	
EXPORTER	SHARE (%)	EXPORTER	SHARE (%)	EXPORTER	SHARE (%)
Top-five exporters to high-income economies, by share of LCT exports					
Germany	25.2	United States	16.9	China	17.2
United States	22.7	Germany	14.5	Germany	14.0
Japan	18.9	Japan	13.3	United States	10.5
Switzerland	5.8	United Kingdom	6.3	Japan	6.1
Netherlands	4.6	France	5.0	Mexico	4.0
Top-five exporters to upper-middle-income economies, by share of LCT exports					
United States	40.2	United States	34.0	United States	13.9
Japan	28.6	Germany	15.4	Korea, Rep.	13.5
Germany	13.3	Japan	9.5	Germany	10.8
Singapore	3.8	Italy	7.4	China	10.7
Switzerland	2.6	Singapore	4.3	Japan	10.4
Top-five exporters to lower-middle-income economies, by share of LCT exports					
Germany	27.6	Japan	19.9	China	32.8
Japan	21.8	Hong Kong SAR, China	13.0	Korea, Rep.	8.3
United States	20.1	Germany	12.1	Germany	7.7
Spain	3.5	United States	12.0	Japan	7.2
Switzerland	3.3	Italy	8.3	United States	6.3
Top-five exporters to low-income economies, by share of LCT exports					
Japan	33.6	Japan	13.3	China	32.2
United States	22.7	United States	11.0	United Arab Emirates	9.8
Germany	16.7	Germany	10.7	India	9.6
Korea, Rep.	5.4	Italy	9.0	United States	6.5
China	3.3	China	7.3	South Africa	6.0

Source: World Bank World Integrated Trade Solution (database), https://wits.worldbank.org.

REFERENCES

Glachant, M., D. Dussaux, Y. Meniere, and A. Dechezlepretre. 2013. "Promoting the International Transfer of Low-Carbon Technologies: Evidence and Policy Challenges." Report for the Commissariat général à la stratégie et à la prospective (French Center for Policy and Planning), MINES ParisTech, October.

World Bank. 2008. *International Trade and Climate Change: Economic, Legal, and Institutional Perspectives.* Washington, DC: World Bank.

APPENDIX C

Chapter 3 Tables and Figures

TABLE C.1 **Developing countries' inward patents and CO$_2$ emissions, 2010–15**

RANK	RECIPIENT COUNTRY	% OF LCT PATENTS RECEIVED	SHARE OF WORLD CO$_2$ EMISSIONS (%)
1	China	25.2	33.7
10	Russian Federation	1.6	6.0
14	Brazil	0.8	1.6
16	Mexico	0.6	1.7
22	South Africa	0.3	1.6
26	Turkey	0.2	1.1
34	Romania	0.2	0.3
35	Ukraine	0.1	1.0
36	Malaysia	0.1	0.8
44	Colombia	0.1	0.3

Source: Calculations based on PATSTAT data.
Note: CO$_2$ = carbon dioxide; LCT = low-carbon technology.

FIGURE C.1

Distribution of China's outbound LCT patents, 2010–15

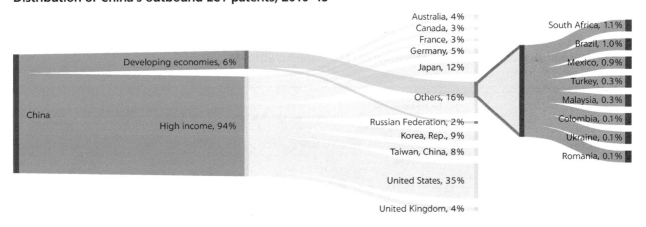

Source: Calculations based on PATSTAT data.

FIGURE C.2

Distribution of the Russian Federation's outbound LCT patents, 2010–15

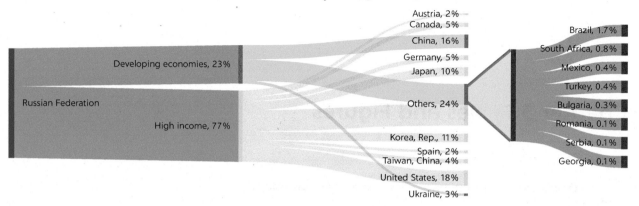

Source: Calculations based on PATSTAT data.

FIGURE C.3

Distribution of China's inbound LCT patents, 2010–15

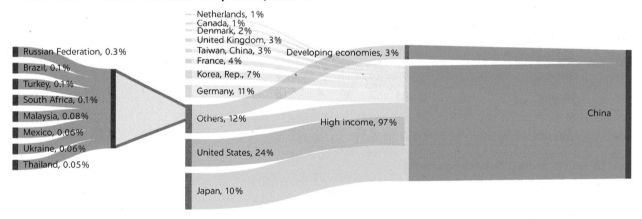

Source: Calculations based on PATSTAT data.

FIGURE C.4

Distribution of the Russian Federation's inbound LCT patents, 2010–15

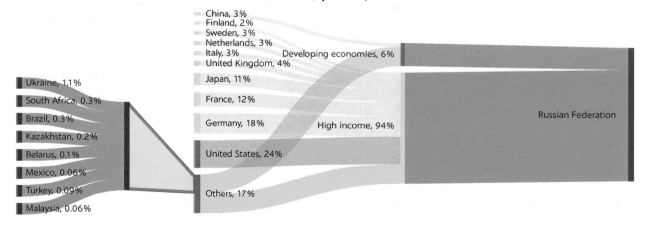

Source: Calculations based on PATSTAT data.

TABLE C.2 **Variable definition and data sources**

VARIABLE	DEFINITION	SOURCE
Intellectual Property Rights stringency	Score from 1 to 7 quantifying the extent of protection of intellectual property. The country-level score is obtained through aggregation of the surveys completed by randomly sampled executives.	World Economic Forum's Executives Opinion Survey
Legal system and property rights	This index is built from the aggregation of four components: (i) legal enforcement of contracts, (ii) judicial independence, (iii) impartial courts, and (iv) the integrity of the legal system.	Fraser Institute's Economic Freedom of the World 2015
"Enforced" Intellectual Property Rights stringency	This index is the multiplication of the World Economic Forum intellectual property right index and the Fraser Institute's legal system and property rights index. It is rescaled from 0 to 10.	World Economic Forum's Global Competitiveness Report and Fraser Institute's Economic Freedom of the World 2015
Log (GDP)	Country's gross domestic product in current US$.	World Bank's World Development Indicators
Log (GDP per capita)	Country's per capita gross domestic product in constant US$.	World Bank's World Development Indicators
Environmental regulations stringency	Environmental Performance Index ranks 180 countries on 24 performance indicators across 10 issue categories covering environmental health and ecosystem vitality.	Yale University
Climate policy stringency	Sub indicator "Climate and Energy" of the Environmental Performance Index.	Yale University
High tariff barriers	The index is constructed through the calculation and aggregation of three indicators: (i) revenues from trade taxes (percent of trade sector), (ii) mean tariff rate, and (iii) standard deviation of tariff rates.	Fraser Institute's Economic Freedom of the World 2015
High nontariff barriers	Based on the Global Competitiveness Report survey question: "In your country, tariff and non-tariff barriers significantly reduce the ability of imported goods to compete in the domestic market. 1–7 (best)." The question's wording has varied slightly over the years.	World Economic Forum's Executives Opinion Survey
Controls on the movement of capital and people (0–10 restrictive)	The index is constructed through the calculation and aggregation of three indicators: (i) foreign ownership/ investment restrictions, (ii) capital controls, and (iii) freedom of foreigners to visit.	Fraser Institute's Economic Freedom of the World 2015
Flexibility of labor regulations (0–10 flexible)	The index is constructed through the calculation and aggregation of six indicators: (i) difficulty of hiring, (ii) flexibility of hiring and firing regulations, (iii) centralization of wage bargaining, (iv) rigidity of working hours, (v) mandated cost of worker dismissal, and (vi) military conscription.	Fraser Institute's Economic Freedom of the World 2015
Flexibility of business regulations (0–10 flexible)	The index is constructed through the calculation and aggregation of six indicators: (i) administrative requirements, (ii) bureaucracy costs, (iii) time and money required to start a business, (iv) extra payments frequency, (v) licensing restrictions, and (vi) cost of tax compliance.	Fraser Institute's Economic Freedom of the World 2015
Flexibility of credit market regulations (0–10 flexible)	The index is constructed through the calculation and aggregation of three indicators: (i) share of privately held deposits, (ii) extent of government borrowings, (iii) interest rate controls/negative real interest rates.	Fraser Institute's Economic Freedom of the World 2015
Log (stock of inventions)	Log of the discounted stock of low-carbon technology inventions.	European Patent Office (EPO) Cooperative Patent Classification scheme and EPO Worldwide Patent Statistical Database (PATSTAT)

TABLE C.3 **Summary statistics**

VARIABLE	OBSERVATIONS	MEAN	STANDARD DEVIATION	MINIMUM	MAXIMUM
Low-carbon technology patents transfer	162,892	0.84	33.44	0.00	4,389.53
Log (stock of inventions)	162,892	1.24	2.04	0.00	9.68
Environmental policy stringency	162,892	6.87	1.38	3.27	9.19
Enforced intellectual property rights stringency	162,892	2.64	1.04	0.55	6.68
Controls on the movement of capital and people	162,892	5.49	1.86	1.00	9.05
Tariff barriers	162,892	2.87	1.22	0.18	6.67
Nontariff barriers	162,892	4.42	1.35	1.86	10.00
Flexibility of business regulations	162,892	16.56	1.48	13.13	21.04
Flexibility of labor regulations	162,892	7.77	1.01	5.39	9.59
Flexibility of credit regulations	162,892	5.70	1.00	2.31	8.51
Log (population)	162,892	6.19	1.33	2.29	9.24
Log (GDP per capita)	162,892	8.15	1.42	2.67	10.00
Trade agreement	162,892	0.09	0.29	0.00	1.00
Contiguity	162,892	0.02	0.14	0.00	1.00
Common official language	162,892	0.15	0.36	0.00	1.00
Colonial tie	162,892	0.01	0.09	0.00	1.00
Log (distance between most populated cities)	162,892	8.77	0.74	4.45	9.90

Note: GDP = gross domestic product.

FIGURE C.5

Environmental performance index and GDP per capita

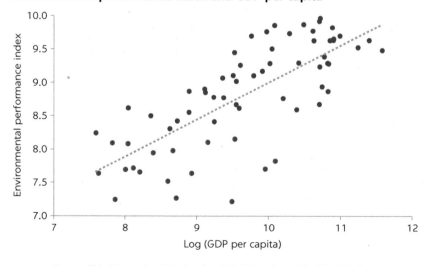

Sources: Calculation using 2014 data from Yale University and the World Bank.
Note: GDP = gross domestic product.

FIGURE C.6

Countries with the highest levels of FDI controls

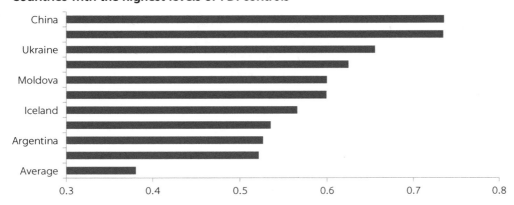

Source: Calculations using 2014 data from the Fraser institute.
Note: We restrict the graph to the top-10 countries in terms of foreign direct investment (FDI) controls.
"Average" means world average. The axis reports the index on FDI controls (0–10 restrictive).

FIGURE C.7

Countries with the highest levels of tariffs

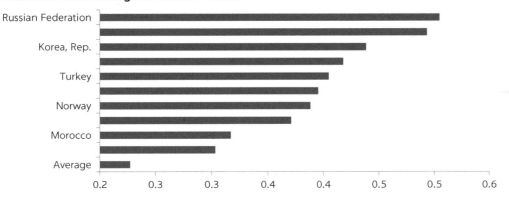

Source: Calculations using 2014 data from the Fraser institute.
Note: We restrict the graph to the top-10 countries in terms of tariffs. "Average" means world
average. The axis reports the index on levels of tariffs (0–10 restrictive).

FIGURE C.8

Countries with the highest levels of nontariff barriers

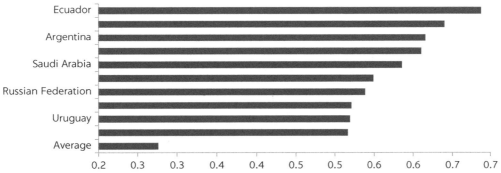

Source: Calculations using 2014 data from the Fraser institute.
Note: We restrict the graph to the top-10 countries in terms of nontariff barriers. "Average" means
world average. The axis reports the index on Levels of nontariff barriers (0–10 restrictive).

TABLE C.4 **Economies included or not included in the econometric analysis**

ECONOMY	CODE	REGION	INCOME GROUP	INCLUDED IN THE ECONOMETRIC ANALYSIS
American Samoa	ASM	East Asia and Pacific	Upper-middle income	
Australia	AUS	East Asia and Pacific	High income	X
Brunei Darussalam	BRN	East Asia and Pacific	High income	
Cambodia	KHM	East Asia and Pacific	Lower-middle income	
China	CHN	East Asia and Pacific	Upper-middle income	X
Fiji	FJI	East Asia and Pacific	Upper-middle income	
French Polynesia	PYF	East Asia and Pacific	High income	
Guam	GUM	East Asia and Pacific	High income	
Hong Kong SAR, China	HKG	East Asia and Pacific	High income	
Indonesia	IDN	East Asia and Pacific	Lower-middle income	
Japan	JPN	East Asia and Pacific	High income	X
Kiribati	KIR	East Asia and Pacific	Lower-middle income	
Korea, Dem. People's Rep.	PRK	East Asia and Pacific	Low income	
Korea, Rep.	KOR	East Asia and Pacific	High income	X
Lao PDR	LAO	East Asia and Pacific	Lower-middle income	
Macao SAR, China	MAC	East Asia and Pacific	High income	
Malaysia	MYS	East Asia and Pacific	Upper-middle income	X
Marshall Islands	MHL	East Asia and Pacific	Upper-middle income	
Micronesia, Fed. Sts.	FSM	East Asia and Pacific	Lower-middle income	
Mongolia	MNG	East Asia and Pacific	Lower-middle income	
Myanmar	MMR	East Asia and Pacific	Lower-middle income	
Nauru	NRU	East Asia and Pacific	Upper-middle income	
New Caledonia	NCL	East Asia and Pacific	High income	
New Zealand	NZL	East Asia and Pacific	High income	X
Northern Mariana Islands	MNP	East Asia and Pacific	High income	
Palau	PLW	East Asia and Pacific	High income	
Papua New Guinea	PNG	East Asia and Pacific	Lower-middle income	
Philippines	PHL	East Asia and Pacific	Lower-middle income	X
Samoa	WSM	East Asia and Pacific	Upper-middle income	
Singapore	SGP	East Asia and Pacific	High income	X
Solomon Islands	SLB	East Asia and Pacific	Lower-middle income	
Thailand	THA	East Asia and Pacific	Upper-middle income	X
Timor-Leste	TLS	East Asia and Pacific	Lower-middle income	
Tonga	TON	East Asia and Pacific	Upper-middle income	
Tuvalu	TUV	East Asia and Pacific	Upper-middle income	
Vanuatu	VUT	East Asia and Pacific	Lower-middle income	
Vietnam	VNM	East Asia and Pacific	Lower-middle income	X
Albania	ALB	Europe and Central Asia	Upper-middle income	X
Andorra	AND	Europe and Central Asia	High income	
Armenia	ARM	Europe and Central Asia	Upper-middle income	
Austria	AUT	Europe and Central Asia	High income	X
Azerbaijan	AZE	Europe and Central Asia	Upper-middle income	

continued

TABLE C.4, *continued*

ECONOMY	CODE	REGION	INCOME GROUP	INCLUDED IN THE ECONOMETRIC ANALYSIS
Belarus	BLR	Europe and Central Asia	Upper-middle income	
Belgium	BEL	Europe and Central Asia	High income	X
Bosnia and Herzegovina	BIH	Europe and Central Asia	Upper-middle income	
Bulgaria	BGR	Europe and Central Asia	Upper-middle income	X
Channel Islands	CHI	Europe and Central Asia	High income	
Croatia	HRV	Europe and Central Asia	High income	X
Cyprus	CYP	Europe and Central Asia	High income	X
Czech Republic	CZE	Europe and Central Asia	High income	X
Denmark	DNK	Europe and Central Asia	High income	X
Estonia	EST	Europe and Central Asia	High income	X
Faroe Islands	FRO	Europe and Central Asia	High income	
Finland	FIN	Europe and Central Asia	High income	X
France	FRA	Europe and Central Asia	High income	X
Georgia	GEO	Europe and Central Asia	Lower-middle income	X
Germany	DEU	Europe and Central Asia	High income	X
Gibraltar	GIB	Europe and Central Asia	High income	
Greece	GRC	Europe and Central Asia	High income	X
Greenland	GRL	Europe and Central Asia	High income	
Hungary	HUN	Europe and Central Asia	High income	X
Iceland	ISL	Europe and Central Asia	High income	X
Ireland	IRL	Europe and Central Asia	High income	X
Isle of Man	IMN	Europe and Central Asia	High income	
Italy	ITA	Europe and Central Asia	High income	X
Kazakhstan	KAZ	Europe and Central Asia	Upper-middle income	X
Kosovo	XKX	Europe and Central Asia	Lower-middle income	
Kyrgyz Republic	KGZ	Europe and Central Asia	Lower-middle income	
Latvia	LVA	Europe and Central Asia	High income	X
Liechtenstein	LIE	Europe and Central Asia	High income	
Lithuania	LTU	Europe and Central Asia	High income	X
Luxembourg	LUX	Europe and Central Asia	High income	X
Moldova	MDA	Europe and Central Asia	Lower-middle income	X
Monaco	MCO	Europe and Central Asia	High income	
Montenegro	MNE	Europe and Central Asia	Upper-middle income	
Netherlands	NLD	Europe and Central Asia	High income	X
North Macedonia	MKD	Europe and Central Asia	Upper-middle income	X
Norway	NOR	Europe and Central Asia	High income	X
Poland	POL	Europe and Central Asia	High income	X
Portugal	PRT	Europe and Central Asia	High income	X
Romania	ROU	Europe and Central Asia	Upper-middle income	X
Russian Federation	RUS	Europe and Central Asia	Upper-middle income	X

continued

TABLE C.4, *continued*

ECONOMY	CODE	REGION	INCOME GROUP	INCLUDED IN THE ECONOMETRIC ANALYSIS
San Marino	SMR	Europe and Central Asia	High income	
Serbia	SRB	Europe and Central Asia	Upper-middle income	
Slovak Republic	SVK	Europe and Central Asia	High income	X
Slovenia	SVN	Europe and Central Asia	High income	X
Spain	ESP	Europe and Central Asia	High income	X
Sweden	SWE	Europe and Central Asia	High income	X
Switzerland	CHE	Europe and Central Asia	High income	X
Tajikistan	TJK	Europe and Central Asia	Low income	
Turkey	TUR	Europe and Central Asia	Upper-middle income	X
Turkmenistan	TKM	Europe and Central Asia	Upper-middle income	
Ukraine	UKR	Europe and Central Asia	Lower-middle income	X
United Kingdom	GBR	Europe and Central Asia	High income	X
Uzbekistan	UZB	Europe and Central Asia	Lower-middle income	
Antigua and Barbuda	ATG	Latin America and the Caribbean	High income	
Argentina	ARG	Latin America and the Caribbean	High income	X
Aruba	ABW	Latin America and the Caribbean	High income	
Bahamas, The	BHS	Latin America and the Caribbean	High income	
Barbados	BRB	Latin America and the Caribbean	High income	
Belize	BLZ	Latin America and the Caribbean	Upper-middle income	
Bolivia	BOL	Latin America and the Caribbean	Lower-middle income	
Brazil	BRA	Latin America and the Caribbean	Upper-middle income	X
British Virgin Islands	VGB	Latin America and the Caribbean	High income	
Cayman Islands	CYM	Latin America and the Caribbean	High income	
Chile	CHL	Latin America and the Caribbean	High income	X
Colombia	COL	Latin America and the Caribbean	Upper-middle income	X
Costa Rica	CRI	Latin America and the Caribbean	Upper-middle income	X
Cuba	CUB	Latin America and the Caribbean	Upper-middle income	
Curaçao	CUW	Latin America and the Caribbean	High income	
Dominica	DMA	Latin America and the Caribbean	Upper-middle income	
Dominican Republic	DOM	Latin America and the Caribbean	Upper-middle income	X
Ecuador	ECU	Latin America and the Caribbean	Upper-middle income	X
El Salvador	SLV	Latin America and the Caribbean	Lower-middle income	X
Grenada	GRD	Latin America and the Caribbean	Upper-middle income	
Guatemala	GTM	Latin America and the Caribbean	Upper-middle income	X
Guyana	GUY	Latin America and the Caribbean	Upper-middle income	
Haiti	HTI	Latin America and the Caribbean	Low income	
Honduras	HND	Latin America and the Caribbean	Lower-middle income	X
Jamaica	JAM	Latin America and the Caribbean	Upper-middle income	
Mexico	MEX	Latin America and the Caribbean	Upper-middle income	X
Nicaragua	NIC	Latin America and the Caribbean	Lower-middle income	X
Panama	PAN	Latin America and the Caribbean	High income	X
Paraguay	PRY	Latin America and the Caribbean	Upper-middle income	

continued

TABLE C.4, *continued*

ECONOMY	CODE	REGION	INCOME GROUP	INCLUDED IN THE ECONOMETRIC ANALYSIS
Peru	PER	Latin America and the Caribbean	Upper-middle income	X
Puerto Rico	PRI	Latin America and the Caribbean	High income	
Sint Maarten (Dutch part)	SXM	Latin America and the Caribbean	High income	
St. Kitts and Nevis	KNA	Latin America and the Caribbean	High income	
St. Lucia	LCA	Latin America and the Caribbean	Upper-middle income	
St. Martin (French part)	MAF	Latin America and the Caribbean	High income	
St. Vincent and the Grenadines	VCT	Latin America and the Caribbean	Upper-middle income	
Suriname	SUR	Latin America and the Caribbean	Upper-middle income	
Trinidad and Tobago	TTO	Latin America and the Caribbean	High income	
Turks and Caicos Islands	TCA	Latin America and the Caribbean	High income	
Uruguay	URY	Latin America and the Caribbean	High income	X
Venezuela, RB	VEN	Latin America and the Caribbean	Upper-middle income	
Virgin Islands (U.S.)	VIR	Latin America and the Caribbean	High income	
Algeria	DZA	Middle East and North Africa	Upper-middle income	X
Bahrain	BHR	Middle East and North Africa	High income	
Djibouti	DJI	Middle East and North Africa	Lower-middle income	
Egypt, Arab Rep.	EGY	Middle East and North Africa	Lower-middle income	X
Iran, Islamic Rep.	IRN	Middle East and North Africa	Upper-middle income	
Iraq	IRQ	Middle East and North Africa	Upper-middle income	
Israel	ISR	Middle East and North Africa	High income	X
Jordan	JOR	Middle East and North Africa	Upper-middle income	X
Kuwait	KWT	Middle East and North Africa	High income	
Lebanon	LBN	Middle East and North Africa	Upper-middle income	
Libya	LBY	Middle East and North Africa	Upper-middle income	
Malta	MLT	Middle East and North Africa	High income	X
Morocco	MAR	Middle East and North Africa	Lower-middle income	X
Oman	OMN	Middle East and North Africa	High income	
Qatar	QAT	Middle East and North Africa	High income	
Saudi Arabia	SAU	Middle East and North Africa	High income	X
Syrian Arab Republic	SYR	Middle East and North Africa	Low income	
Tunisia	TUN	Middle East and North Africa	Lower-middle income	X
United Arab Emirates	ARE	Middle East and North Africa	High income	
West Bank and Gaza	PSE	Middle East and North Africa	Lower-middle income	
Yemen, Rep.	YEM	Middle East and North Africa	Low income	
Bermuda	BMU	North America	High income	
Canada	CAN	North America	High income	X
United States	USA	North America	High income	X
Afghanistan	AFG	South Asia	Low income	
Bangladesh	BGD	South Asia	Lower-middle income	
Bhutan	BTN	South Asia	Lower-middle income	
India	IND	South Asia	Lower-middle income	

continued

TABLE C.4, *continued*

ECONOMY	CODE	REGION	INCOME GROUP	INCLUDED IN THE ECONOMETRIC ANALYSIS
Maldives	MDV	South Asia	Upper-middle income	
Nepal	NPL	South Asia	Low income	
Pakistan	PAK	South Asia	Lower-middle income	
Sri Lanka	LKA	South Asia	Lower-middle income	
Angola	AGO	Sub-Saharan Africa	Lower-middle income	
Benin	BEN	Sub-Saharan Africa	Low income	
Botswana	BWA	Sub-Saharan Africa	Upper-middle income	
Burkina Faso	BFA	Sub-Saharan Africa	Low income	
Burundi	BDI	Sub-Saharan Africa	Low income	
Cabo Verde	CPV	Sub-Saharan Africa	Lower-middle income	
Cameroon	CMR	Sub-Saharan Africa	Lower-middle income	
Central African Republic	CAF	Sub-Saharan Africa	Low income	
Chad	TCD	Sub-Saharan Africa	Low income	
Comoros	COM	Sub-Saharan Africa	Low income	
Congo, Dem. Rep.	COD	Sub-Saharan Africa	Low income	
Congo, Rep.	COG	Sub-Saharan Africa	Lower-middle income	
Côte d'Ivoire	CIV	Sub-Saharan Africa	Lower-middle income	
Equatorial Guinea	GNQ	Sub-Saharan Africa	Upper-middle income	
Eritrea	ERI	Sub-Saharan Africa	Low income	
Ethiopia	ETH	Sub-Saharan Africa	Low income	
Gabon	GAB	Sub-Saharan Africa	Upper-middle income	X
Gambia, The	GMB	Sub-Saharan Africa	Low income	
Ghana	GHA	Sub-Saharan Africa	Lower-middle income	
Guinea	GIN	Sub-Saharan Africa	Low income	
Guinea-Bissau	GNB	Sub-Saharan Africa	Low income	
Kenya	KEN	Sub-Saharan Africa	Lower-middle income	
Lesotho	LSO	Sub-Saharan Africa	Lower-middle income	
Liberia	LBR	Sub-Saharan Africa	Low income	
Madagascar	MDG	Sub-Saharan Africa	Low income	
Malawi	MWI	Sub-Saharan Africa	Low income	
Mali	MLI	Sub-Saharan Africa	Low income	
Mauritania	MRT	Sub-Saharan Africa	Lower-middle income	
Mauritius	MUS	Sub-Saharan Africa	Upper-middle income	
Mozambique	MOZ	Sub-Saharan Africa	Low income	
Namibia	NAM	Sub-Saharan Africa	Upper-middle income	
Niger	NER	Sub-Saharan Africa	Low income	
Nigeria	NGA	Sub-Saharan Africa	Lower-middle income	
Rwanda	RWA	Sub-Saharan Africa	Low income	
São Tomé and Príncipe	STP	Sub-Saharan Africa	Lower-middle income	
Senegal	SEN	Sub-Saharan Africa	Low income	
Seychelles	SYC	Sub-Saharan Africa	High income	
Sierra Leone	SLE	Sub-Saharan Africa	Low income	
Somalia	SOM	Sub-Saharan Africa	Low income	

continued

TABLE C.4, *continued*

ECONOMY	CODE	REGION	INCOME GROUP	INCLUDED IN THE ECONOMETRIC ANALYSIS
South Africa	ZAF	Sub-Saharan Africa	Upper-middle income	X
South Sudan	SSD	Sub-Saharan Africa	Low income	
Sudan	SDN	Sub-Saharan Africa	Lower-middle income	
Swaziland	SWZ	Sub-Saharan Africa	Lower-middle income	
Tanzania	TZA	Sub-Saharan Africa	Low income	
Togo	TGO	Sub-Saharan Africa	Low income	
Uganda	UGA	Sub-Saharan Africa	Low income	
Zambia	ZMB	Sub-Saharan Africa	Lower-middle income	
Zimbabwe	ZWE	Sub-Saharan Africa	Low income	

TABLE C.5 **Main results of the literature on the determinants of LCT transfer**

	DECHEZLEPRÊTRE, GLACHANT, AND MÉNIÈRE (2013)	DUSSAUX, DECHEZLEPRÊTRE, AND GLACHANT (2018)		THIS REPORT	
Dependent variable	Patent	Trade	FDI	Patent	
Sourcing economies	All economies	All economies		High income	Developing
Scope of recipient economies	96 developed or developing economies	140 developed or developing economies		33 developing economies	
Low-carbon technologies covered	Hydro, solar PV, solar thermal, heating, insulation, lighting, cleaner vehicles, CCS, cleaner coal, fuel cells	Hydro, solar PV, solar thermal, wind, heating, insulation, lighting, cleaner vehicles		All technologies: Buildings, CCS, ICT, energy, manufacturing, transportation, wastewater treatment and management	
Period	1995–2007	2006–15		2006–15	
Economy-pair fixed effects	Yes	Yes	No	Yes	Yes
Exporter-year fixed effects	No	Yes	No	Yes	Yes
Local absorptive capacities	(Specific) Negative for most technologies	(Generic) Mostly insignificant but negative for two fields	(Generic) Positive or insignificant	(Specific) Insignificant	(Specific) Positive
Environmental policy stringency	Positive for half of the technologies	Insignificant for most technologies	Insignificant for most technologies	Negative	Negative
Enforced IPR stringency	Positive for all technologies	Positive for half of the technologies, insignificant for the others	Positive for half of the technologies, insignificant for the others	Insignificant	Insignificant
Controls of the movement of capital and people	Negative for all technologies		Mostly insignificant but negative for two fields	Negative	Negative
Tariff barriers	Negative for half of the technologies, insignificant for the others	Negative for half of the technologies, insignificant for the others		Negative	Negative
Nontariff barriers		Mostly insignificant		Positive	Positive
Market size	Positive or insignificant	Positive or insignificant	Positive for all technologies	Positive	Positive

Note: CCS = carbon capture and storage; FDI = foreign direct investment; ICT = information and communication technology; IPR = intellectual property rights; LCT = low-carbon technology; PV = photovoltaic.

TABLE C.6 **Determinants of LCT transfer to developing economies from high-income economies**

	BUILDINGS	ICT	ENERGY	MANUFACTURING	TRANSPORT	WASTE
Log (stock of inventions)	−0.415**	−0.027	−0.015	−0.263**	−0.154	−0.350**
	(0.194)	(0.308)	(0.086)	(0.129)	(0.242)	(0.145)
Environmental policy stringency	−0.381	−0.58	−0.986***	−0.670**	−1.028***	−0.363
	(0.479)	(0.519)	(0.294)	(0.296)	(0.253)	(0.290)
Enforced IPR stringency	−0.261***	−0.323	−0.1	−0.168	−0.029	−0.097
	(0.101)	(0.219)	(0.103)	(0.112)	(0.158)	(0.091)
Controls of the movement of capital and people	−0.06	−0.175	−0.09	−0.175**	−0.153*	−0.177*
	(0.091)	(0.136)	(0.095)	(0.083)	(0.087)	(0.101)
Tariff barriers	−0.131**	−0.015	−0.141*	−0.157**	−0.088	−0.158**
	(0.053)	(0.152)	(0.073)	(0.065)	(0.075)	(0.066)
Nontariff barriers	0.135*	0.045	0.248***	0.200***	0.174***	0.184***
	(0.075)	(0.142)	(0.064)	(0.055)	(0.058)	(0.062)
Log (population)	−5.471*	−2.463	0.536	−0.566	−3.298*	−0.001
	(2.962)	(3.485)	(1.725)	(1.170)	(1.837)	(1.241)
Log (GDP per capita)	0.701	1.626**	0.419	1.441***	1.613**	1.170**
	(0.527)	(0.677)	(0.367)	(0.483)	(0.789)	(0.471)
Flexibility of business regulations	0.204	0.008	0.156	0.1	0.049	0.121*
	(0.132)	(0.194)	(0.101)	(0.098)	(0.189)	(0.071)
Flexibility of labor regulations	−0.098	−0.425	−0.141	−0.2	−0.513**	−0.251**
	(0.192)	(0.286)	(0.166)	(0.152)	(0.237)	(0.117)
Flexibility of credit regulations	−0.207*	−0.053	−0.353***	−0.169**	−0.163	−0.153*
	(0.109)	(0.117)	(0.101)	(0.078)	(0.104)	(0.084)
Economy pair in trade agreement (0/1)	−0.07	0.285	0.002	0.076	−0.111	0.545***
	(0.144)	(0.202)	(0.104)	(0.089)	(0.242)	(0.172)
Exporter-year fixed effects	X	X	X	X	X	X
Importer fixed effects	X	X	X	X	X	X
Economy pair fixed effects	X	X	X	X	X	X
Observations	3,985	2,362	7,676	8,515	4,142	5,376
Number of economies	420	248	806	869	436	567

Note: Marginal effects for upper-middle-income, lower-middle-income, and low-income economies. See table C.2 for definitions of variables. See table C.3 for summary statistics. ICT = information and communication technology; IPR = intellectual property rights. Robust standard errors clustered at the economy level.
* $p < 0.10$ ** $p < 0.05$ *** $p < 0.01$

TABLE C.7 **Determinants of LCT transfer to developing economies from developing economies**

	BUILDINGS	ICT	ENERGY	MANUFACTURING	TRANSPORT	WASTE
Log (stock of inventions)	0.388	1.164***	−0.095	0.322*	0.114	0.038
	(0.380)	(0.376)	(0.176)	(0.189)	(0.781)	(0.279)
Environmental policy stringency	0.445	−1.626*	−1.122**	−0.905***	−1.494*	−1.199*
	(0.796)	(0.926)	(0.474)	(0.338)	(0.901)	(0.676)
Enforced IPR stringency	−0.506**	−0.618**	−0.005	0.083	−0.368	0.227
	(0.242)	(0.264)	(0.146)	(0.129)	(0.325)	(0.191)
Controls of the movement of capital and people	−0.154	−0.169	−0.211*	−0.294***	0.101	−0.541**
	(0.233)	(0.141)	(0.123)	(0.064)	(0.252)	(0.217)
Tariff barriers	−0.598**	−0.346	−0.028	−0.320***	−0.231	−0.21
	(0.234)	(0.213)	(0.147)	(0.059)	(0.215)	(0.181)
Nontariff barriers	0.176	0.019	0.257***	0.104	0.457**	0.375***
	(0.146)	(0.225)	(0.096)	(0.077)	(0.186)	(0.124)
Log (population)	−2.259	10.928**	2.098	4.665**	−14.484**	7.430*
	(2.677)	(4.924)	(2.502)	(2.178)	(5.695)	(4.443)
Log (GDP per capita)	2.777**	−0.965	1.951***	0.228	3.135*	0.503
	(1.331)	(2.701)	(0.666)	(0.589)	(1.760)	(0.868)
Flexibility of business regulations	−0.008	0.843**	0.016	−0.107	−0.411	0.058
	(0.210)	(0.418)	(0.176)	(0.090)	(0.366)	(0.168)
Flexibility of labor regulations	−0.239	0.346	−0.259	−0.129	−0.896**	−0.861**
	(0.622)	(0.666)	(0.244)	(0.134)	(0.379)	(0.342)
Flexibility of credit regulations	−0.509**	−0.487**	−0.348*	−0.219**	−0.054	−0.144
	(0.216)	(0.227)	(0.197)	(0.092)	(0.268)	(0.165)
Economy pair in trade agreement (0/1)	−1.719*	−14.082***	−1.028*	−0.063	12.566***	1.607**
	(0.932)	(0.538)	(0.579)	(0.620)	(0.593)	(0.656)
Exporter-year fixed effects	X	X	X	X	X	X
Importer fixed effects	X	X	X	X	X	X
Economy pair fixed effects	X	X	X	X	X	X
Observations	577	432	1,905	2,445	658	869
Number of economies	82	59	247	286	86	120

Note: Marginal effects for upper-middle-income, lower-middle-income, and low-income economies. See table C.2 for definitions of variables. See table C.3 for summary statistics. ICT = information and communication technology; IPR = intellectual property rights. Robust standard errors clustered at the economy level.
* $p < 0.10$ ** $p < 0.05$ *** $p < 0.01$

TABLE C.8 **Regression results when excluding China**

	FROM HIGH-INCOME ECONOMIES		FROM DEVELOPING ECONOMIES	
	BASELINE	EXCLUDING CHINA	BASELINE	EXCLUDING CHINA
Log (stock of inventions)	−0.153	−0.211	0.302*	0.065
	(0.113)	(0.178)	(0.162)	(0.267)
Environmental policy stringency	−0.759***	−0.591**	−1.082***	−0.993***
	(0.289)	(0.291)	(0.214)	(0.377)
Enforced IPR stringency	−0.115	−0.196*	−0.052	0.035
	(0.110)	(0.106)	(0.105)	(0.176)
Controls of the movement of capital and people	−0.138*	−0.257***	−0.283***	−0.241***
	(0.081)	(0.098)	(0.068)	(0.090)
Tariff barriers	−0.133**	−0.071	−0.243***	−0.255***
	(0.057)	(0.095)	(0.071)	(0.095)
Nontariff barriers	0.193***	0.197***	0.148***	0.048
	(0.052)	(0.062)	(0.057)	(0.072)
Log (population)	−1.283	−1.288	3.082*	2.762
	(1.385)	(1.410)	(1.792)	(1.809)
Log (GDP per capita)	1.247**	0.877	1.233***	−0.896
	(0.503)	(0.898)	(0.463)	(0.787)
Flexibility of business regulations	0.074	−0.081	−0.066	−0.218*
	(0.116)	(0.115)	(0.082)	(0.116)
Flexibility of labor regulations	−0.252	−0.208	−0.276*	−0.224
	(0.166)	(0.131)	(0.159)	(0.157)
Flexibility of credit regulations	−0.195**	−0.236**	−0.222**	−0.250**
	(0.090)	(0.094)	(0.105)	(0.112)
Economy pair in trade agreement (0/1)	0.045	0.233**	0.158	0.46
	(0.086)	(0.106)	(0.352)	(0.469)
Exporter-year fixed effects	X	X	X	X
Importer fixed effects	X	X	X	X
Economy pair fixed effects	X	X	X	X
Observations	11,339	9,574	3,730	2,581
Number of economy pairs	1,142	993	426	333

Note: Marginal effects for upper-middle-income, lower-middle-income, and low-income economies. See table C.2 for definitions of variables. See table C.3 for summary statistics. ICT = information and communication technology; IPR = intellectual property rights. Robust standard errors clustered at the country level.
* $p < 0.10$ ** $p < 0.05$ *** $p < 0.01$

TABLE C.9 **Catalogue of LCT-related encouraged industries for foreign investment in China**

I. Agriculture, Forestry, Animal Husbandry and Fishery

9	Construction and operation of environment protection projects, such as the planting of trees and grass to combat desertification and soil erosion

III. Manufacturing Industries

(I) Agricultural and Sideline Food Processing

16	Development and production of safe, efficient and environment-friendly fodder and additives (containing methionine)

(IV) Textile Industry

24	Dyeing and after finishing processing of high-end textiles, using advanced energy conservation and emission reduction technologies and equipment
25	Processing of special natural fibers (including but not limited to cashmere and other special animal fibers, bamboo fiber and bastose, silk, and colored cotton) that satisfy the ecological, comprehensive resource utilization and environmental protection requirements

(X) Manufacturing of Chemical Raw Materials and Chemical Products

50	Comprehensive utilization, treatment and disposal of waste gas, liquid waste and waste residue

(XIII) Rubber and Plastic Products

69	Recycle and reutilization of plastic waste

(XIV) Nonmetallic Mineral Products

71	Development and production of building materials featuring energy conservation, environmental protection, waste recycling, light-weight, high-strength, high performance and multiple functions
72	Production of energy-saving and high-efficiency chemical building materials using plastic to replace steel or wood

(XVII) General Equipment Manufacturing

113	Manufacturing of the third and more generation car wheel hub bearings, bearings for high or medium-grade CNC machine tools or processing centers, high-speed wire rod or plate rolling mill bearings, high-speed railway bearings, low-noise bearings with vibration below Z4, P4 or P2 level bearings of various bearings, bearings of wind turbine generator set, and aircraft bearings
115	Manufacturing of gear transmission used for wind power or high speed rail, gear transmission agent with adjustable blades used for vessels, and large-sized and heavy-load gear boxes

(XVIII) Special-Purpose Equipment Manufacturing

178	Manufacturing of equipment specially for producing solar cells
180	Manufacturing of water pollution prevention and control equipment: horizontal spiral centrifugal dehydrators, membrane and membrane materials, ozone generators with a capacity of more than 50 kg/h, chlorine dioxide generators with a capacity of more than 10 kg/h, ultraviolet disinfection devices, small domestic sewage treatment equipment used in rural areas, and heavy metal wastewater treatment equipment
181	Manufacturing of solid waste treatment and disposal equipment: sewage plant sludge disposal and resource recycling equipment, complete sets of refuse incineration equipment with a daily treatment capacity of 500 tons or more, landfill leachate treatment technology equipment, anti-seepage geo-membranes in landfills, building waste treatment and resource recovery utilization equipment, devices for disposal of hazardous waste, devices for power generation with biogas in landfills, treatment equipment for ferrous wastes, and soil remediation equipment
188	Environmental protection technology for aquatic ecosystems and the manufacturing of relevant equipment
190	Unconventional water treatment or recycling equipment and water quality monitoring instruments
198	Manufacturing of equipment for hydrogen energy preparation, storage and transportation and inspection systems
200	Manufacturing of devices for recovery of marine oil spilling
202	Development and utilization of clean coal technologies and products as well as manufacturing of relevant equipment (coal gasification and liquefaction, coal water slurry and industry shape-coal)

(XIX) Automobile Manufacturing

209	Manufacturing of key parts and components of new energy automobiles: battery separators (thickness of 15-40 µm, porosity of 40%-60%); battery management system, motor management system, electronic control integration of electric vehicles; driving motors of electric vehicles (peak power density ≥ 2.5 kW/kg, high-efficiency area: 65%, efficiency in working area ≥ 80%), vehicle DC/DC (input voltage of 100 V – 400 V), high-power electronic devices (IGBT, voltage class ≥ 600 V, current ≥ 300 A); and plug-in hybrid electromechanical coupling drive systems; low-platinum catalyst for fuel cell, composite membranes, membrane electrodes, humidifier control valves, air compressors, hydrogen circulating pumps, and 70 MPa hydrogen cylinders.

continued

TABLE C.9, *continued*

(XXI) Electric Machinery and Equipment Manufacturing	
231	Manufacturing of key auxiliary equipment for hydropower generating units232
232	Manufacturing of power transmission and transformation equipment
233	Manufacturing of complete sets of equipment or key equipment for new energy power generation: equipment for photovoltaic power generation, geothermal power generation, tidal power generation, wave power generation, garbage power generation, biogas power generation, and wind power generation with a capacity of 2.5 megawatts or more
236	Manufacturing of high-tech green batteries: nickel-metal hydride (Ni-MH) batteries, nickel-zinc batteries, silver-zinc batteries, lithium-ion batteries, solar batteries, fuel batteries, etc. (excluding energy type of new energy vehicle batteries)
(XXIV) Comprehensive Utilization of Waste Resources	
284	Production of completely biodegradable materials
285	Recycling and treatment of waste and used electrical and electronic products, automobiles, electromechanical equipment, rubbers, metals, and batteries
IV. Production and Supply of Electric Power, Heating Power, Fuel Gas and Water	
289	Construction and operation of integrated gasification combined cycle power generation and other clean coal power generation projects
291	Construction and operation of hydropower stations for the primary purpose of power generation
292	Construction and operation of nuclear power stations
293	Construction and operation of new energy power stations (including but not limited to solar energy, wind energy, geothermal energy, tidal energy, tidal current energy, wave energy, and biomass energy)
294	Construction and operation of power grid
299	Construction and operation of vehicle charging stations and battery replacement stations
300	Construction and operation of hydrogen refueling stations
V. Transportation, Warehousing and Postal Service Industries	
301	Construction and operation of network of trunk railway lines
302	Construction and operation of intercity railway, urban (suburban) railway, resource-oriented development railway, branch railway lines, and relater bridges, tunnels, ferries and station facilities
303	3Comprehensive maintenance of infrastructures of high-speed railway lines and intercity railways
VII. Leasing and Commercial Service Industries	
318	International economic, science and technology, environmental protection, and logistical information consulting services
VIII. Scientific Research and Technical Services	
328	Offshore oil pollution cleaning and ecological restoration technology and relevant product development, technology for prevention and treatment of seawater eutrophication, technology for prevention and treatment of marine life explosive growth disaster, and coastal zone ecological environment restoration technology
329	Development of energy saving and environmental protection technologies and related services
330	Development and application of technologies for recycling and comprehensive utilization of resources and for recycling of emissions and discharges from enterprise production
331	Environmental pollution treatment and monitoring technologies
332	New technologies for energy efficiency in chemical fiber production and printing and dyeing processing and for the treatment of exhaust gas, waste liquid and waste residue
333	Desertification prevention and desert treatment technologies
IX. Water Conservancy, Environmental, and Public Facility Management Industries	
341	Construction and operation of urban subway, light railway and other track transport
342	Construction and operation of sewage and garbage treatment plants, hazardous waste treatment and disposal plants (incineration plants and landfills), and environmental pollution treatment and control facilities

Source: Invest in China web page, http://www.fdi.gov.cn/1800000121_39_4851_0_7.html.

TABLE C.10 **Correlation coefficients between explanatory variables**

	LOG (STOCK OF INVENTIONS)	ENVIRON-MENTAL POLICY STRINGENCY	ENFORCED IPR STRINGENCY	CONTROLS ON THE MOVEMENT OF CAPITAL AND PEOPLE	TARIFF BARRIERS	NONTARIFF BARRIERS	FLEXIBILITY OF BUSINESS REGULATIONS	FLEXIBILITY OF LABOR REGULATIONS	FLEXIBILITY OF CREDIT REGULATIONS	LOG (POPULATION)	LOG (GDP PER CAPITA)	TRADE AGREEMENT
Log (stock of inventions)	1											
Environmental policy stringency	0.3664*	1										
Enforced IPR stringency	0.0530*	0.2837*	1									
Controls on the movement of capital and people	−0.0875*	−0.1655*	−0.1669*	1								
Tariff barriers	−0.2149*	−0.2007*	0.0071*	0.0663*	1							
Nontariff barriers	0.1483*	0.0479*	0.0185*	−0.0736*	0.0095*	1						
Flexibility of business regulations	0.4154*	0.5172*	0.2256*	−0.1637*	−0.2229*	0.1201*	1					
Flexibility of labor regulations	0.4885*	0.5667*	0.4043*	−0.1541*	−0.2256*	−0.0344*	0.5369*	1				
Flexibility of credit regulations	0.3618*	0.4108*	0.3690*	−0.0597*	−0.2146*	−0.1658*	0.3151*	0.5297*	1			
Log (population)	0.1395*	0.0902*	0.0803*	−0.0735*	−0.1081*	−0.0495*	0.0277*	0.1582*	0.1582*	1		
Log (GDP per capita)	−0.0125*	−0.1235*	0.0399*	−0.0315*	0.0937*	−0.0028	−0.1340*	−0.0563*	−0.0147*	0.1486*	1	
Trade agreement	0.0873*	0.1334*	0.0922*	−0.0164*	−0.0641*	0.0119*	0.0821*	0.1342*	0.0969*	0.0066*	−0.0177*	1

Note: The variables are demeaned as in the economy-pair fixed effects model. IPR = intellectual property rights; * $p < 0.10$ where p is the probability value.

REFERENCES

Dechezleprêtre, A., M. Glachant, and Y. Ménière. 2013. "What Drives the International Transfer of Climate Change Mitigation Technologies? Empirical Evidence from Patent Data." *Environmental and Resource Economics* 54 (2): 161–78.

Dussaux, D., A. Dechezleprêtre, and M. Glachant. 2018. "Intellectual Property Rights Protection and the International Transfer of Low-Carbon Technologies." Working Paper 288, January, Grantham Research Center for Climate Change and the Environment.

Low-Carbon Technology in Emerging Countries

THE REPUBLIC OF KOREA'S APPROACH TO DEVELOPING NEW ENERGY TECHNOLOGIES

Like many economies, the Republic of Korea began focusing on the development of new energy technologies in response to the global oil crises of the 1970s. Korea has very few energy resources beyond some modest reserves of anthracite coal, and with rapid industrialization came the major policy challenge of accommodating an ever-growing demand for electricity by firms and consumers. In the 1970s, Korea was still very much a developing economy, and large-scale investment in the energy sector—for both infrastructure and research and development (R&D)—remained almost exclusively within the purview of the public sector.

Throughout the 1970s and 1980s, successive administrations prioritized energy security. The government elaborated and revised the laws and regulations governing the energy sector, created supportive tax and tariff codes, expanded financial support to build generation and distribution capacity, and implemented technology development and education programs. The 1979 Energy Use Rationalization Act has been continuously revised and updated, steadily increasing the government's financial support for energy conservation and the development of new energy technologies. These policies have helped create demand for new energy technologies, spurring complementary private investment in energy-technology R&D.

Decades of investment and sustained government support ultimately enabled Korea to become an exporter of energy technologies to the global market. The country's success reflects a steady focus on institutional, economic, and technical capacity building to manage the risks involved in technology development and dissemination. Although the public sector has played a key role in this process, rising private sector interest and investment in energy technologies have been vital to the sustainability of energy R&D. The benefits of reducing firms' exposure to volatile oil prices drove much of the early private investment in new energy technology, but new energy technologies were increasingly incorporated into the business-diversification strategies of large conglomerates such as Chaebol. Although initial public support for new energy technology was motivated by oil prices, by the 2000s a growing body of evidence on the role of carbon in climate change became a major force behind public investment in the energy sector.[1]

Korea's approach to developing new energy technologies is not without its drawbacks, however. For example, the government-led project selection process has focused more on the application of existing technology rather than original research, and Korea's innovation output is relatively low compared to that of Japan. Limited domestic innovation capacity could inhibit Korea's ability to develop state-of-the-art technologies in the future. In addition, the rigid structure of the energy industry, which is dominated by public utilities such as KEPCO and KOGAS, combined with excessively burdensome regulations and non-market-based pricing policies and business practices has slowed private investment in the development and dissemination of new energy technologies.

Energy storage systems (ESSs) are critical to energy efficiency, because technical limitations on the storage and retrieval of excess power are a major source of energy losses. ESSs include batteries and other devices, either chemical or mechanical, that can help overcome the time difference between energy production and consumption. ESS functions can be divided into three main areas: frequency adjustments to stabilize power-supply systems, the stabilization of output from inherently variable energy sources such as wind and solar power, and the storage of excess power for home and commercial use and its retrieval during periods of peak demand.[2]

The wide and expanding range of ESS technologies includes electrochemical storage methods such as a lithium-ion batteries, lead-acid batteries, and hydrogen fuel cells as well as physical storage mechanisms such as flywheel systems and pumped hydropower reserves. Modern lithium-ion batteries are a large-capacity version of the batteries used in smartphones and other consumer electronics. Although the concept of ESS may bring to mind this type of chemical battery, physical storage mechanisms are also an important ESS technology, especially at large scales. For example, pumped hydropower reserves are reservoirs of water filled by pumps powered by excess electricity; to retrieve the stored mechanical energy, these reserves are run through hydropower dams.[3] Hydrogen fuel cells are an emerging ESS technology and are currently being tested for use in small-scale smart grids.

The rapid growth of the global ESS market is driving increased demand for ESS technology in Korea. Korea's ESS capacity grew from 265 megawatt-hours in 2016 to 1.2 gigawatt-hours (GWh) in 2017 and reached nearly 4.8 GWh in 2018. Remarkably, Korea's ESS industry now accounts for nearly 50 percent of the global ESS market. In 2018, Samsung SDI and LG Chem are expected to account for 43 and 37 percent of the global ESS market, respectively—a combined global market share of 80 percent. By contrast, in 2014 these two companies had a combined global market share of 59 percent.

Korea's lithium-ion battery industry has benefitted from significant government support, both directly and as a result of support to precursor industries. Beginning in the 1990s, the authorities strategically fostered the growth of semiconductor, computer, and mobile-device manufacturing. As large firms such as Samsung and LG began to mass produce semiconductors and smartphones, the public and private sectors increasingly focused on the development and mass production of lithium-ion batteries, which are critical to cost competitiveness in the semiconductor and smartphone industries.

The government's response to climate change and the expansion of the smart grid have greatly contributed to the growing demand for ESSs, and public support played a major role in mitigating the risks involved in new ESS projects. New ESS technologies have been installed at a rapid pace since January 2017, when the government introduced a special fare system for ESS, created various financial incentives, and mandated the use of ESS technologies in public buildings. In part because of these policies, Korea now has 4.8 GWh of installed ESS capacity, roughly equivalent to the output of four nuclear power plants.

In addition to public support, a range of factors contributed to the growth of the Korean ESS industry. Korean firms were able to draw on existing international technologies to develop their first-generation lithium-ion batteries, and their capacity to absorb inbound technology transfer reduced the need for domestic investment in R&D. In addition, Korea has a large number of small firms that can produce ESS components, and competition between these firms has helped to keep costs low.

Despite its impressive progress, Korea's ESS industry faces significant challenges. They include the establishment of model codes and interoperability safety standards, which are vital to enter global markets. Recent accidents involving installed ESS technologies underscore the importance of reinforcing safety measures before deploying these technologies on a large scale.

Korea's experience with ESS development yields three important lessons. First, forward and backward linkages between existing industries and new ESS technologies are crucial, because investments in ESSs are subject to large sunk costs, long lead times, and high levels of market risk. Small-scale investment modalities, such as venture capital, are not well suited to the ESS industry, and the intrinsic costs and risks involved can only be mitigated by backward linkages to ESS-intensive industries such as smartphone manufacturing. Second, the public and private sectors must avoid implementing ambitious projects without first imposing adequate technical verification requirements and safety standards at the manufacturing, transportation, installation, and operation stages. Prioritizing short-term performance over regulatory integrity can lead to serious liability issues. Third, after an initial period of robust public investment the government should scale back its role to focus on creating an enabling policy environment, expanding the ESS market through deregulation and privatization, and mitigating business risks by providing technology and financial support to strengthen the competitiveness of the ESS industry.

EXAMPLES OF SOUTH–SOUTH TECHNOLOGY TRANSFER

Korea's experience highlights some of the most important challenges involved in LCT transfer. Korea, as well as a few emerging countries in the South, has been a pioneer in South–South collaboration. Do South–South exchanges of knowledge, technical assistance, and technology transfer differ and, if so, in what way from North–South exchanges? This appendix provides a few, illuminating examples of these issues.

Huh and Kim (2018) discuss two projects, the introduction of carbon-capture-and-utilization technology to Bantayan Island in the Philippines and a waste-to-energy project in the city of Santiago in the Dominican Republic. Both projects were implemented by Korea's Green Technology Center between June 2014 and May 2016, in collaboration with domestic and international partners. Both rojects failed to successfully transfer their respective technologies, but the experience proved instructive, because it revealed the risks posed by what the study termed "uninformed transfer." The projects were undermined by a lack of cooperation between national and local governments within the target countries, reflecting varying levels of commitment among stakeholder groups.

The analysis found that technology transfer must be informed by a comprehensive understanding of the recipient country's social, political, and economic context, because uneven levels of local ownership can prove as serious a threat to a project's success as any technical difficulty it may encounter.

China's experience with building dams in developing countries sheds light on several important challenges involved in South–South technology transfer. Dam projects are often controversial. They require large amounts of financing, which can have adverse implications for debt sustainability; they entail serious risks to ecosystems and communities; and they are usually driven by a combination of business interests and geopolitical considerations. China's construction of the Bui Dam in Ghana and the Kamchay Dam in Cambodia illustrates the importance of these issues—even for a world leader in the construction of dams in developing economies such as China.

Commissioned in 2013, the Bui Dam was built by the Chinese firm Sinohydro as a turnkey project funded by China EximBank. Sinohydro employed about 3,000 largely unskilled Ghanaian workers, but it provided no additional training or employment assistance after the end of the construction phase. Chinese staff held most of the highly skilled positions, even though the Ghanaian workforce has significant experience in hydraulic engineering. Although the Ghanaian government did not adhere to the requirements of the resettlement planning framework, Sinohydro also failed to respect the construction management plan laid out in the environmental and social impact assessment. Similarly, China EximBank followed its own environmental guidelines, not Ghana's, and it did so in form only (Hensengert 2018).

The Kamchay Dam in Cambodia was also financed by China EximBank and constructed by Sinohydro. The project was based on a build-operate-transfer arrangement under which Sinohydro would build the dam and manage it for 44 years before transferring ownership to the Cambodian government in 2050. Technology transfer via the project was essentially limited to capital goods and equipment, and the project imparted very little in the way of skills, knowledge, or expertise that would enable the Cambodian workforce to independently operate and maintain the dam or to implement similar projects in the future (Urban 2018; Urban et al. 2016). The preconstruction consultation process was incomplete, and it involved little participation from local stakeholders. The dam was successfully installed, but the limited transfer of complementary knowledge and expertise reflected an inadequate supply of workforce skills and organizational competencies in Cambodia, as well as the project's lack of investment in building these capabilities.

A more recent study (Chen 2018) compares two wind power projects in Ethiopia, one by a Chinese firm and another by a French firm, to identify differences between South–South and North–South technology transfer. The two projects are the Adama Wind Farm constructed by HydroChina and the Ashegoda Wind Farm constructed by the French firm Vergnet. The study evaluates three dimensions of technology transfer: (i) the transfer of capital goods and equipment, (ii) the direct and indirect transfer of skills, and (iii) the transfer of knowledge and expertise. Through interviews with key stakeholders and a detailed analysis of the negotiation and construction processes for both projects, the study found that, although HydroChina shared a greater degree of knowledge and expertise with local engineers and university scholars during the construction phase, Vergnet formed stronger long-term links with local universities and employed a larger share of local workers. The study highlights the important role of the Ethiopian government in negotiating how the technology was transferred and in maximizing its impact. The differing demands and expectations of the Ethiopian government relative to the two foreign firms were primarily responsible for the observed differences in the scope and sustainability of technology transfer that occurred via the two projects.

NOTES

1. Korea has also benefitted from technological cooperation with Japan, which was further along in the industrialization process for much of the 20th century.
2. ESS technologies typically consist of four parts, a power-conversion unit (PCU), a battery, a battery-management system (BMS), and an operating system. The PCU transfers power to and from the battery; the BMS monitors voltage, temperature, storage capacity, and battery life; and the operating system communicates information between the PCU, the PMS, and the user.
3. Norway is a leader in pumped hydropower storage, because its geography is naturally suited to the technology.

REFERENCES

Chen, Y. 2018. "Comparing North–South Technology Transfer and South–South Technology Transfer: The Technology Transfer Impact of Ethiopian Wind Farms." *Energy Policy* 116 (2018): 1–9.

Hensengert O. 2018. "South–South Technology Transfer: Who Benefits? A Case Study of the Chinese-Built Bui Dam in Ghana." *Energy Policy* 114 (March): 499–507.

Huh, T., and H.-J. Kim. 2018. "Korean Experimentation of Knowledge and Technology Transfer to Address Climate Change in Developing Countries." *Sustainability* 10 (4): 1263.

Urban, F. 2018. "China's Rise: Challenging the North–South Technology Transfer Paradigm for Climate Change Mitigation and Low Carbon Energy." *Energy Policy* 113 (February): 320–30.

Urban, F., G. Siciliano, K. Sour, P. D. Lonn, M. Tan-Mullins, and G. Mang. 2016. "South–South Technology Transfer of Low-Carbon Innovation: Large Chinese Hydropower Dams in Cambodia." *Sustainable Development* 23 (4): 232–44.

Empirical Evaluations of Innovation Policy Instruments

The following table summarizes empirical findings on innovation policy instruments on the basis of 1,600 empirical studies.

MEASURE OR INSTRUMENTS	TYPE	PURPOSE	MARKET FAILURE	FINDINGS		EMPIRICAL EVIDENCE
				PROS	CONS	
Fiscal instruments: Tax incentives for R&D within firms	Economic instruments	Tech-push	KS, IPR	Can be targeted (strategic sectors, geographical regions). More generous schemes, volume-based incentives, and tax credits can be effective at inducing R&D.	Can entail very high costs. Could crowd out private investment. Less effective for large firms. Effects may diminish over time. May stimulate R&D with lower marginal returns. High variability in outcomes.	Ambivalent
Public finance: Grants and loans for R&D within firms	Economic instruments	Tech-push	KS, IPR	Can address underinvestment by firms where there are nonappropriable positive spillovers.	Measures tend not to be well-targeted. Needs to be administratively simple with low bureaucracy. Direct support may need to be complemented by indirect support (advisory services, coaching/ training).	Mostly positive
Public finance: Publicly supported venture capital and government-backed loan guarantees	Economic instruments	Tech-push	Fin	Credit guarantee schemes have contributed to relaxing financial constraints for SMEs in many countries and help firms grow. Supporting VCs can make this form of funding less susceptible to economic downturns.	Some schemes did not impact of firm productivity, R&D or investment intensity. Supporting struggling firms may ultimately stifle innovative forces. Can create moral hazard issues. VC support can be after innovation.	Mostly positive
Competition enhancing and securing regulation	Regulation (economic)	Systemic	KS, NE	Increases and secures incentives to invest in innovation	Reduces rents for innovators	Ambivalent
Antitrust regulation	Regulation (economic)	Systemic	KS, IRS	Allows competitors to enter the market and put pressure on dominant companies	Prohibits R&D cooperation	Only anecdotal evidence

continued

MEASURE OR INSTRUMENTS	TYPE	PURPOSE	MARKET FAILURE	FINDINGS		EMPIRICAL EVIDENCE
				PROS	CONS	
Mergers and acquisitions (M&A)	Regulation (economic)	Systemic	IPR, IRS	M&A allows efficient takeover of innovative companies; M&A restrictions protect management from short-term market pressures	Dominant (innovative) companies have limited incentives to invest further in R&D	Ambivalent (U-shape)
Market entry regulation	Regulation (economic)	Systemic	IPR, IRS	Reduces competition for incumbents, for example, for infant industries	M&A restrictions limit takeover pressure and incentive to innovate	Only indirect evidence of entry pushing innovation in technology advanced sectors
Price regulation	Regulation (economic)	Systemic	IRS	Minimum prices secure minimum turnovers and decrease risks; completely free prices allow monopoly pricing	Prohibits market entry of probably innovative newcomers	Not available
Regulation of natural monopolies and public enterprises	Regulation (economic)	Systemic	IRS	Incentives to achieve progress in productivity in case of rate of return regulation	Price caps reduce innovation incentives	Positive in case of deregulation
Competition enhancing and securing regulation	Regulation (economic)	Systemic	KS, IPR	Increases and secures incentives to invest in innovation	High price pressure and low gains allow no investments into R&D in case of marginal cost pricing	Ambivalent
Antitrust regulation	Regulation (economic)	Systemic	Inf	Allows competitors to enter the market and put pressure on dominant companies	Reduces rents for innovators	Only anecdotal evidence
Environmental protection	Regulation (social)	Systemic	Inf	Creates incentives for development of new eco-friendly processes and products (incl. environmental technologies) by creating temporary market entry barriers	Restricts innovation and creates compliance costs	Mainly positive
Worker health and safety protection	Regulation (social)	Systemic	Inf, KS	Creates incentives for development of processes with higher workers' safety by creating temporary market entry barriers and monopoly gains	Restricts innovation and creates compliance costs	—
Product and consumer safety	Regulation (social)	Systemic	Inf	Increases the acceptance of new products among consumers and promotes their diffusion creating innovation incentives	Restricts innovation and creates compliance costs	Limited ambivalent evidence

continued

MEASURE OR INSTRUMENTS	TYPE	PURPOSE	MARKET FAILURE	FINDINGS		EMPIRICAL EVIDENCE
				PROS	CONS	
Liability law	Regulation (institutional)	Systemic	Inf	Increases the acceptance of new products among customers and promotes their diffusion creating innovation incentives	Too high liability risks reduce the incentives to develop and market innovative products	Ambivalent
Employment protection legislation	Regulation (institutional)	Systemic	KS	Can positively affect incremental innovation in certain contexts. Employment protection can encourage investments in human capital.	Less flexible labor laws can impede productivity growth in certain, but not all, contexts. No clear view of which parts of labor legislation fit with what parts of innovation policies.	Ambivalent
Immigration (for example, high-skilled international labor migration)	Regulation (institutional)	Systemic	Inf	Immigration of foreign workers brings in new ideas while increasing pressure on domestic workers	Integration costs	No significant impacts
Bankruptcy laws	Regulation (institutional)	Systemic	Fin	Increased confidence of creditors to invest in innovation	Restrictions to acquire external funds for risky investments	Negative
Intellectual property rights	Regulation (institutional)	Systemic	IPR, IRS, KS	Create additional incentives to invest in R&D by appropriating temporary monopoly rights (plus increasing R&D efficiency by disclosure of technological knowhow)	Restricts the development (for example, via patent thickets) and the diffusion of new technologies and products.	Ambivalent
IPR exploitation support (for example Technology Transfer Offices or National Patent Offices)	Information	Tech-push	IPR, IRS, KS	Can provide direct targeted support to strategic sectors e.g. by helping universities to commercialize IPR	One size does not fit all; tailoring is essential; patenting not always the right strategic choice	—
Innovation training for firms (for example, provided by higher educational institutions)	Information	Tech-push	Inf	Flexible pathways between educational institutions and workplace training programs appear to have positive outcomes for adaptability and raising of skill levels	Higher educational institutions may be limited in their ability to train firms; difficult to assess impact	Mostly positive
Clustering policies (for example, high-tech spaces within cities)	Information	Tech-push	Inf, KS	Cluster policies provide the resources and framework to advance the innovation potential of different interest groups; effective at leveraging private funding	Needs direct management team and long-term provision of support services; difficult to balance between hands-off and direct steering of clusters	Ambivalent
Collaboration support for R&D between academia and firms or across firms	Information	Tech-push	Inf, KS, IRS	Collaboration can save costs and help firms achieve economies of scale. Stable, long-term commitment by government can help internalize informational spillovers.	Only works when mutual trust established, with strong governance and audit arrangements, and minimal bureaucracy	Mostly positive

continued

MEASURE OR INSTRUMENTS	TYPE	PURPOSE	MARKET FAILURE	FINDINGS		EMPIRICAL EVIDENCE
				PROS	CONS	
Networks among firms (for example, marketing networks among SMEs in the same industry)	Information	Tech-push	Inf, KS, IRS	Networks can have very positive effects on the stimulation of learning processes and the enhancement of skills levels. Policy instruments that facilitate network formation and development (such as support for network brokers or other intermediary organizations) are often successful.	Strong network management and leadership (such as through a board of directors), coupled with transparent and efficient administrative processes are overwhelmingly cited as essential contributory factors for network success. Can fail if trust is low. Difficult to predict path of network.	Mostly positive
Entrepreneurship policies (education to individuals, advice to startups)	Information	Tech-push	Inf, KS, NE, IRS	Educational programs on entrepreneurship can encourage uptake of entrepreneurship, incubators could help entrepreneurs share knowledge.	Any benefits are long-term in nature. Effects vary: at school level, there is a negative and significant effect; at the college level, the effect is low; at the university level, the effect is positive.	Ambivalent
Public procurement (general, strategic, cooperative, catalytic)	Economic instruments	Demand-pull	IRS, NE	Lack of demand is a key barrier to investments in green products. Public procurement can help address this.	Uses scarce resources of government that may be more socially desirable to be allocated elsewhere.	—
Direct support for private demand (tax incentives and subsidies)	Economic instruments	Demand-pull	IRS, NE	There is strong theoretical reasoning and empirical evidence that demand is crucial for innovation activities. Demand subsidies have a positive impact on the uptake of eco-innovation,	There is not a clear "best" approach. Other factors may be more important, for example, R&D subsidies may be more effective at raising innovation. The innovation effect spills over to foreign markets	Mostly positive
Indirect support for private demand (awareness building, labels, training, user-producer interaction)	Information	Demand-pull	Inf	Increasing awareness for an innovation accelerate diffusion, thus feeding back to innovation effects, while transparency through labelling increases competition and innovation.	Limited evidence for the innovation and diffusion effects from indirect support. Can be status-quo oriented in not rewarding innovation.	Ambivalent

Sources: Summarized and adapted from Edler and Shapira 2013. Blind 2012; Cunningham 2012a, 2012b; Cunningham et al. 2013; Cunningham and Ramlogan 2012; Edler 2013; Edler et al. 2013; Gök 2013; Harper 2013; Jones 2012; Jones and Grimshaw 2012; Köhler, Laredo, and Rammer 2012; Pfeiffer and Mulder 2013; Rai and Funkhouser 2015; Rai, Schultz, and Funkhouser 2014; Ramlogan and Rigby 2012; Rigby and Ramlogan 2013; Shapira and Youtie 2013; Uyarra 2012; Zhao, Tang, and Wang 2013).

Note: Under the neoclassical paradigm, innovation policy instruments are described in terms of the market failures they seek to address. Market failures are described in table 5.6 and abbreviated as follows: Fin = financial market frictions and mismatches; Inf = imperfect information and inattention; IPR = incomplete property rights; IRS = increasing returns to scale; KS = knowledge spillovers; NE = network externalities; — = not available.

REFERENCES

Blind, K. 2012. "The Impact of Regulation on Innovation." In *Compendium of Evidence on the Effectiveness of Innovation Policy*. Manchester Institute of Innovation Research, University of Manchester, U.K. http://www.innovation-policy.org.uk/share/NESTA_Compendium_Regulation_20120124_linked.pdf.

Cunningham, P. 2012a. "The Impact and Effectiveness of Policies to Support Collaboration for R&D and Innovation." In *Compendium of Evidence on the Effectiveness of Innovation Policy*. Manchester Institute of Innovation Research, University of Manchester, U.K. http://www.innovation-policy.org.uk/share/06_The%20Impact%20and%20Effectiveness%20of%20Policies%20to%20Support%20Collaboration%20for%20R&D%20and%20Innovation.pdf.

———. 2012b. "The Impact of Direct Support to R&D and Innovation in Firms." In *Compendium of Evidence on the Effectiveness of Innovation Policy*. Manchester Institute of Innovation Research, University of Manchester, U.K. http://www.innovation-policy.org.uk/share/09_Impact%20of%20Direct%20Support%20to%20R&D%20and%20Innovation%20in%20Firms.pdf.

Cunningham, P., J. Edler, K. Flanagan, and P. Larédo. 2013. "Innovation Policy Mix and Instrument Interaction." In *Compendium of Evidence on the Effectiveness of Innovation Policy*. Manchester Institute of Innovation Research, University of Manchester, U.K. http://www.innovation-policy.org.uk/share/19_Policy%20mix_linked.pdf.

Cunningham, P., and R. Ramlogan. 2012. "The Effects of Innovation Network Policies." In *Compendium of Evidence on the Effectiveness of Innovation Policy*. Manchester Institute of Innovation Research, University of Manchester, U.K. https://media.nesta.org.uk/documents/the_effects_of_innovation_network_policies.pdf.

Edler, J. 2013. "Review of Policy Measures to Stimulate Private Demand for Innovation: Concepts and Effects." In *Compendium of Evidence on the Effectiveness of Innovation Policy*. Manchester Institute of Innovation Research, University of Manchester, U.K. http://www.innovation-policy.org.uk/share/12_Review%20of%20Policy%20Measures%20to%20Stimulate%20Private%20Demand%20for%20Innovation.%20Concepts%20and%20Effects.pdf.

Edler, J., P. Cunningham, A. Gök, P. Shapira, and K. Blind. 2013. "The Impact of Standardisation and Standards on Innovation." In *Compendium of Evidence on the Effectiveness of Innovation Policy*. Manchester Institute of Innovation Research, University of Manchester, U.K. http://www.innovation-policy.org.uk/share/14_The%20Impact%20of%20Standardization%20and%20Standards%20on%20Innovation.pdf.

Edler, J., and P. Shapira. 2013. "Impacts of Innovation Policy: Synthesis and Conclusion." In *Compendium of Evidence on the Effectiveness of Innovation Policy*. Manchester Institute of Innovation Research, University of Manchester, U.K. http://www.innovation-policy.org.uk/compendium/.

Gök, A. 2013. "The Impact of Innovation Inducement Prizes." In *Compendium of Evidence on the Effectiveness of Innovation Policy*. Manchester Institute of Innovation Research, University of Manchester, U.K. http://www.innovation-policy.org.uk/share/17-%20impact%20of%20innovation%20inducement%20prizes.pdf.

Harper, J. C. 2013. "Impact of Technology Foresight." In *Compendium of Evidence on the Effectiveness of Innovation Policy*. Manchester Institute of Innovation Research, University of Manchester, U.K. http://www.innovation-policy.org.uk/share/15_Impact%20of%20Technology%20Foresight.pdf.

Jones, B. 2012. "Innovation and Human Resources: Migration Policies and Employment Protection Policies." In *Compendium of Evidence on the Effectiveness of Innovation Policy*. Manchester Institute of Innovation Research, University of Manchester, U.K. http://www.innovation-policy.org.uk/share/08_Innovation%20and%20Human%20Resources%20Migration%20and%20Employment%20Protection.pdf.

Jones, B., and D. Grimshaw. 2012. "The Effects of Policies for Training and Skills on Improving Innovation Capabilities in Firms." In *Compendium of Evidence on the Effectiveness of Innovation Policy*. Manchester Institute of Innovation Research, University of Manchester, U.K. http://www.innovation-policy.org.uk/share/04_The%20Effects%20of%20Policies%20for%20Training%20and%20Skills%20on%20Improving%20Innovation%20Capabilities%20in%20Firms.pdf.

Köhler, C., P. Laredo, and C. Rammer. 2012. "The Impact and Effectiveness of Fiscal Incentives for R&D." In *Compendium of Evidence on the Effectiveness of Innovation Policy*. Manchester Institute of Innovation Research, University of Manchester, U.K. https://media.nesta.org .uk/documents/the_impact_and_effectiveness_of_fiscal_incentives.pdf.

Pfeiffer, B., and P. Mulder. 2013. "Explaining the Diffusion of Renewable Energy Technology in Developing Countries." *Energy Economics* 40 (November): 285–96. https://doi.org/10.1016/j .eneco.2013.07.005.

Rai, V., and E. Funkhouser. 2015. "Emerging Insights on the Dynamic Drivers of International Low-Carbon Technology Transfer." *Renewable and Sustainable Energy Reviews* 49 (September): 350–364.

Rai, V., K. Schultz, and E. Funkhouser. 2014. "International Low Carbon Technology Transfer: Do Intellectual Property Regimes Matter?" *Global Environmental Change* 24 (1): 60–74. doi.org/10.1016/j.gloenvcha.2013.10.004.

Ramlogan, R., and J. Rigby. 2012. "Access to Finance: Impacts of Publicly Supported Venture Capital and Loan Guarantees." In *Compendium of Evidence on the Effectiveness of Innovation Policy*. Manchester Institute of Innovation Research, University of Manchester, U.K.

Rigby, J., and R. Ramlogan. 2013. "The Impact and Effectiveness of Entrepreneurship Policy." In *Compendium of Evidence on the Effectiveness of Innovation Policy*. Manchester Institute of Innovation Research, University of Manchester, U.K.

Shapira, P., and J. Youtie. 2013. "Impact of Technology and Innovation Advisory Services." In *Compendium of Evidence on the Effectiveness of Innovation Policy*. Manchester Institute of Innovation Research, University of Manchester, U.K.

Uyarra, E. 2012. "Review of Measures in Support of Public Procurement of Innovation." In *Compendium of Evidence on the Effectiveness of Innovation Policy*. Manchester Institute of Innovation Research, University of Manchester, U.K.

Zhao, Y., K. K. Tang, and L.-L. Wang. 2013. "Do Renewable Electricity Policies Promote Renewable Electricity Generation? Evidence from Panel Data." *Energy Policy* 62 (November): 887–97. doi.org/10.1016/j.enpol.2013.07.072.